Unnatural Monopolies

Unnatural Monopolies

The Case for Deregulating Public Utilities

Edited by

Robert W. Poole, Jr.
The Reason Foundation

Lexington Books
D.C. Heath and Company/Lexington, Massachusetts/Toronto

Allen County Public Library
Ft. Wayne, Indiana

Library of Congress Cataloging in Publication Data

Main entry under title:

    Unnatural monopolies

    Includes index.
    1. Public utilities—United States—Addresses, essays, lectures. 2. Monopolies—United
States—Addresses, essays, lectures. I. Poole, Robert W., 1944–
HD2766.U57   1985   338.8′ 2613636′ 0973   84–40828
ISBN 0-669-10126-5 (alk. paper)

Published simultaneously in Canada
Printed in the United States of America on acid-free paper
International Standard Book Number: 0-669-10126-5
Library of Congress Catalog Card Number: 84-40828

Contents
5012599

Tables and Figures

Tables

Figure

Preface and Acknowledgments

This book derives its origins from a clipping sent in by a reader of *Reason* magazine in 1980. That clipping was of a wire-service story reporting the surprising fact that Lubbock, Texas, is served by two complete electric utility systems, between which residents can switch at will. We published that information in *Reason*'s "Trends" column as a unique example—proof, by counterexample, that electricity is not necessarily a natural monopoly.

Shortly thereafter we received a letter from economist Gordon Tullock, pointing out that electric utility duopolies existed in several dozen U.S. cities and that this phenomenon had been studied extensively by economist Walter Primeaux (a contributor to this book). Before long *Reason* undertook an investigative journalism project on competing electric companies. The resulting article, "Two Utilities Are Better Than One" (October 1981), received the 1981 John Hancock Award for Excellence in Business and Financial Journalism.

Perhaps more important, the research that we had done for the electricity article stimulated our thinking at The Reason Foundation. The more we looked into other so-called natural monopolies, the more we saw increasing opportunities for competition. After commissioning and publishing two further *Reason* articles, one on cable television franchising by Thomas Hazlett and the other on telephone competition by Peter Samuel (both contributors to this book), we had come across enough solid analysis in the journals of law, economics, and regulation to decide that the time was ripe for a book that would take a fresh look at public utility regulation. Drawing on people with whom we had come in contact researching the *Reason* articles, as well as a growing network of other contacts in academia, think tanks, and consulting firms, we put together an outline and recruited qualified people to write each chapter. In part because of a grant from the Alex C. Walker Educational and Charitable Foundation, we were able to bring this project to a fruitful conclusion.

Although the idea for this book and the selection of the contributors are the work of its editor, its timely completion would not have been possible without the efforts of manuscript editor Lynn Scarlett. She worked with each of the contributors, editing their manuscripts and helping to shape the individual chapters into parts of a coherent whole. Besides her technical skill as an editor, she brought to this task a broad substantive knowledge of political economy, which greatly added to her role as manuscript editor.

The contributors do not agree with one another on all the specifics of their proposals, but all agree that traditional public utility regulation is long overdue for reexamination.

The views expressed in these pages do not necessarily represent the views of any individual trustee, officer, or advisory board member of the Reason Foundation.

Introduction

Throughout most of the twentieth century, public utility regulation went virtually unchallenged. Even when deregulation of other industries, especially in transportation services, began achieving widespread support, most policymakers and economists continued to argue for regulation of public utilities.

Proponents of regulation have claimed that public utilities are different from other enterprises because these industries are "natural monopolies"; that is, a single supplier in these industries is assumed to be able to operate at a lower unit cost than two or more smaller suppliers serving the same geographical area. Under these circumstances, the marketplace is deemed inadequate to ensure efficient allocation of services at competitive prices. In an unregulated marketplace, natural monopolies would be able to capture a given market area and charge monopoly prices to consumers.

Using this logic, proponents of public utility regulation have supported the need for regulatory agencies to control entry into the industry and to regulate rates. In exchange for guaranteeing an exclusive territory to the public utility supplier, the regulatory agency is supposed to control rates through regulation to prevent the supplier from exploiting its monopoly position. Other arguments have supplemented this fundamental natural monopoly thesis. Public utilities have come to be considered essential services. Only regulation, it is argued, can ensure that everyone has access to, say, telephone service or electricity at reasonable prices.

By the late 1970s, the impulse toward deregulation of many industries had begun to accelerate. Even public utility regulation began to come under scrutiny. A number of factors prompted this reevaluation.

First, the general political climate had changed. The thrust toward big government had abated. Soaring federal deficits, widespread charges of government waste and inefficiency, the Watergate debacle, the erosion of individual privacy, and other issues eroded faith in government as the vehicle for promoting progress and prosperity. The deregulation push is a natural component of this increasingly skeptical political climate.

A second factor fueled the impetus toward deregulation. In addition to a general malaise about government operations, there was a mounting perception that regulation was not working. This included a failure of regulation to function effectively in the domain of public utilities. Rate-of-return regulation, which has characterized public utility regulatory policy, has provided strong incentives for firms to overinvest in capital stock so as to increase the value of the rate base on which their allowable rate of return is calculated. Protection from competition has shielded public utility firms from the discipline of the marketplace, making them slow to adopt innovations and less responsive to consumers than might be desirable. Moreover, regulatory lag in obtaining rate increases has made it difficult for regulated firms to respond promptly to changing conditions with investment in new types of equipment.

Technology itself provided a third force toward reevaluating the wisdom of public utility regulation. In the electricity, telephone, and cable television industries, recent technological changes have opened the door to possible competition. Alternative energy systems—such as fuel cells, turbine total energy systems, small hydropower, and windpower—in some cases can produce electricity at lower cost than additional increments of central station supply. In local telecommunications, both radio-based systems (for example, cellular radio, microwave) and hard-wired systems (two-way cable, fiber optics) are being designed to provide telephone bypass service in competition with the local telephone monopoly. And a number of alternatives exist to provide the various services offered by cable systems: master antenna systems for apartment buildings, over-the-air pay television, and telephone-based information services, to name a few.

These three objective conditions—changes in the political climate, regulatory failures, and technological innovation—are joined by a fourth theoretical development that bolsters the case for public utility deregulation. During the 1970s, economists became increasingly critical of natural monopoly theory itself. Empirical studies have now thrown into doubt assertions that monopoly is more efficient than competition in the provision of public utility services. In addition, a review of the historical record has begun to shed doubt on whether natural monopoly theory was ever correct in this regard.

Several recent legal decisions may also have strengthened the case for deregulation. For example, in January 1982 the U.S. Supreme Court ruled that the award of an exclusive franchise for a Boulder, Colorado, cable television system was a potential violation of federal antitrust laws, since city governments are not exempt from those laws (as are state governments). Although this decision does not affect state regulation of electric companies or telephone companies, it has sweeping implications for cable firms and for local telephone or electricity distribution systems, should they at some point be turned over to local regulators due to deregulation at the state level.

Thus the stage is set for a fundamental rethinking of public policy toward public utility services. Conventional exclusive franchising with rate-of-return regulation increasingly is being viewed as an impediment to modernization and more responsible service. Still, there are many unanswered questions. If existing regulatory arrangements are unsatisfactory, what role, if any, should government play in dealing with these rapidly changing industries? How far should deregulation go? What are the opportunities and pitfalls that might accompany this process? These are the questions that the contributors to this book address.

In chapter 1, economist Tom Hazlett looks at the intellectual history of natural monopoly. He revivifies the work of turn-of-the-century scholars who foresaw marketplace solutions to problems generated by the concentration of economic power envisioned in natural monopoly theory. In addition, Hazlett challenges the prevailing wisdom that regulatory policy arose to meet failures of the marketplace to function effectively.

Economists Nina Cornell and Douglas Webbink take on a more specific aspect of public utilities regulation in chapter 2, in which they criticize rate-of-return regulation. The relationship between antitrust law and public utility deregulation is examined by legal scholars William Mellor and Malcolm Allen in chapter 3.

Chapter 4, by Thomas Hazlett, serves as a transition between the more theoretical first three chapters and the remaining chapters that analyze specific public utilities. Hazlett first develops a theoretical model that shows how long-term private contracts could serve to overcome scale-economy, information, free-rider, and other problems often associated with public-utility-type industries. He then provides an empirical study of the relatively new cable television industry to illustrate how the sort of market arrangements his model describes have begun to be utilized.

In chapter 5, economist Walter Primeaux, Jr., analyzes the electric utility industry and shows that competition in both the generation and distribution of electricity is not only feasible but desirable.

In chapter 6, Charles Jackson considers the possibilities of competition in the cable television industry, focusing primarily on the technological alternatives that render the industry competitive in character.

Finally, Peter Samuel makes the case for complete deregulation of the telecommunications industry in chapter 7, pointing especially to the proliferation of many competitive technological alternatives to existing hard-wired telephone services.

Although each of the authors criticizes public utility regulation, their proposals for change vary somewhat in the role they accord to governments in the deregulation process. Some authors see total deregulation as genuinely possible and desirable. Others argue for deregulation in most aspects of public utility provision but believe that a continued government role may be essential in limited ways, especially during the transition from regulation to deregulation.

That the issues involved in public utility deregulation are complex is amply illustrated by the knowledgeable comments that accompany the chapters (from Ithiel de Sola Pool, William Berry, Linda Cohen, Patrick Wiggins, Sue Blumenfeld, and Leland Johnson). Their critical remarks highlight the fact that, even among those sympathetic to deregulation, debate is substantial. For example, should generation, transmission, and distribution of electric power all be deregulated? Or should generation alone be deregulated? Will telephone deregulation result in higher prices for local service? Will those prices thwart the achievement of universal telephone service? Is universal service in fact desirable? Can long-term private contracts function to make the private provision of public utilities feasible? Will antitrust laws enhance or hinder efforts to deregulate public utilities? These are the kinds of questions addressed by the commentators.

In a political and economic environment that has been marked for so long by public utility regulation, deregulation will no doubt bring with it unforeseen consequences. Nonetheless, considerable evidence exists to show that the current system has not achieved its goals of providing high-quality service at competitive prices in the most efficient manner. This book is designed to present that evidence and to offer theoretical and empirical support for deregulation.

1
The Curious Evolution of Natural Monopoly Theory

Thomas Hazlett

The most traditional economic case for regulation assumes the existence of natural monopoly—that is, where economies of scale are so
persistent that a single firm can serve the market at lower unit cost than
two or more firms. Reasonably clear examples include electric power
and gas distribution, local telephone service, railroading between
pairs of small- to medium-sized metropolitan areas, and the long-
distance transportation of petroleum and gas in pipelines. Regulation
is said to be necessary in such instances to protect consumers from the
monopoly pricing behavior that achieving all scale economies renders
virtually inevitable.

> F.M. Scherer, *Industrial Market
> Structure and Economic Performance*

Professor Scherer's view would hardly startle contemporary economists.
But economic history offers at least one surprise for this perspective:
the modern regulation of U.S. industry did not begin in an industry
naturally monopolistic by anyone's definition. Early on the key issue delimit-
ing government's right to intervene in commerce was the public nature of the
business involved. As economist Alfred Kahn notes, "There is no trace of the
concept of natural monopoly in the landmark constitutional cases delineating
the category of businesses 'affected with a public interest.'"[1]

In *Munn* v. *Illinois* (1877), the historic U.S. Supreme Court decision establishing a legislature's legal authority to control the market prices of grain
elevators in Chicago, the Court held that when "one devotes his property to a
use in which the public has an interest, he must submit to be controlled by the
public for the common good."[2] Moreover, "*Munn* decided that history and
economics could determine whether a business was a public calling."[3] As
James Nelson surmises, the natural monopoly rationale is nowhere to be
found in the *Munn* decision:

> In a transportation center the size of Chicago, there is no technical or eco-
> nomic reason why numerous companies should not operate grain elevators.

In short, *Munn* vs. *Illinois* involved a representative industry from the stand-point of establishing the *right to regulate*, but its industrial background was singularly inappropriate as a source of answers to questions about *types of regulation*.[4]

Nelson's premise is unassailable (there existed fourteen grain elevators, owned by nine competing firms). His conclusion—that *Munn* v. *Illinois* throws no light on the regulatory question—however, is suggestive of just the hypothesis that this chapter questions: the concept of natural monopoly is theoretically well defined as an economic problem demanding a (public) regulatory solution. As an alternative hypothesis, I shall argue that the fundamental importance of natural monopoly is as a legalistic entity that facilitates the efforts of political coalitions to restrict output in the manner predicted in the capture view of regulation.

Genesis of Natural Monopoly Theory

> It seems then that the word monopoly was never used in English law, except when there was a royal grant authorizing some one or more persons only to deal in or sell a certian commodity or article. If a number of individuals were to unite for the purpose of producing any particular article or commodity, and if they should succeed in selling such article very extensively, and almost solely, such individuals in popular language would be said to have a monopoly. Now, as those individuals have no advantages given them by the law over other persons, it is clear they can only sell more of their commodity than other persons by producing the commodity cheaper and better.
> *Penny Encyclopedia* (1839), 15:341.

The modern theory of natural monopoly traces its roots to the mid-nineteenth century; however, contemporaneous to the writings of early monopoly theorists such as Antoine Cournot and Rene Dupuit, there existed a perspective in both popular and academic circles that the "monopoly problem" was fading from view. Adam Smith, claims George Stigler, paid "no attention to the formal theory of monopoly" and categorized "the serious monopolies of his time with the grants of exclusive power by the state."[5] This view held sway over opinions of the day and for decades thereafter, as the passage from the *Penny Encyclopedia* of 1839 attests.

John Stuart Mill had an even stronger contention, however, by mid-century: that monopoly as had been manifested was being eliminated by grander forms of competitive enterprise. Mill, who introduced the idea and term *natural monopoly* in his *Principles of Political Economy*, noted that competition was "making itself felt more and more through the principal branches of retail trade in the large towns."[6] The pleasant fact was that "the rapidity and cheapness of transport, by making consumers less dependent on the dealers in their immediate neighborhood," were "tending to assimilate more and more the whole country to a large town."[7] The vestiges of local monopoly, Mill saw, were being swept away by the technical and economic advantages of the industrial revolution.

By the late 1800s, this view of monopoly in retreat had reached the level of an orthodoxy among U.S. economists. To the extent that monopoly was a problem, it was a problem of state-enforced franchises. Arthur L. Perry, whose popular 1865 text, *Elements of Political Economy*, would enjoy "at least 19 printings before 1890," cited such nonmarket controls as "trade unions and labor legislation, usury laws, paper money and protective tariffs."[8] Moreover, such economists saw the new rivalry among large-scale producers as inherently antimonopolistic. Well-known Columbia University sociologist Franklin Giddings, writing in 1887, claimed that "combinations have not prevented investment of new capital, or sustained prices." In fact, he pointed to "the general decline of prices" since 1870—"that is, during the period within which combinations have had their phenomenal growth."[9] A particularly sophisticated observation of Giddings was contained in his critiques of "ruinous competition" and "barriers to entry":

> Other things being equal, new capital will hesitate longest about entering into competition with established producers in those industries in which each producer must have a plant that is costly in proportion to the value of the total product of all producers. But the combination that would reap advantage from this hesitancy must face the fact that it is precisely this expensiveness of plant that entails heavy fixed charges—which must be met at whatever sacrifice of profits—and impels competition to a ruinous extreme if more capital is tempted into the business than the normal social need requires. . . . Hence, as combinations learn their unalterable limitations in "the nature of things," they must adjust prices and production, by a conscious policy, to the normal basis that otherwise will be reached in a more wasteful way. They must permit the full satisfaction of normal demands and allow prices to gravitate to an equality with cost of production.[10]

Hence Giddings adopted a global view of competition that encompassed the mercurial properties of this ubiquitous force. His conclusion as to "the persistence of competition" may be more fully understood today than it was in his time:

> That competition in some form is a permanent economic process, is an implication of the conservation of energy. . . . Therefore, when market competition seems to have been suppressed, we should inquire what has become of the forces by which it was generated. We should inquire, further, to what degree market competition actually is suppressed or converted into other forms.[11]

David A. Wells, whose 1889 *Recent Economic Changes* is described by Hans Thorelli as "by far the most popular work along somewhat heterodox lines," leaves no doubt as to his perspective on the correlation between higher living standards and industrial concentration.[12]

> Society has practically abandoned—and from the very necessity of the case has got to abandon, unless it proposes to war against progress and civilization—the prohibition of industrial concentration and combinations. The world demands abundance of commodities, and demands them cheaply; and experience shows that it can have them only by the employment of great capital upon extensive scale.[13]

Most important, Wells did not see these new methods as any large departure from the competitive constraints of old, a notion that has dominated thinking on large-scale enterprise, and particularly natural monopoly, in the century since he wrote. Wells saw competitive forces lurking implicitly, but effectively, to constrain monopoly behavior. Dramatic increases in society's wealth had created "a desire to convert this wealth into the form of negotiable securities. . . . Hence, a stimulus for the undertaking of new enterprises which can create and market securities."[14] The salubrious result for consumers was

> the tendency and the interest of every successful manufacturing combination . . . to put the prices of its products down to a figure where it will not pay for speculators to form new competitive stock companies to be bought off or crushed by it. For, if it did keep up high profit-assuring prices, one of two things would eventually happen: either new factories would be started; or the inventive spirit of the age would devise cheaper methods of production, or some substitute for the product they furnished, and so ruin the first combination beyond the possibility of redemption. And hence we have here another permanent agency, antagonistic to the maintenance of high and remunerative prices.[15]

John Bates Clark, while early in his career a moralistic critic of the orthodox economists, was soon to join mainstream thinking on the monopoly question. Although industrial combinations did exist, they were neither designed to nor guilty of inefficient restriction of output. Rather they were "the product of a social evolution," and "residual competition of the actual kind subsists between productive establishments of comparatively equal strength in combination with each other; and residual competition of the potential kind is maintained between the entire combination and the remainder of society."[16] This was an effective constraint on large firms or combinations, selected "primarily" for their "comparative advantage in economical production" and assured that "capital and labor may still transfer themselves to and from the industry they try to control."

Here again we see a striking portrayal of competition as a global, irrepressible phenomenon. This view has lain dormant through most of this century's economic theory, Joseph Schumpeter being the one noteworthy exception until recently. The danger present in the more common twentieth-century view, expressed succinctly in the passage by Scherer, is that all models of monopoly distortion underlying the rationale for public utility regulation assume a market of local monopoly (spatially and by product), which may be identified, analyzed, and remedied by some reliable administrative policy. The global notion of competition presents a readily insoluble dilemma: competitive forces may not be so easily dismissed, even where indetectable to the naked eye, and monopoly inefficiency may not be so handily improved on.

Two other analysts that merit discussion here are George Gunton and Henry Wood. Gunton keenly observed the efficiencies taking place in the marketplace of his late-nineteenth-century world:

> Strictly speaking, concentration of capital does not drive small capitalists out of business, but simply integrates them into larger and more complex systems of production, in which they are enabled to produce wealth more cheaply for the community and obtain a larger income for themselves. . . . The competition between trusts naturally tends to reduce the profits to a closer margin than did the competition between corporations for the reason that the larger the business transacted, the smaller the percentage profit necessary to its success. Thus, instead of concentration of capital tending to destroy competition the reverse is true. . . . By the use of large capital, improved machinery and better facilities the trust can and does undersell the corporation.[17]

Gunton recommended that the gathering political movement in favor of regulating big business be calmed so as to "ascertain whether we are really engaging a public enemy or simply pursuing an industrial phantom."[18] He was careful in his analysis to focus on the falling level of prices in industries commonly held to be dominated by trusts, including the petroleum industry.[19]

Henry Wood was another contemporary analyst whose views appear to have preceded much of the latter-day new learning in industrial organization. He was able to slice a clear distinction between concentration to restrict output and concentration that expanded it much in the tradition of Oliver Williamson or Robert Bork.[20] "As a general rule," he wrote in 1888, "any consolidation which reduces the cost of production is legitimate, and contributes to the public welfare. On the other hand, any combination whose primary object is the forcing of abnormal prices is temporarily harmful to the community."[21] Wood's policy prescription was that combinations "need not excite public alarm for they have in them the elements of inharmony and dissolution and are not worthy of legislative attention." Indeed they were "in the end, usually unprofitable to the promoters."[22]

This brief sampling of some previously well known but now long-for-gotten purveyors of the rise of natural monopoly is introduced to establish the existence of an alternative explanation for the phenomenon of industry dominated by massive scale economies that was widely discussed within the historical context of the times. Most important, this view was sophisticated and Schumpeterian in its acceptance of the global nature of competitive forces. Attempts by some historians to categorize these writers (or the more famous Herbert Spencer and William Graham Sumner) as unaware of the great trans-formation then underway must be explained as a slick academic ploy to discredit and bury a school that, with few credible followers until recent decades, has had little opportunity to fight back.

The importance of this scholarly misdeal is that the contemporary view of monopoly in general and natural monopoly in particular pins much of its veracity on the historical record, a record that includes the allegedly universally unsatisfactory performance of competition unconstrained by antitrust laws (for oligopolistic industries) and public utility regulation (for natural monopolies).

Hans Thorelli, a modern analyst who has examined this record, dismisses the widespread belief of late-nineteenth-century U.S. economists in the proconsumer consequences of concentration. Thorelli accuses orthodox believers in laissez-faire of unwittingly wrapping themselves in a knot of contradiction: "The logical outcome of 'survival of the fittest' thinking was monopoly, while the static analysis of classical economics envisaged a timeless equilibrium of perfect competition."[23] Yet Thorelli fails to comprehend the extent to which Giddings, Clark, and others had given up on the timeless equilibrium of Ricardian economics, more than happy to trade it in for what Joseph Schumpeter was to dub the "gale of creative destruction." We may thus conclude that it is Thorelli's orthodoxy that requires amendment, as critical examination of the received theory of natural monopoly has revealed troubling inadequacies.

Harold Demsetz has noted that existing neoclassical price theory, contrary to prevailing opinion, presents no fully logical explanation as to why the existence of one supplier in a market "renders monopoly pricing behavior . . . virtually inevitable" (to use F.M. Scherer's words). Industrial organization economists have taken Demsetz's cue by more fully including competitive forces in some monopolistic but "contestable" markets.[24] Nonetheless, the presumption that regulation of so-called natural monopoly is in the public interest has scarcely budged due to an uncritical acceptance of the view that unregulated monopolistic firms of the late nineteenth century ravaged their consumers, workers, and investors.

We may thus conclude that there were at least two distinct schools of thought in the early days of large-scale industry. One accepted the newer market forces simply as empirical amendments to the traditional Ricardian view of competition as the omnipresent and beneficent regulator of economic activity. Another strain soon developed that opposed and eclipsed this view.[25] This latter school discarded the universality of the competitive assumption, focusing on instances in which competition was thought to be too weak a regulator to maximize consumer welfare. In the United States, this view would materialize from two premises: that large corporations were, as concentrations of great wealth, immoral in a strongly normative sense; and, in a positive framework, that in particular natural monopoly markets, competition was not an efficient but a wasteful allocator of resources.

Yet the Schumpeterian vision of large-scale rivals battling in hard-fought "competition for the field," as Edwin Chadwick (1859) termed it, survives as a competing hypothesis to the traditional view equating market share with market power, and large scale with deadweight loss. When Thorelli maintains that "the problem of monopoly was relatively or entirely neglected by members of the orthodox school," his contradiction is revealing.[26] Only paragraphs before (and after) he was informing as to the views of the orthodox school on the dynamic, proconsumer consequences of large-scale enterprise. The orthodox writers were not silent; rather they were loudly supportive of the increasing concentration of some industrial markets, which they saw as evidence of a superior, more efficient environment. They neglected only to deal with monopoly in terms of what was soon to be a new orthodoxy replacing the classical view.

This new perspective began to identify monopoly as the central failing of a market economy, and even its theoretical elements soon splintered into two directions. First, among the more formal economic theorists, the phenomenon of monopoly came to be identified with a downward sloping demand curve for the firm. French economists Antoine Cournot and Rene Dupuit associated the monopolist with a less than perfectly elastic demand curve; additionally, Dupuit noted the possible benefits of monopoly price discrimination in the case of a public good.[27]

This approach gradually crept into English-language writings with the later work of Francis Edgeworth, Henry Sidgwick, and Alfred Marshall.[28] Yet the critique of monopoly in general and natural monopoly in particular did not wait for the scholarly development of formal theory. In fact, the classical defenders of large-scale enterprise did seek to extend Ricardian analysis of competition to the events and circumstances of the new era.

At the same time, critics of (unregulated private) monopoly generally departed from classical economic theory altogether in their writings. This large group of writings (representing a decidedly minority academic viewpoint) may be broken into two subsets: those who attacked trusts on normative grounds and those who focused on the wasteful duplication inherent in natural monopoly markets. Neither group was particularly systematic in its formulations, but this fact is clearly more distressing in the latter for the natural monopoly theorists purported to be engaged in positive empirical and theoretical analysis and laid the groundwork for views of natural monopoly that have survived for a century. Thus, although this group is clearly the more important subject of my study, I will first outline the views of the normative antagonists to the trusts to illustrate some key motivations underlying the animosity to large-scale enterprise.

According to Thorelli, the American Economic Association (AEA) was designed in 1885 by it founders as a counterweight to the prevailing orthodoxy that combinations presented no clear or present danger. The chief founder, Richard T. Ely, was particularly distressed by the disappearance of the small traders of a less combative—or affluent—day gone by. "Manufactures were carried on in the last century in insignificant shops by men of little wealth and no great social importance," bemoaned Ely in 1887.[29] "The word manufacturer, in Adam Smith's *Wealth of Nations*, did not mean a great proprietor but a man who worked with his own hands—a humble artisan."

It was on a blatantly moralistic note that the AEA was formed by Ely, J.B. Clark, Simon Patten, and others. An emergent social gospel was being propounded by such men as Washington Gladden, who, in revolt of the classicists, believed that "the whole object of the Christian scheme of ethics . . . is to counteract injuries wrought by the survival of the fittest."[30] Thorelli asserts that the AEA founders wanted to redirect the "spontaneous" social forces toward

> establishment of a "cooperative brotherhood," a society governed by the principles of "Christian Socialism" in a most elated, idealistic, nondogmatic and, it might be added, rather esoteric sense. . . . Inevitably, the members of the new guild of economists came to recognize the state as the vehicle with which to give their social gospel and push the general welfare beyond its existing limits. Nowhere was this more distinctly stated than in the by-laws of the American Economic Association.[31]

The contemporary economic argument that monopoly tends to create inefficiency by leaving some gains from trade unexploited was not evident in nineteenth-century writings. But the critique of monopoly surely had more to its credit than a religious-based appeal to the social gospel. In fact, Ely himself was ready to concede that efficiency had forced firms to integrate to larger size: "Owing to discoveries and inventions . . . it became necessary to prosecute enterprises of great magnitude."[32] And so he quickly shifted his focus to the greatest source of evil:

> What are the corporations of which one thinks when people talk about the abuses of corporated powers? . . . First and foremost are the railways. Then follow express companies, telegraph companies, street-car companies, gas-

light companies, water-supply companies, and others. But there is something common about all these productive agencies which are conspicuous for the abuse of corporate power. They are beyond the regular, normal action of competition. They are natural monopolies.[33]

Ely thus bridges the gap between the normative and positive arguments against monopoly and distinguishes the dangerous ground of natural monopoly from a hostility toward large-scale business organizations in general: "It is not true that private corporations are a bad form of industrial organization: it is true that their sphere has been unduly extended."[34] Ely's solution to the natural monopoly problem, however, was to abandon private property in favor of public ownership. His level of confidence in the efficacy of government enterprise was metered by his somewhat ebullient endorsement of the coming benefits of a recent regulatory innovation: "When the evolution recently promoted by the Inter-State Commerce Law is carried so far that railways are essentially public undertakings, we will hear as little of strikes of railway employees as we now do of post-office employees."[35]

Henry Carter Adams is credited with associating the natural monopoly problem with large, fixed investment and hence declining average cost (or, equivalently, increasing returns). In separating industries into three categories, those experiencing decreasing, constant, or increasing returns, Adams essentially was creating the research program that has defined the field of industrial organization for nearly three-quarters of a century. His analysis was most important in a fundamental, methodological sense. In focusing on cost conditions of potential producers in a market in an abstract and nonbehavioral model, Adams was implicitly assuming certain modes of market competition ineffectual, as in Edwin Chadwick's "Competition *for* the market."[36] Moreover, Adams set industrial organization questions into a technical engineering framework of measuring physical input-output relations. This, in turn, firmly placed the study of market structure at a distance from the economic forces at work in that market, which, along with technological or engineering constraints, were themselves determining that structure—hence the tendency of traditional industrial organization economists to judge the efficiency of particular markets taking that structure as given and atomistic perfect competition as ideal, rather than to explain why different efficient market structures evolve under varying circumstances.[37]

A second implicit assumption contained in Adams's analysis, which would soon become entrenched as a tradition, was embodied in the habit of looking at a class of firms in similar product markets as homogeneous. In speaking of a decreasing-cost industry, all interfirm differentiation is assumed away. Cost curves and output characteristics must be identical between rivals and potential rivals (if firms have distinct quality products, for instance, their cost curves cannot be viewed in the same price-quantity space and the decreasing-costs designation is meaningless).[38] The key importance of this assumption is that the entire rationale for competition's being an efficient regulator of economic activity points to its role as a selection process sorting differentiated firms.[39] It is difficult indeed to construct a viable rationale for competitive behavior, and the duplicative effort (here by definition) it expends, should the assumption that firms are identical be consistently employed. It is not surprising, therefore, that the natural monopoly model has, on these terms, successfully convinced scholars of the waste of market rivalry for nearly a century. How the model's key assumptions have gone so little challenged remains the mystery.

The impotency (or uselessness) of competitive market forces under these assumptions was soon recognized. Ely, in creating a brief for public utility regulation, leaned on Ferrer's five conditions indicative of natural monopoly:

1. What they supply is a necessary.
2. They occupy peculiarly favored spots or lines of land.
3. The article or convenience they supply is used at the place where, and in connection with the plant or machinery by which, it is supplied.
4. This article or convenience can in general be largely, if not indefinitely, increased without proportionate increase in plant and capital.
5. Certainty and harmonious arrangement, which can only be attained by unity, are paramount considerations.[40]

Ely then discusses the "more scientific" formulation of the natural monopoly problem put forth by Henry Carter Adams. Here is the categorization of competitive possibilities that Carter deduced from the "technology of supply":[41]

1. Industries of the first class are such as to demand a proportional increase in capital and labor to secure a given increase in product.
2. Industries of the second class . . . a given increment of capital and labor.
3. Industries of the third class . . . conform to the class of increasing, rather than to the law of constant or decreasing, returns.[42]

Adams argued that industries of the first and second class were best left to "unregulated" market forces; competition in its normal course was up to the task of directing resources optimally. But such forces were no match for the industries of the third class: "It is certainly absurd to say that a business superior to the regulatory influence of competition, conducted according to the principle that the highest possible price should be demanded for services rendered, can be managed in a spirit of fairness to the public."[43]

Adams's writing is littered with errors of logic and written in a tone of ad hominem attack on corporate capitalism rather than a measured presentation of the inefficiency in unregulated private monopoly. Interestingly, however,

Adams created a lasting tradition with his assertion that a firm experiencing increasing returns finds itself in possession of "exclusive privileges administered for personal profit."[44] Here he did not mean privileges granted in law, to which he was not opposed: "Such monopolies as exist should rest in law and be established in the interests of the public; a well-organized society will include no extra-legal monopolies of any sort." Adams cites at least six reasons for ruling these "extralegal" monopolies antisocial:

1. "The principle of free competition is powerless to exercise a healthy regulatory influence . . . because it is easier for an established business to extend its facilities than for a new industry to spring into competitive existence."

2. Monopolies will not produce the efficiencies generally expected of private enterprise vs. state-run institutions, because they "usually exist in the form of corporations . . . the stockholders are more frequently interested in the manipulation of stock than in the management of details of the business; and . . . the responsibility and care for the detailed management of great concerns must of necessity be assigned to superintendents and agents."

3. The simple fact that some ventures of the third class appear profitable. Objecting to Edward Atkinson's defense of railroads on the basis of falling shipping rates, Adams claims "it is an error to judge of the efficiency of competition in the railroad industry solely on the basis of freight schedules. There are other tests equally as clear and much more simple." Adams proposes a test wherein we observe whether or not there exist sufficient profits in an industry to buy out potential competitors: "If it be true that competition rules the railroad business, the chief purpose of building new lines within the territory of an established line, should not be to make money by selling out to the stockholders of the line already doing the business. There can be no money in such speculation unless the net receipts of the old road are far in excess of the normal return."

4. Competition in industries of classes (1) and (2) allow men to profit by "depressing the cost of rendering a service below the average necessary price," while monopolies make their fortune "from the excess of the market price over the necessary cost of production."

5. Competition does not regulate those businesses where great discrepancies of personal income are permanently maintained among men of equal talent.

6. Their economic benefits could be harnessed for society, without the costs entailed in (1)–(5), by "a monopoly established by law and managed in the interests of the public."[45]

Defining Natural Monopoly: A Critique

Each of these six explanations is inadequate for defining characteristics of natural monopoly.

First, if the expansion of output with less than a proportional increase in inputs were the defining characteristic of natural monopoly, then it would appear that all multiplant firms with some element of fixed cost general to the business as a whole (which we suspect whenever we observe multiplant firms surviving the rigors of the market) would be so classified. For example, let us consider the production function of a national retail chain such as McDonald's. This business would appear to have significant fixed costs associated largely with the entire national organization, including a national advertising campaign, accumulated brand name capital, marketing research, legal staff, product development, management control techniques, and capital budgeting procedures.

Under such cost conditions and given the key implicit assumption of interfirm homogeneity over cost and output, the notion that an incumbent firm may always expand output at lower cost than an entrant holds at the single-plant level of entry or higher. Since it is at the plant or multiplant level at which it is coherent to speak of entry into this market, we can only understand Adams's criterion to classify as naturally monopolistic any firm with fixed charges spread across plants. Since this quite evidently encompasses all major industries to one degree or another, we find no unique content in this condition defining natural monopoly.[46]

The second criterion is simply the old canard that corporations, which natural monopolies are asserted to become more often than other businesses, are inefficient due to the separation of ownership and control. In fact, Ely went so far as to castigate the chances of corporations surviving in the competitive marketplace, comparing the post office's efficiency properties quite favorably to those of private corporations. At this late date, little need be said here, save mention of the curious contradiction that we regulate the hopelessly inefficient out of business; the selection process of market forces is inexplicably omitted.

Item 3 presents Adams's evidence that monopoly returns existed in the railroad industry, yet the story remains uncompelling. If monopoly prices were earning an incumbent firm monopoly profits and entrants were being paid (purchased) to protect such returns, quite evidently the incumbent would be in a position of having to pay off an endless stream of entrants, surrendering all of its rents and quasi-rents to such firms. A better way to deter entry, in that at least the incumbant's quasi-rents would survive, would be simply to price such entrants out of the market by setting rates equal to (or just under) long-run average cost (for whatever level of output an entrant might hope to capture). Such a policy would prove more effective over the long run, certainly, than the policy of inviting entry with monopoly pricing, only to pay firms to shut down on entry, and then repeating the process all over again (because only one firm is bought off at a time). A competitive price structure would permanently deter entry while allowing capture of at least the incumbent's quasi-rents because any firm threatening to enter at prices not covering its long-run average costs would not be taken seriously.

There is, however, a plausible explanation for behavior such as reported by Adams (whether paying firms just to cease operation was, in fact, done is not to be disputed here), which is suggested by Adams himself. In discussing the railroad industry, he notes "The two hundred and fifteen millions of acres of public lands granted by the federal government to these corporations; the one hundred and eighty-five millions [of dollars, presumably] of municipal bonds issued for the building of railroads; the many instances of local taxes paid to construction companies."[47] Adams uses this to show that "it was a mistake to suppose that private capital was adequate to meet the needs of a growing country." This puts Adams on record as accusing the railroads of sufficient monopoly profits to buy off potential competitors and in need of government subsidy to complete the job at hand. The paradox can be resolved, quite contrary to the spirit of Adams's argument, by viewing the federal, state, and local government subsidies as overinvestment into a field with heavy sunk investment. If firms were given rights-of-way, franchises, and other resources contingent on their building railroads not warranted had costs been internalized by the firm, then overbuilding and consolidation, perhaps with some firms' investments retired from operation, would be the logical conclusion. William Sharkey claims this explicitly: "Government subsidization of early railroad expansion was in part responsible for the first episode of destructive competition."[48]

Adams's fourth point contrasting the competitor's mission with that of the monopolist reduces to the truism that profit is the margin between price and average cost (times quantity). Moreover, while the perfect competitor faces a parametric price (one determined exogenously to the firm), by definition it also faces, according to the assumptions of the modern price theorist, a parametric cost function.[49] It is actually the price searching firm that vigorously strives to lower cost in the pursuit of profit maximization—indeed, Joseph Schumpeter argues forcefully that the price searcher endeavors more vigorously because of better-established property rights to the discovery of cost-saving technologies and modes of organization.[50] (In the limit, the price taker has no property right to cost-saving innovation.) If we remember that, for a given demand curve, the monopolist has but one profit-maximizing price (speaking generally and abstracting from discrimination), then the monopolist finds itself striving on a daily basis to accrue profits solely by resort to a lower cost curve. In this endeavor, the firm's management will be disciplined by competitive capital markets.

The one slight sense in which this statement has operational meaning is illustrated by recalling the implicit homogeneity assumption made for natural monopoly markets. If all potential monopoly suppliers are assumed to possess identical cost curves, then there is some plausibility to the notion that these firms strive only to raise prices and do not attempt to lower costs. Yet this conclusion is purely a creation of our strong assumptions. In fact, our assumptions over competitive markets were to become much stronger than those made in Adams's day. Hence, the idea that perfectly competitive firms seek to lower costs or to engage in any other rivalrous behavior whatever has become ruled out by definition.[51]

The fifth point made by Adams is a blatantly normative appeal to the alleged wealth effects of monopoly enterprise that has no positive content. Yet the appeal is characteristic of the motivation of early crusaders against monopoly such as those who initiated the AEA. Their only contemporary importance is that their arguments in favor of public franchising and/or regulation and/or ownership of natural monopolies are still common currency among both the public and the economics professions.

Adams's sixth argument in behalf of regulation—that the problems associated with natural monopoly are solvable by the mere assumption of government intervention in the public interest—began a long tradition that is finally encountering the scrutiny a proposition of such import deserves. The argument for regulation must not only show evidence of monopoly, by whatever standard; clearly it must also show "that consumers or society are better off if there is regulation of entry, exit, rate of return, specific rates, expenditures and conditions of service, rather than if those were left unregulated."[52]

Most of Adams's views on natural monopoly would now be judged quite crude by economists, and some are considered analytically incorrect (for example, his denunciation of the corporate property rights structure as inherently inefficient). Yet, curiously, his pronouncement that industries displaying increasing returns are prima facie candidates for public regulation or nationalization remained a widespread view of industrial organization economists until recently.

The notion of increasing returns tends to be associated with the concept of large permanent investment, which Arthur T. Hadley had noted was the crux of the monopoly problem and demanded a regulatory solution in his 1886 *Quarterly Journal of Economics* article, "Private Monopolies and Public Rights."[53] Hence Hadley saw not only railroads as inherently monopolistic but industries such as oil, coal, and steel rails, "which involve large capital, under concentrated management," thus rendering "the old theory of free competition . . . as untenable as it was in the case of railroads." The large fixed investment already sunk "when a factory is well-established" led to increasing returns. There was a widespread demand for regulation, which applied the term *virtual monopoly* to a wide variety of industrial markets said to affect a public use: "The definition of public use was extremely vague; but the monopoly character, due to the organization of modern industry, seems to have been the distinguishing ground which the Court applied the term to in the business of the Chicago grain elevators."

Modern Monopoly Theories

The earlier view of the notion of increasing returns may have been closer to theoretical consistency than the modern. As the natural monopoly idea has evolved, the alleged necessary and sufficient condition of increasing returns has stayed alive and well, if somewhat altered. That is, the decreasing average cost notion has been replaced with the more general idea of subadditivity. Subadditivity refers to the notion that a natural monopoly can exist with decreasing returns if any specified required rate of output can be supplied most economically by a single firm or single system.[54] The reformulation simply inserts the divisibility problem into the increasing returns argument.

It is important to clarify a common confusion remaining in this analysis: that natural monopoly (or natural oligopoly) "depends upon two key variables: the relevant technology, and the size of the market (that is, output that would be demanded at a price just sufficient to cover minimum unit cost)."[55] This assertion is troublesome, particularly in the light of the development of the economic view of transactions (and, hence, market structure).[56] The important conclusion of this approach is that economic structures are determined by efficient survivors of economic selection, with costs of various market transactions determining these surviving institutions.

Seen in this light, the technology explanation of scale economies is unsatisfactory. While a given technology of decreasing cost (or subadditivity) may be necessary for natural monopoly, it is far from sufficient. The transactions cost framework immediately shifts out of focus from the declining average cost issue to the broader question of what contractual or other market arrangements might be employed to produce outcomes consistent with economic performance in other competitive markets. Such institutions might include buyers' cooperatives or other bargaining agencies, private long-term contracting directly between consumers and producers, vertical integration by customers of the natural monopoly, or some type of rental or joint ownership (by rival firms that continue to compete in the output market) of the fixed investment facility that yields a declining average cost technology. That market forces will not sustain such an alternative to the classic natural monopoly market structure is no more due solely to technical reasons than that firm X decides to contract with an outside law firm for its legal work rather than support an in-house staff. Both market arrangements must be analyzed as economic cost-benefit trade-offs, where subjectively evaluated costs and benefits include such items as the relative possibilities of opportunistic behavior and asymmetric information.[57]

Considering the widespread influence of the transactions costs literature, the continuance of an unamended technology argument to explain natural monopoly is a marked anomaly.[58] And although this error may appear benign in the particular instance where a firm's cost curve is the subject of study, the preoccupation with technical cost conditions, to the exclusion of full consideration of types of economic transactions that have been and could be undertaken to produce and distribute that technology, will soon prove the undoing of much of what remains of natural monopoly theory.

Returning to the issue of subadditivity, this refinement led economists to the fruitful notion of contestability, in which markets are analyzed as naturally monopolistic not on the mere presence of large, fixed cost but large, fixed, nonsalvageable cost. In other words, for a true natural monopoly to exist, there must be a barrier to exit, an impediment preventing an incumbent firm from easily (in the limit, costlessly) transferring its fixed investment to some alternative employment. In this manner, the trucking and, particularly, the airline industries are now generally seen by economists as competitive in the contestability sense in that substantial fixed costs do give rise to declining average costs but are salvageable (and therefore not truly sunk) by virtue of their easy fungibility between markets. This narrows the appropriateness of the traditional declining average cost explanation of natural monopoly by excluding so-called contestable markets.

Still, the notion that a market is naturally monopolistic "if and only if a single firm can produce the desired output at a lower cost than any combination of two or more firms" is not at all what economic theorists mean to say.[59] This definition leaves every surviving firm a natural monopolist over its market. It has been shown by market selection that it can produce "the desired output at a lower cost than any combination of two or more firms."

What the monopoly theory means to say is that the space in which the firm establishes its natural monopoly (that is, that range of customers the firm monopolizes) is more precisely defined geographically than other firms' markets (although it appears that all firms use some spatial coordinates in defining their output vectors). The true natural monopoly survives by bunching its customers over a geographic dimension more so than do other firms.[60] This gives the physical appearance of eliminating competitive forces. Market rivalry may or may not serve customers well when operative over a geographic plane, but there is no a priori economic theory that allows us to state the inherent weakness of this sort of competitive battleground versus those extant in other output characteristics.

Carl Kaysen and Donald Turner demonstrate the prevailing tendency to treat spatial competition as a fundamentally distinct phenomenon from other sorts of market rivalry. Hence their primary rationale for public utility regulation is based on "situations in which competition, as a practical matter, cannot exist or survive for long, and in which, therefore, an unregulated market will not produce competitive results."[61] This explanation not only jumps, without explanation, to a conclusion that competition is not present because numerous firms operating in the same physical territory are not observed but fails to provide a clue as to which firms will be excluded from the natural monopoly designation because all have monopolized some market by some definition.

We are pushed into a framework in which we are forced to estimate the effectiveness of competitive forces governing constraining spatial variables in firm outputs versus (analytically identical) competitive forces governing other output characteristics. There has been at least an implicit recognition of this fact, as evidenced by the frequent citation of a stylized version of our "actual experience" with "competitive" natural monopoly markets. For example, Alfred Kahn surmises that the U.S. competitive era in public utility provision (roughly 1850–1910) was, "it seems generally conceded, a failure."[62] Kahn notes that

> it was out of this experience that the concept of "natural monopoly" gradually emerged, as an attempt on the one hand to explain the persistent tendency of competition to produce inferior results and to disappear and, on the other, to justify its abandonment. . . . There remains to this day a widespread consensus that at least some part of these businesses is, in truth, a natural monopoly, in the sense that direct competition is likely in most instances to involve unbearably great inefficiencies.[63]

The dual significance of this statement is, first, that the historical record, such as it developed, became the actual foundation for an ill-specified theory of natural monopoly. Second, the political push to regulate preceded rather than followed the development of the theory of natural monopoly distortion (in the sense of underproduction and deadweight loss).[64] This points to the need for an examination of the emergence of natural monopoly regulation in the historical epoch in which it emerged.

Uncontestable Markets

The subadditivity criterion for natural monopoly has not led to a reexamination of the traditional core of natural monopoly theory concerning so-called public utilities (that is, those industries that do involve significant nonsalvageable investment). Kahn believes, for such industries, that economies of scale remain a necessary and sufficient rationale for regulation: "The critical and— if properly defined—all-embracing characteristic of natural monopoly is an inherent tendency to decreasing unit costs over the entire extent of the market."[65] But Kahn, unlike others, is careful to specify this "decreasing unit cost" property as appropriately belonging not necessarily to the quantity of output dimension but to the quantity of suppliers dimension. That is, even in a market where unit costs increase as output expands (his example is telephone service, which has been recognized as an increasing cost industry since at least the first decade of this century), "monopoly is still natural because one company can serve any *given* number of subscribers (for example, all in a community) at lower cost than two."[66]

To illustrate, he raises the possibility that two locally overlapping telephone companies would make it necessary for the consumer to pay for "two instruments, two lines into his home, two bills."[67] Kahn explains this paradox of increasing returns wedded to natural monopoly by noting that the quality of a telephone unit increases with the quantity supplied by the system; that is, there exists a positive externality (which will be internalized by the phone seller), which the quantity dimension generates for users of telephones. The more people there are to call or to receive calls from, the more valued any single instrument will be. So, Kahn argues, in quality-adjusted terms, the average cost of telephone service falls as quantity supplied increases.

This is true enough; increasing average cost in local telephone service will not invite a telephone company on every block (abstracting from the possibility of interconnection) because most consumers desire an instrument to call people on and off their block. Kahn implicitly makes the key assumption that such rival firms' services are identical to each other; hence no utility is gained from having one service rather than another. This assumption is much stronger than the typical product homogeneity idea; it says that a second firm's output is not only identical to the first, it is of zero marginal value. Thus we arrive at the pure duplication argument for natural monopoly.

If consumers in figure 1–1 are no better off with a second telephone system connected to their homes, then instead of firm 2's adding units along the quantity axis to industry output, it simply adds higher costs to units already provided by firm 1. Hence, it is apparent that two firms serving the same market are wasteful; entry by a second firm adds only to costs and not at all to the supply of goods. Clearly the key to deriving this wasteful-duplication argument is not that increasing returns are present but that the output of a second firm produces no increment of output.[68]

This awareness of the costliness of duplication has widely been cited as an argument in favor of allowing monopoly in natural monopoly markets and in favor of mandating (through exclusive public franchise awards) one seller in such markets. The first argument is straightforward. It argues for realizing the economical advantages in monopoly market structure where they arise. The second argument is an enigma, however: why should we need to prevent entry when the market's own verdict is that only one firm shall survive? How is it that political agents are quicker and surer in their estimations of monopoly market structure than capital markets? Why the waste of duplication is not internalized by private investors remains a question haunting this literature.

Before proceeding to discuss it, I will quickly bring up two related arguments. First there exists an argument concerning cream-skimming, which is relevant but will not be discussed here (see chapter 4 for a discussion of cream

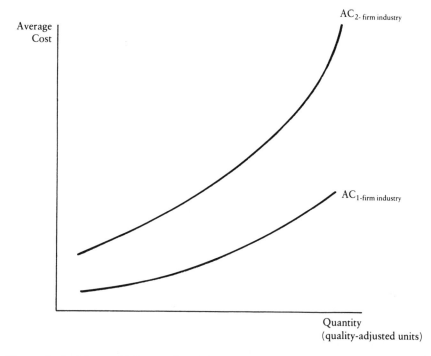

Figure 1–1. Natural Monopoly with Increasing Returns: Pure Duplication

skimming pertaining to duplicative entry into the cable television market). Second, the wasteful-duplication argument, which clearly does entail an externalities problem, is one embodied in the complaint that multiple public utility providers would cause excessive inconvenience by duplicating street disruptions, utility pole space, unsightly overground wires, administrative paperwork to use public rights-of-way, and so on.

Demsetz correctly identifies this problem as an externalities issue prompted by "the failure of communities to set a proper price on the use of these scarce resources."[69] Excessive disruption may occur under a sole supplier in the event these goods are priced below their social opportunity cost. The problem is not specific to a monopoly market structure. This, however, is not the classic, front-line wasteful-duplication argument that is a recurring theme in the natural monopoly literature. That argument deals with the waste of private investment, not public disruption. In tying this view to the declining costs theme, Burton Behling writes:

> The possibility of handling additional business without a proportional increase in cost applies particularly to the distribution of services such as elec-

tricity and gas, since any given equipment can bear an increasing load. . . .
Also, since the cost of distribution becomes greater as the distance between
the point of production and the place of use increases, density of service
without a compact area is desirable. Hence, competition is wasteful for the
reason that concentration or density of service is diminished when there is
rivalry between duplicate enterprises in the same area.[70]

The most intriguing aspect of the wasteful-duplication argument as presented by Behling is its longevity in the face of its obvious inconsistency. The
thought that private firms will frivolously enter a market already captured by
an efficient monopolist implies that these doomed entrants fail to internalize
the easily anticipated costs associated with entry. Moreover, the argument,
which generally ensues, for state-issued and, possibly but not inevitably,
regulated exclusive franchises (either exclusive in law or by virtue of the issuance of a sole, nominally nonexclusive, license) implies that legal authorities
are better able to spot this market phenomenon than capitalists. Yet since the
1880s, the issue has had staying power.

The mystery as to why a monopoly must be assured where monopoly is a
certainty thickens. Behling notes that creation of monopoly market structures
has been a clear intent and effect of the law: "It is plainly apparent that the
public utility commissions, in the exercise of their discretion under the law,
have contributed in several ways to the existing monopolistic structure of the
industries."[71] In a passage perhaps more revealing than Behling knew, he observes that "society committed itself almost unconditionally to monopoly in
the conduct of public utility enterprise . . . without assuring itself that the
benefits of monopoly would accrue to the public." This state of affairs does
not appear suspect to Behling but only naive.

Victor Goldberg, on the other hand, would view it, perhaps, as shrewd.
In his contemporary writings, in which he attempts to resuscitate a "plausible"
proconsumer rationale for public regulation, he argues that monopoly franchising and regulation may be economically efficient in that legal monopoly
will encourage investment in the nonsalvageble plant that is the sine qua non
of natural monopoly, perhaps to the optimal level.[72] So Goldberg argues just
the reverse of the historical position endorsing regulation and entry barriers,
which criticized a regime of laissez-faire as inviting overinvestment. Goldberg
writes:

> Two closely related criticisms of regulation are that it unduly restricts entry
> and that it discourages technological change by protecting existing producers
> from competing technologies. . . . Entry barriers do enable the producer to
> charge a higher price in the short run than he could without the barriers;
> likewise, the regulator who, for example, protects UHF station owners from
> CATV [cable television] competition is undoubtedly in error within this
> framework. But this short-run analysis ignores the importance of the pro-

tection of the right to serve. Would the firm have come into the market initially without some protection from competition? Would it have come in on terms as favorable as it did? What will be the rate of supply of innovations in the future if potential suppliers realize they will not be protected by the regulator? That is, if we view the protection afforded by the regulatory agent as *forward looking*, we can see it as a goad to innovation rather than a hindrance. Restrictions on entry by firms with identical or competing technologies provide a (possibly beneficial) haven from the Schumpeterian gale of creative destruction.[73]

Although the implication of Goldberg's view is precisely contrary to what earlier advocates of public utility regulation advanced as a defense, he has managed to put the argument in support of regulation on consumer welfare grounds into more subtle, contemporary terms. In so doing, he abandons Adams's increasing returns argument altogether. Goldberg builds on Demsetz's "debunking of the standard natural monopoly justification for regulation—namely the allegation there might be room for only one efficient producer." Hence, the traditional natural monopoly theory seems to have been eclipsed by a more modern view, which lists scale economies as a necessary but insufficient condition for the existence of monopoly power. This current approach does not equate market structure with market power. Moreover, it focuses much of its analysis on the sorts of institutions and transactions that a market may creatively employ to discipline firms toward the goal of a consumer welfare maximization.

As we abandon the now-obsolete scale economies theories of natural monopoly, it is best to reflect on the historical and somewhat hysterical progression of natural monopoly theory. The economists' analysis of the inefficiency of unregulated natural monopoly markets did not spring from a scientific or particularly scholarly research program but in response to "a growing clamor for more government."[74] Indeed many of the early natural monopoly writers had attacked the problem because of personal ideological agendas; their politics preceded their studies.

Yet at the same time, there existed a clear consensus among most economists that the rivalry of markets left unfettered by government was in the interests of consumers, workers, and investors alike. Thorelli mistakenly insists that "the problem of monopoly was relatively or entirely neglected by members of the orthodox school," a charge that simply reveals a latter-day economist's complete dissatisfaction in seeing the monopoly question dealt with in such responsive tones.[75] Such analysts as David A. Wells, Franklin H. Giddings, and John Bates Clark dealt with the questions in a manner highly sophisticated for their time (and, it may appear, for our own). Yet the views of the economics fraternity came quickly around; as political forces moved legal institutions, scholarly documentation of the social benefits of regulation of monopoly was not far behind.

Whereas the economic analysis once suggested monopoly franchising and public regulation as an antidote to overinvestment and wasteful duplication, it now recommends it as beneficial in guaranteeing specific capital investments where laissez-faire would lead to too little entry. The model may have entirely reversed its rationale, yet the policy recommendation lives on: political agency is the solution to the natural monopoly problem.

Notes

1. Alfred Kahn, *The Economics of Regulation* (New York: John Wiley and Sons, 1971), p. 118.
2. *Munn* v. *Illinois*, 94 U.S. 126 (1877).
3. Bernard Siegan, *Economic Liberties and the Constitution* (Chicago: University of Chicago Press, 1980), p. 180.
4. James R. Nelson, "The Pole of Competition in the Regulated Industries," *Antitrust Bulletin* 2 (January–April 1966):1–36.
5. George Stigler, "Economists and the Problem of Monopoly," *American Economic Review* 72 (May 1982):1.
6. John Stuart Mill, *Principles of Political Economy* (1848; reprint ed., New York: Augustus M. Kelley, 1961).
7. Franklin H. Giddings, "The Persistence of Competition," *Political Science Quarterly* 2 (March 1887):62.
8. Hans Thorelli, *The Federal Antitrust Policy* (Baltimore: Johns Hopkins Press, 1955), p. 110.
9. Giddings, "Persistence of Competition," p. 67.
10. Ibid., p. 76.
11. Ibid., p. 66.
12. David A. Wells, *Recent Economic Changes* (1889; reprint ed., New York: DaCapo Press, 1970), p. 111.
13. Ibid., p. 74.
14. Ibid., p. 75.
15. Ibid., pp. 75–76.
16. For this and following quotations in this paragraph, see John Bates Clark, "The Limits of Competition," *Political Science Quarterly* 2 (March 1887):58–59.
17. George Gunton, "The Economics and Social Aspect of Trusts," *Political Science Quarterly* 3 (Sept. 1888):385–408.
18. Ibid., p. 390.
19. Sanford Gordon, "The Significance of Public Opinion in the Passage of the Sherman Act" (Ph.D. diss., New York University, 1953), p. 178.
20. See Oliver E. Williamson, "Economies as an Antitrust Defense: The Welfare Trade-Offs," *American Economic Review* 58 (1968), and Robert H. Bork, "Legislative Intent and the Policy of the Sherman Act," *Journal of Law and Economics* 9 (October 1966):7–48.
21. Gordon, "Significance of Public Opinion," p. 176.
22. Ibid.
23. Thorelli, *Federal Antitrust Policy*, p. 116.

24. The notion of contestability has emerged recently in the industrial organization literature as a theoretical advance over the structure-conduct-performance paradigm. Whereas the latter takes concentrated industry structure per se to prompt output-restricting behavior, the contestability analysis focuses on the level of entry and exit costs necessary to compete in any given concentrated industry. The airline industry is singled out as a market with concentrated supply and high fixed (entry) costs but of competitive (or contestable) structure due to low exit costs (the easy transferability of airline resources into alternative markets). This theoretical insight is of significance in economic analysis of contestable markets but has not had an effect on the analysis of markets wherein fixed costs are nonsalvageable (exit costs are high); this is the criterion that currently defines the public utility market.

25. Thorelli, *Federal Antitrust Policy*, p. 119.

26. Ibid., p. 112.

27. William Sharkey, *The Theory of Natural Monopoly* (New York: Cambridge University Press, 1982), pp. 13–14.

28. Stigler, "Economists and the Problem of Monopoly," p. 3.

29. For this and following quotations in this paragraph, see Richard T. Ely, "The Growth of Corporations," *Harper's* (June 1887):71–79. At times, Ely appears a critic not of monopoly but of population expansion; he laments that "the evolution of the race has reached the point where the supremacy of the individual is neither needed nor desired," using the increasing propensity of scholars to form such organizations as the American Historical Association, the Modern Language Association, and the American Economic Association as illustrations.

30. Cited by Thorelli, *Federal Antitrust Policy*, p. 118.

31. Ibid., p. 119. Thorelli adds, "A sign of the times was the fact that among the numerous prominent Social Gospelers who joined the association in its first years were several ministers, including Lyman Abbot and Washington Gladdens" (p. 120).

32. Ely, "Growth of Corporations," p. 75.

33. Richard Ely, "The Future of Corporations," *Harper's* (July 1887):260. Edward Lowry argues that while John Stuart Mill, Thomas Ferrer, and Henry C. Adams developed the basic theory underlying the natural monopoly concept, it "was Richard T. Ely . . . who labeled and widely disseminated this concept." Lowry, "Justification for Regulation: The Case for Natural Monopoly," *Public Utilities Fortnightly*, November 8, 1973, p. 19. While Mill had actually been the one to label the concept (see his *Principles*, p. 410), we trust Lowry's judgment on the latter assertion.

34. Ely, "Future of Corporations," p. 261.

35. Ibid., p. 265.

36. Edwin Chadwick, "Results of Different Principles of Legislation and Administration of Europe; of Competition for the Field, as Compared with Competition Within the Field of Service," *Royal Statistical Society Journal* 22 (1859).

37. That this tendency among economists is rapidly changing of late, to the great frustration of the antitrust bar, is nicely illustrated in Suzanne Weaver, "Antitrust Division Department," in *The Politics of Regulation*, ed. James Q. Wilson (New York: Basic Books, 1980).

38. Ford and GM, for instance, could be compared in a "characteristics space" for, say, "transportation units," but declining average costs would not necessarily give one firm a monopoly over this market so long as consumers evaluated these units

heterogeneously. The ambiguity for consumers of any scale constructed in such a manner makes a declining average-cost curve necessary but insufficient criterion for the presence of natural monopoly.

39. On this, the overwhelmingly strong assumptions of the model of perfect competition have only succeeded in obscuring. See F.A. Hayek, "The Meaning of Competition," in Hayek, *Individualism and Economic Order* (Chicago: Henry Regnery, 1948); Joseph Schumpeter, *Capitalism, Socialism, and Democracy* (New York: Harper and Row, 1942); and Paul McNulty, "Economic Theory and the Meaning of Competition," *Quarterly Journal of Economics* 82 (1968), reprinted in *The Competitive Economy: Selected Readings*, ed. Yale Brozen (Morristown, N.J.: General Learning Press, 1975).

40. Ely, "Future of Corporations," p. 261.

41. This term is taken from Richard Posner, "Natural Monopoly and Its Regulation," *Stanford Law Review* 21 (1969):548.

42. This and the following categories are described by Henry Carter Adams, *Relation of the State to Industrial Action and Economics and Jurisprudence* (1887; reprint, ed., New York: Columbia University Press, 1954), pp. 105, 107, 109.

43. Ibid., p. 103.

44. Ibid., p. 104.

45. The six reasons cited from Henry Carter Adams, *Relation of the State to Industrial Action and Economics and Jurisprudence* (two essays), Columbia Bicentennial Editions and Studies (New York: Columbia University Press, 1954), pp. 110, 111, 112–113, 107, and 114.

46. Of course, as a national firm expands its local retail outlets, to continue with the generic example, costs of coordinating these disparate enterprises may increase, thus offsetting, in part or in whole, these scale economies. Still, the weakness of Adams's assertion is in entirely neglecting such considerations. His approach theoretically, and in a policy sense, fails to consider the generality throughout all industries of this trade-off between scale economies and the costliness of centralized monitoring. Indeed the national retailer would appear more monopolistic than the local power supplier, which owns just one generating station.

47. Adams, *Relation of the State*, p. 118.

48. Sharkey, *Theory of Natural Monopoly*, p. 27.

49. See Hayek, "Meaning of Competition," and Israel Kirzner, *Competition and Entrepreneurship* (Chicago: University of Chicago Press, 1973).

50. Schumpeter, *Capitalism, Socialism, and Democracy*.

51. See Hayek, "Meaning of Competition," and McNulty, "Economic Theory and the Meaning of Competition."

52. See Douglas Webbink, "Should Cable TV Be Regulated as a Public Utility?" *Public Utilities Fortnightly* (June 22, 1973), p. 34.

53. For this and other quotations in this paragraph, see Arthur Hadley, "Private Monopolies and Public Rights," *Quarterly Journal of Economics* 1 (October 1886): 28–44.

54. James Bonbright, *Principles of Public Utility Rates* (New York: Columbia University Press, 1961), pp. 14–15.

55. F.M. Scherer, *Industrial Market Structure and Economic Performance* (Chicago: Rand McNally, 1980), p. 90.

56. See Ronald Coase's famous 1937 article, "The Nature of the Firm," *Economica* 4 (November 1937), F.A. Hayek's insightful "The Use of Knowledge in Society" *American Economic Review* 25 (September 1945), and Oliver Williamson, *Markets and Hierarchies* (New York: Free Press, 1975).

57. Williamson, *Markets and Hierarchies*.

58. "The term 'plant subadditivity' is used to describe subadditivity that ensues from the purely technical aspects of production." See Sharkey, *Theory of Natural Monopoly*, p. 57.

59. Ibid., p. 54.

60. General Telephone is considered a monopolist, whereas General Motors is not, not because GTE faces fewer U.S. competitors or serves greater numbers of customers as a proportion of its product market but because the customers it does serve are not interspersed spatially with customers of rival telephone companies, the way Ford owners live next door to Chevy buyers.

61. Cited by Sharkey, *Theory of Natural Monopoly*, p. 17.

62. Alfred Kahn, *The Economics of Regulation* (New York: John Wiley, 1971), 2:118.

63. Ibid., pp. 118–119.

64. See Thomas Hazlett, "Three Essays on Monopoly" (Ph.D. diss., University of California, Los Angeles, 1984), chap. 3, p. 41, for further discussion of this issue.

65. Kahn, *Economics of Regulation*, p. 119.

66. Ibid., p. 123.

67. Ibid.

68. We see this, correctly, as similar to the classic public good case; however, whereas a public good has $MC = 0$, the purely duplicative natural monopoly is distinguished by $MP = 0$ for firms $(2 - n)$. Analogous to the public good, which estimates its social value by a vertical summation over the quantity of output supplied, the duplicative natural monopoly derives its social cost by vertically summing the cost curves over the output supplied by the first supplier. Conversely, however, the public good problem is one of underinvestment; the duplicative natural monopoly is claimed to be one of overinvestment.

69. Harold Demsetz, "Why Regulate Utilities?" *Journal of Law and Economics* 11 (April 1968):62.

70. Burton Behling, *Competition and Monopoly in Public Utility Industries* (Urbana: University of Illinois Press, 1938), p. 30.

71. For this and following quotations, see, ibid., pp. 72, 73.

72. For the precise assumptions necessary, but not sufficient, to achieve optimality, see Robert Ekelund and Richard Higgins, "Capital Fixity, Innovations, and Long-term Contracting: An Intertemporal Economic Theory of Regulation," *American Economic Review* 72 (March 1982).

73. Victor Goldberg, "Regulation and Administered Contracts," *Bell Journal of Economics* 7 (Autumn 1976):434–435. Copyright 1976, The Rand Corporation. Reprinted with permission from *The Bell Journal of Economics*.

74. Adams, *Relation of the State to Industrial Action*, p. 64.

75. Thorelli, *Federal Antitrust Policy*, p. 112.

2
Public Utility Rate-Of-Return Regulation: Can It Ever Protect Customers?

Nina W. Cornell
Douglas W. Webbink

W hen should an industry be subject to classical public utility regulation—that is, the setting of an allowable rate of return on an approved rate base, with controls on price and entry and exit? Many people argue that this form of regulation should be imposed whenever an industry offers some vital service to the public but has monopoly power over its customers. But our answer is "never." Our reason is simple: this form of regulation, widely viewed as protecting the public from abuse of monopoly power, in fact never has done so, almost never could, and never will. Indeed, over the long run, use of public utility regulation may well hurt the public more than if virtually all of the industries to which it has been applied had been totally unregulated.

Yet the perception lags far behind the reality of failure. Interstate telephone, natural gas, electrical power, and some railroad shipments still are subject to federal public utility regulation. In some states or at the local level, these same industries plus others, such as water, cable television, and taxi companies, also are subject to public utility regulation. And even as some industries—airlines, railroads, and interstate telephone, for example—are being wholly or partly freed from such regulation, there are calls for its retention or wider application to others, particularly to the natural gas industry and to cable television.[1]

It continues to be relevant to examine why public utility regulation not only fails to protect consumers from abuse of monopoly power but has actually

This chapter is an updated, expanded version of Nina W. Cornell, "Rate-of-Return Regulation: Protecting Whom from What?" *Regulation* (November–December 1980):36–41, 49. Although we often use examples from the telephone industry because of previous work at the Federal Communications Commission, we believe that our conclusions have much broader applicability. We wish to thank Michael D. Pelcovits and Steven R. Brenner for a number of helpful suggestions.

quite the opposite effect: it tends to protect firms that are not natural monopolies from competition and in the process harms consumers.

We are not the first to point out the failings of public utility regulation.[2] If ever there is to be an end to it, however, more must be said than simply that its costs outweigh its benefits. Monopoly exists and is likely to be abused, and we believe that society is right in trying to prevent that abuse. But public utility regulation is not the way.

Model of Public Utility Regulation

Rate-of-return regulation is supposed to ensure that public utility prices do not exceed costs; that is, it is supposed to act as a check or constraint on the expected behavior of an unregulated monopolist. Indeed the railroads' practice in the late nineteenth century of charging higher per-mile rates for short hauls than for long hauls (where there were competing railroad routes) led to the first major federal public utility regulation.[3]

If a firm were truly a natural monopoly, it would have no actual competitors and thus face only limited pressure from potential entrants to charge customers the lowest cost for its output, even in the absence of regulation.[4] A natural monopoly is an industry in which one firm is able to produce all the output demanded in a given market—either a single output or a bundle of related outputs—at less cost than if several firms together produced the same total quantity of output.[5] Usually industries thought to represent natural monopoly situations tend to be quite capital intensive.[6] (Of course, some industries such as taxicabs that are clearly not natural monopolies have also been subject to public utility regulation.)

Many of the industries, such as railroads, that have been subjected to public utility regulation are very capital intensive. Once a firm has installed plant and equipment, that investment may deter other firms from entering the market easily, and thus the first entrant has some degree of market power. In addition, the more that customers view the service as indispensable—something they must have even if it is very expensive, such as telephone service—the higher the monopolist can raise price above cost. These characteristics are stated here in overly simple form and not as they arise in individual cases, but they fit the generally held notion of the type of industry that ought to be regulated as a public utility.[7]

The public utility regulatory process involves setting an allowable rate of return on a predetermined investment or rate base.[8] The regulator first must determine an appropriate rate of return: should the utility earn 9, 10, or 11 percent on its investments? Then the regulator must determine how much output will be demanded—for example, how many gallons of water per person per day will be consumed—and the precise costs of producing that amount of output. With these three pieces of information, the regulator can determine the revenue that the firm should be allowed to earn and the price per unit of output that the firm should charge.

Price controls are supposed to serve two functions. One function is to ensure that the price is such that the firm earns no more than the allowable rate of return. Hence the first kind of price control is intended to put a ceiling on prices. The second is intended to prevent price discrimination. In order to attempt to prevent price discrimination, regulatory agencies may put ceilings on some prices and floors on other prices.[9]

Additionally regulatory agencies impose entry and exit controls. Entry controls are also supposed to serve two purposes. One is to prevent the monopoly from overinvesting and then charging the ratepayers for that overage. Thus, for example, interstate telephone companies must get permission before adding to their transmission facilities, and the additional facilities have to be justified by service and demand projections. Entry controls are also justified as a way to ensure that monopolists (or just a few firms) provide services to everyone equally, if necessary by protecting high profits from one service in order to provide a source of funds for the more costly ones. Much has been made, for example, of the need to block entry into trucking and airlines in order to maintain service to small towns by existing firms.[10] More recently, a whole new body of economic literature was developed that implied that regulatory bodies should limit entry into the telephone industry so that the monopolist could take advantage of economies-of-scope cost savings that may result from joint production of a number of different outputs.[11]

Hand in hand with entry controls go exit controls. If a regulated monopoly firm provides one or many services that consumers believe to be essential, then one of the quid pro quos for a monopoly franchise is that the monopolist not be able to abandon unprofitable service at will. Indeed the history of regulation is full of instances in which railroads, airlines, Western Union, and even American Telephone and Telegraph (AT&T) were now allowed to abandon unprofitable services when they wished to do so.[12] Of course, as long as a regulated monopolist is required to provide any service that is truly unprofitable, some other consumer or group of consumers will end up paying more to make up the loss.

The public utility regulatory model might work if four key assumptions were correct, all based on the notion that the world is static:

1. The firm produces only a single kind of output or service that can be uniquely defined.
2. Demand never changes significantly; consumers do not change in number, income levels, or tastes and preferences and they demand the same amount of output year after year.

3. The method of providing that amount of output—the technology—never changes.
4. The firm will cooperate with the regulatory agency.

If the first three conditions are met, it is possible that an industry could now be and remain a natural monopoly. Under those circumstances, the single firm in that industry might be run efficiently under public utility regulation. But that is possible only if the regulatory agency can get the necessary information. That information, however, can come only from one source, the regulated firm itself, and only after that firm has begun operations and made at least a first approximation at getting to the proper size. Thus, the importance of the fourth assumption: the firm has to cooperate with the regulatory agency.

These four key assumptions fit virtually no industries, except perhaps water distribution. Most industries, and perhaps particularly most industries to which the model has been applied, violate all four. Under these conditions, trying to perform the chores demanded of the regulator is mind boggling. Even if demand and technology were unchanging, just consider any of the industries that is currently regulated and list all the inputs that have to be costed. The system of accounts necessary to give that cost information is very large indeed, even if the firm were eager to establish its accounts in the exact way the regulator wanted.[13] In today's dynamic world, however, where both demand and technology change, sometimes quite rapidly, and where the regulated firms face many incentives to try to evade or circumvent effective regulation, the possibility of obtaining the required data in usable form all but disappears.

Problems with the Model: Dynamic Reality

Changing Demand

Consumer demand changes, and, as it does, the problem of calculating costs becomes enormous. Each time demand changes, all costs have to be recalculated because, for an industry to be a natural monopoly, the cost per unit cannot be constant without regard to the amount supplied. Rather, the unit cost must decline as the size of plant is increased over some range of output levels. The regulatory agency must get information on cost per unit, but it is not estimating a single cost per unit that it can use over and over again to make prescriptions. Instead it has to get the cost per unit when output is 100 units, when it is 101 units, 102, and so on.

If the agency can accurately estimate costs at output levels other than the firm's present one, the job is still only half done. In order to fix the proper rates that would result in the allowable rate of return for the next year, the agency has to predict future demand; that is, it must be able to predict that demand will be such that if the firm produces x units of output at predicted cost y and sells them at predicted price z, the firm will earn its allowable rate of return and no more.

This kind of prediction is at best extremely difficult; it requires predicting how changes in price will change the demand for output. Once again the regulator can get the relevant data on costs associated with price changes only from the regulated firm. And because the firm must supply a wide variety of different cost estimates that depend on multiple contingencies, it is much tougher, if not impossible, to verify the accuracy of the data.

No matter how well the regulated firm projects demand, its estimates may turn out to be inaccurate. For example, when airline deregulation expanded competition and lowered air fares a few years ago, passengers increased more than the airlines had expected.[14] Similarly, when the Federal Communications Commission (FCC) required AT&T to lower interstate evening and weekend telephone rates in the 1960s, demand grew more rapidly than expected. Because both the passenger and telephone call increases were met by making better use of equipment during relatively slack periods, increased usage added more to revenues than to costs—more so than had been expected—and thus raised the actual rate of return earned.

Finally, as demand grows—assuming no change in technology and no change in costs of inputs—the quantity demanded at some point will outrun the amount a single supplier can produce at least cost. Thus we will no longer be in the presence of a natural monopoly.

Changing Technology

All of these problems are minor compared to those the regulator faces once we relax the assumption that technology never changes. Firms do not tear out a whole operating plant and replace it with the latest version. Instead they introduce change incrementally. AT&T, for example, has been installing electronic switches (which make possible new services such as call forwarding) in its local exchanges since the mid-1960s and hoped to have all traffic on digital equipment by the end of this century. The type of switching equipment being installed, moreover, has changed significantly over these years. This process of gradual substitution results in a very large number of choices of technologies that the firm may employ. The regulators must match each of these choices to all possible levels of demand if they are to ensure that the profits earned are equivalent or even close to the outcomes of competitive markets.

With data problems of these magnitudes, to derive some prices to play with is patently impossible, and we have not even begun to consider the problem of ensuring that the costs are efficient ones and not subject to waste.

Furthermore, whatever data the agency does get will be rapidly out of date and thus of little value for predicting the future.

Production of Multiple Outputs or Services

The early versions of the traditional public utility regulation model also assumed that the regulated firm produced only a single kind of output or service so that the amount of output and, hence, the cost and revenue per unit of output could be measured along a single dimension. In fact, almost all regulated utilities produce multiple outputs, and the costs of producing each of those outputs should be estimated separately. Sometimes those outputs are very distinct—such as telephone instruments and telephone service—while other times they are essentially the same service priced differently—message toll service (MTS) and wide-area toll service (WATS), both of which use the same plant and equipment in virtually the same way. The job of the utility regulator is to check the utility's estimates of the amount produced of these different offerings and then check the estimates of the costs of producing the predicted quantity of each of those outputs.[15] If, given changing demand and technology, costing just one service is extremely difficult, having to cost a number of services magnifies the problem.[16]

Opposite Goals of Regulated Firms and Regulators

Firms are in business to make as large profits as possible. Regulators are supposed to prevent them from earning as much as the market would allow. The regulators can succeed only if they get the right information from the firms. Obviously, however, firms are not anxious to provide all the information the regulators may need. Instead, knowing it has to give some information to the regulators, the regulated firm has a strong incentive to bias or manipulate the information it provides to further its own internal goals. Firms in all the regulated industries mentioned previously in this chapter operate in unregulated markets and face competition of varying degrees from alternative sources or modes. One major way firms can both evade regulation and increase total profits is to shift accounting costs from unregulated to regulated services and to shift accounting revenues from regulated to unregulated services. The firm has great freedom to make such shifts of costs by the way it allocates the costs of plant used in both regulated and unregulated markets. Moreover, the regulated firm is likely to choose the plant and equipment that it employs based not only on what, by itself in the absence of regulation, would be the least-cost technology but also on whether the choice of one technology over another will make it easier to evade regulation or to block competition.

Such manipulations do not give regulators the information they need even to begin to do the job expected of them. Moreover, if the regulator is to do the job, the cost information has to be developed in a way that enables the agency to prevent wasteful use of inputs. Thus, the regulatory agency must ask "what if" questions: what if the firm's plant were twice as large, or only half as large, or if it used a different mix of labor and capital. And yet such questions offer the regulated firm even more opportunities to manipulate data in ways that support its own policy positions.

Meanwhile the regulator has no independent source of cost data. It is especially ironic that many people who believe that public utility regulation is necessary to protect consumers from the abuses of an unfettered monopolist eagerly accept without verification the cost and demand projections of such a firm when it becomes regulated.

Actual Effects of Rate-of-Return Regulation

As the unrealistic assumptions are replaced by actual conditions, it becomes apparent why public utility regulation never could have held monopoly profits to or even near the competitive level. The amazing point is that anyone ever expected it to. Those who expected public utility regulation to work forgot or ignored the ability of business people to manipulate the investments they make, the services they produce, the prices they charge, and the accounting data they provide in order to evade the intention of the regulations imposed on them.[17] If the only outcome of applying an unworkable model to the control of monopoly were that monopoly power went uncurbed, however, little would be lost except illusions. Unfortunately the actual effects are not so benign.

First, rate base rate-of-return regulation results in static inefficiencies, as has been shown in a large and ever-growing economic literature. Firms have been shown to overinvest by buying more expensive capital equipment than would unregulated firms, by building equipment of higher reliability than consumers would choose if given the choice, and by substituting capital for labor.[18] In addition, the direct administrative costs of the regulatory process itself to both regulated firms and taxpayers are quite significant.[19] Hence, even before considering all the dynamic costs imposed by regulation, it is likely to be true that the static costs of public utility regulation often outweigh the benefits.

More important, however, rate-of-return regulation, by impeding or blocking entry and innovation, has maintained some industries as monopolies and prevented the search for truly effective alternative means to control monopoly power long after competition in the provision of at least some services was possible. These costs are the hardest to measure because they involve the valuation of what did not happen—goods and services not made available to consumers.

Rate-of-return regulation with price and entry controls has the effect of slowing product innovation and technological change by regulated firms, by firms that might want to enter the market, using a better idea to make the same output, and by firms that might develop new products to serve the same basic functions. Such regulation also has a way of expanding from one service or industry to other alternative competing services or industries.

Technology

Regulated firms deploy new technology more slowly than unregulated firms. In the absence of competition, neither a regulated firm nor the regulatory agency has any reason to depreciate and replace any faster than physically necessary the plant and equipment that in a competitive industry would be economically obsolete long before it wears out. In many regulated industries, the physical life of much equipment is very long, often between twenty and fifty years or more.[20] Moreover, unlike in an unregulated industry, rate-of-return regulation means that prices charged by the regulated firm are directly affected by the rate of depreciation it chooses to take. The failure to replace equipment before the end of its physical life benefits society only if no cheaper means of accomplishing the same purpose has been found—that is, if there does not exist some new technique that can perform at sufficiently lower cost to pay back the cost of removing the old equipment before its physical life is over. The cost that must be paid back, however, depends on the rate of depreciation the firm has chosen.

The effects of long depreciation periods can be illustrated in telephone switching equipment. Central office telephone panel switches were the first automatic switches developed to replace operators in larger cities in the 1920s. A few panel switches were still in use in the mid-1970s, fifty years later. In the same period, at least three new generations of switching equipment, including all digital switches, had been developed. Each of these new generations of technology permitted more rapid connections among telephones connected to the same switch or an increase in the number of connections a single switch could handle, as well as the ability to perform new functions at much lower cost and with much simplified maintenance. Yet from the 1920s to the 1970s, telephones connected to panel switches never used any of these newer technologies.

If a regulated firm uses a very long depreciation period and retains the old equipment even when new, improved equipment becomes available, its customers may have to pay more than the lowest possible costs of providing a given output. If the firm in these circumstances faces no pressure to install the new, improved, and lower-cost equipment while writing off the undepreciated part of the old, it will not do so, and its customers will pay for the technological lag.

This situation may well be occurring now with local telephone service. Many local telephone companies are requesting and receiving from state regulatory agencies substantial increases in local rates. Many of those companies are claiming that their costs are rising because of increasing competition in telephone service and Judge Harold Greene's acceptance of divestiture of the local operating companies from AT&T. In fact, however, local telephone companies may be asking for rate increases because they have a great deal of undepreciated and out-of-date, if not obsolete, plant that should have been depreciated long ago.[21] In order to depreciate that plant faster while earning the same allowed rate of return, they must raise rates. The decision to depreciate the plant so slowly in the face of increasing availability of new technologies represented a poor business judgment (although an understandable one for a regulated firm). A competitive firm that had underdepreciated and obsolete assets would have to take a loss to be absorbed by its stockholders. In the absence of protected monopoly status and regulation, local telephone companies would have to do the same.[22]

If old equipment cannot provide new services that new equipment makes possible, the loss to customers becomes much larger and harder to measure besides. Not only are customers potentially paying more than the minimum cost for the output they do receive, but they also cannot receive outputs that are technically possible and for which they might be willing to pay.

Telephone switching equipment illustrates this cost also. Before the advent of switches using digital technology, each new generation of switches offered mainly speedier connections or much simplified maintenance, both of which lower the costs of interconnecting telephones. With the use of digital technology, however, more than just speed and cost economies are possible. Now the switch can be made smart—that is, it can offer forwarding services, call waiting, and international direct dialing, among other services. If the divested operating companies adhere to AT&T's plan to convert all local exchanges to digital switching equipment only by about the turn of the century, then the first time some customers will be able to buy such services will be more than twenty-five years after the relevant technology was developed.

Delay in the deployment of new technologies is not the only barrier to innovation imposed by rate-of-return regulation. Insofar as a regulatory agency does succeed in holding down the rate of return to normal levels, it takes away some of the incentive for the regulated firm to engage in high-risk research and development. Such activities pay off only if a high rate of return can be earned on the successful inventions.

Innovation

Innovation by firms outside the industry is hindered. Rate-of-return regulation slows innovation by firms not in the industry that might have discovered a better means of providing the regulated output. Any firm wanting to offer such service legally usually must apply to the regulatory agency for permission to enter. In making application, the firm has to reveal much of the detail about its new idea, thus providing valuable information to those already in the industry. Frequently the existing firms can block the would-be entrant by adopting the proposed innovation first and by using legal procedures to slow or prevent entry by any potential competitor.[23]

An example occurred in the telephone industry in the 1950s. The telephone companies planned to expand the long-distance network mainly by the use of cable, which would have meant substantially higher long-distance rates. In response, the television networks considered building their own interconnections using much less expensive microwave technology, which had been developed by the military during World War II. The telephone companies promptly decided that they should use microwave technology and asked the FCC to bar anyone other than telephone companies from building such networks. The commission initially agreed with the telephone companies; subsequently it allowed private microwave systems as well.[24]

Thus, because of the regulatory process, potential new firms may never get into the industry at all and almost certainly cannot inject ideas into the market before existing firms learn of them and even adopt them. It is scarcely surprising, therefore, that few firms are willing to innovate in regulated areas unless these innovations are likely to be so massively profitable that they still would pay off even if the original innovating firm were not first into the market.

Predatory Behavior

Regulated firms have incentives to behave in a predatory manner in unregulated, competitive markets. Firms whose monopoly prices are restrained by regulation can increase their profits by entering competitive markets, shifting costs from those competitive markets to the monopoly ones while shifting revenues the other way. Such shifting allows the regulated firm to ask for and receive additional revenue from its monopoly markets without appearing to earn more than its allowed rate of return.

As regulated firms have become bigger factors in unregulated, competitive markets, competitors have begun to raise a new kind of price discrimination issue. The fear in the past was that some prices would be set far above costs where monopoly power was particularly strong; now the fear is that a monopoly firm may price services in competitive markets far below costs and make up the loss from its remaining monopoly markets. This concern is evident in the regulatory activity at the FCC over the past ten years. During this period, much of the FCC's attention has been on Computer II (determining and defining the delineation between regulated and nonregulated services) and costing dockets, which have focused on methods for preventing such predatory cross-subsidies. Although some economists have argued that predatory pricing is not a profitable strategy for an unregulated oligopolist, clearly predatory pricing can be profitable for a regulated firm.[25] Such predatory cross-subsidy behavior is exceedingly hard to detect and nearly impossible to prevent.[26] Among the methods considered to prevent predatory pricing has been the Computer II requirement to establish separate subsidiaries and keep separate books of account for the unregulated competitive and regulated monopoly services.[27] The establishment of separate subsidiaries and accounting rules, however, does not prevent cross-subsidies and predatory behavior; it only makes such behavior easier to detect.[28]

If such predatory behavior is successful, the firm could not only evade regulatory constraints in the regulated market but also could monopolize the previously unregulated market. Because all of the regulated firm's various activities, regulated and unregulated, use in common at least some of the same inputs—at a minimum, the firm's overhead—the firm may be able to cover common costs in the price of the regulated output and gain immediate advantage in the previously unregulated sphere. Indeed regulated firms may purposely choose technologies (such as electronic switches) that make it difficult to separate out the costs of regulated and unregulated services and hence enable the firms to manipulate the data more easily. Thus more regulation is needed to block unwanted cross-subsidies. Regulation tends to creep from one service to other substitute services.

Intermodal Competition

Intermodal competition that would erode the monopoly power is hampered. Entirely aside from the desire of a specific regulated firm to provide unregulated services to evade regulation, the regulatory process itself encourages further regulatory creep.[29] As similar services are discovered or instituted, they too become subject to regulation. In the process, regulation blocks the very activities that could curb monopoly power at its source—the market. The spread of regulation from railroads to trucking and barges is an outstanding example of such regulatory creep.

The most certain way to reduce the potential for abuse of monopoly power, particularly in the face of inelastic demand, is actively to encourage the search for substitutes. This means encouraging innovation. Innovation is most likely to be encouraged if there are alternative sources of supply—that is, if there is lively competition. Compare, for example, the degree of change since World War II in the telephone instrument, on the one hand, and the desk calculator on the other. The contrast is all the more striking because roughly the same technology could have been used to upgrade both products.

Demand for any service tends to be inelastic in the absence of substitutes that can serve the same or almost the same function and that provide users with a choice. Gasoline provides a good example. As long as all of us have cars, we must have a liquid fuel that does not destroy internal combustion or diesel engines. There are few substitutes for gasoline or diesel fuel. Moreover, because alternative modes of transportation are so poorly developed, particularly for short-haul movement of people, not only is there no alternative choice of fuel but also no alternative mode of transportation for many people. It is not surprising therefore that demand for gasoline is relatively inelastic. (The conventional wisdom, now proved erroneous, had been that demand for gasoline was totally inelastic. During the upheavals in the oil market, very high gasoline prices in fact reduced consumption as consumers switched to smaller cars that used less gasoline per mile and also drove fewer miles.)

Innovation in ways to supply a high-priced product will take place unless it is curbed by regulation; so also innovation to find close substitute products that might curb the monopoly power will take place unless the regulatory agency prevents it. Unfortunately, regulation often curbs both kinds of innovation.

Alternative Approaches to Curbing Monopoly Power

Traditional rate-of-return regulation does not work, creates distinctly bad side effects, and takes on the status of a self-fulfilling prophesy. There is no possibility of keeping profits at the competitive level and, worse, two of monopolies' major counteracting forces, competition and innovation, have in effect been nullified. Indeed one of the strangest things about the choice of rate-of-return regulation to cope with monopoly power is that it is equivalent to saying, "Because in an unfettered market you might exercise or you have in fact exercised your monopoly power, we're going to give it to you in perpetuity. In addition, we will let you control the relevant information so we cannot tell whether you are abusing your monopoly power."

Monopoly power does exist and can be abused. If governmental action is going to be taken against it, ways must be found to produce the desired output competitively and to produce alternative outputs that meet the same basic need. In brief, what is called for are government actions that end the monopoly but do no more than that, leaving market forces free to act in all other normal ways. There may not be any one universally available solution, but a few examples suggest routes to follow in at least some cases.

Test Whether a Regulated Industry Is a Natural Monopoly

In many industries where there is heavy investment in physical transmission facilities or networks, generally it has been assumed that the industry is a natural monopoly. The usual examples include electricity distribution, local telephone exchange, cable television, water and natural gas distribution, and railroads. In these examples people usually make commonsense reference to the cost of digging up streets repeatedly, stringing duplicate wires, or laying duplicate tracks. Whenever a city or state franchises only a single provider of such a service, however, it guarantees that there will be monopoly supply, regardless of whether economies of scale or scope exist, at least until other competing modes of supply are developed.[30]

An alternative to granting an exclusive franchise is to franchise two or more competing companies but to make each responsible for repairing any damage it may do to streets and private property. Only by allowing competition and observing what happens is it possible to determine the extent to which any industry is really a natural monopoly, even in the short-run static sense.[31] This is also a method for gaining objective information about the underlying costs of operating in a market without asking the single regulated firm to provide those data.

A variation on the theme of allowing competition in the provision of services that appear to be natural monopolies is to deregulate and allow competition in any parts of an industry where the possibility of competition appears feasible. Thus, the FCC deregulated telephone instruments in its Computer II decision and has begun deregulation of inside wiring (though not all issues have been decided).[32] Similarly much has been written in recent years about deregulating electricity generation (as opposed to electricity distribution), and there is a continuing debate over fully deregulating old as well as new natural gas production (while continuing to regulate natural gas distribution).[33]

The process of deregulating a previously regulated industry is not simple. In the transition period there will be many gainers and losers. The issue of whether and, if so, how losers should be compensated is a complex economic and political issue. Questions such as how assets should be valued and transferred and how to prevent cross-subsidies and predatory behavior by firms operating in both sectors after deregulation are not trivial.[34]

One of the strongest arguments against imposing public utility regulation in the first place is the difficulty of the transition process to deregulation later. When utilities have sunk large capital investments in physical plant, whether for telephone switches and wires, railroad lines, or nuclear reactors, that are no longer justified, the question of who should absorb the costs of writing off that equipment becomes important and difficult to answer. If utility regulation law does not allow stockholders to bear the loss, ratepayers will have to absorb it. The hope of avoiding paying the price to cover those costs may be sufficiently strong that it may make it politically impossible ever to deregulate that industry fully.

Make Interconnection Mandatory

When society deals with firms engaged in providing network services—railroads, telephones, electric utilities, and the like—structuring the market with a few carefully drawn rules could be much more effective than applying rate-of-return regulation. One such rule should be mandatory interconnection of all those locations in the area where multiple lines come together; examples are requiring all railroads entering a city to transfer cars to any other railroad at all other railway terminals in the city or requiring all local telephone exchange switches to pass message traffic to all other local exchange switches.[35]

Encourage Intermodal Competition

Not only competition within the existing industry but also competition among similar industries offers consumers better protection from monopoly power than rate-of-return regulation. In the early days of railroads, for example, more public attention to the state of the highways might have generated earlier and better alternatives to the railroads for short hauls. Ultimately the advent of trucks provided precisely that kind of competition, and then they were regulated also.

Similar competitive possibilities are arising today in communications. Competition to traditional local telephone companies that interconnect telephone by wire could come from wireless systems—two-way radios that operate on new frequencies—or systems that combine radio and wire links. A few relatively modest changes in regulatory restrictions on the use of existing radio systems could open the way to such competition. Similarly new video technologies such as cassettes and discs, as well as more relaxed rules on low-power television and multipoint distribution service stations, could be more effective antimonopoly techniques than state or local rate regulation of cable television systems. Again, this is a far better way to test whether a firm is operating efficiently than to have it provide data that it can manipulate for its own benefit.

Apply Antitrust Restrictions

When a monopoly offers a multiplicity of closely related services, its power to abuse can be held in check by antitrust restrictions against tie-ins and refusals to deal. For example, government could require that, insofar as a firm is a monopoly, its various services be offered individually and be subject to resale. These two techniques—unbundling (requiring, for example, that the telephone service and the telephone set be offered separately) and resale (allowing the customer to share purchase with other users and to charge for that sharing)—would impose pressures to keep charges close to costs and induce competitive offerings of at least some services.[36]

Conclusions

Each of these four suggested alternatives to traditional utility regulation relies on providing alternatives to a single regulated monopoly firm or modifies some of the incentives of such a monopoly firm. None relies on the willingness of the monopoly firm to provide the information necessary to restrain its behavior. Hence, all seem far more practical than traditional public utility regulation, which inevitably relies on the existence of such information in order to work.

Society does have techniques available for reducing monopoly power. These alternatives all require governmental intervention in markets. Some even involve regulation—but not rate-of-return regulation. No consumer has yet been protected from abuses of monopoly power or ever will be. It is both a snare and a delusion—and an unacceptable fraud on the public.

Notes

1. For recent deregulatory legislation, see, for example, Airline Deregulation Act of 1978, Public Law 95-504, 92 Stat. 1705 (1978); Railroad Revitalization and Regulatory Reform Act, Public Law 94-210, 90 Stat. 31 (1976), Motor Carrier Act of 1980, Public Law 96-296, 94 Stat. 793 (1980); Staggers Rail Act of 1980, Public Law 96-448, 594 Stat. 1895 (1980); and Natural Gas Policy Act of 1978, Public Law 95-621, 15 U.S.C. 3301 (Supp. II, 1978).

The Nebraska Public Service recently ruled that an Omaha cable television system that was transmitting voice and data was a common carrier subject to state regulation. Other states and the FCC are now also considering the issue of state or local common carrier regulation of data and voice services over cable television. See *Cablevision,* May 9, 1983, p. 15; *Cablevision,* May 16, 1983, p. 65; *Broadcasting,* July 11, 1983, p. 36.

A bill recently passed by the U.S. Congress would forbid the regulation of cable television as a common carrier or public utility. See Communications Act of 1984, Public Law 98-549.

The Reagan administration has proposed to deregulate all remaining natural gas, but some members of Congress are even proposing to reregulate that so-called new gas, which is currently unregulated. See Robert D. Hershey, Jr., "Natural Gas: A Winter of Discontent," *New York Times,* February 6, 1983, sec. 3, p. 1; and Robert D. Hershey, Jr., "Gas Price Decontrol Supported," *New York Times,* April 22, 1983, pp. D1, D2.

2. Much of the writing on public utility regulation suggests that such regulation was never intended to duplicate the workings of a competitive marketplace but was designed for other goals, such as protecting regulated firms from competition or cross-subsidizing certain groups of customers or classes of service. See, for example, Roger G. Noll and Bruce M. Owen, *The Political Economy of Deregulation: Interest Groups in the Regulatory Process* (Washington, D.C.: American Enterprise Institute, 1983); Roger G. Noll and Paul L. Joskow, "Regulation in Theory and Practice: An Overview," in Gary Fromm, ed., *Studies in Public Regulation* (Cambridge, Mass.: MIT Press, 1981); Bruce M. Owen and Ronald Braeutigam, *The Regulation Game: Strategic Use of the Administrative Process* (Cambridge, Mass.: Ballinger, 1978); Sam Peltzman, "Toward a More General Theory of Regulation," *Journal of Law and Economics* 19 (August 1976):211–240; Richard A. Posner, "Theories of Economic

Regulation," *Bell Journal of Economics and Management Science* 5 (Autumn 1974): 335–358; Roger G. Noll, "The Behavior of Regulatory Agencies," *Review of Social Economy* 29 (March 1971):15–19; Richard A. Posner, "Taxation by Regulation," *Bell Journal of Economics and Management Science* 2 (Spring 1971):22–50; and George J. Stigler, "The Theory of Economic Regulation," *Bell Journal of Economics and Management Science* 2 (Spring 1971):2–21. See also Louis DeAlessi, "An Economic Analysis of Government Ownership and Regulation: Theory and Evidence from the Electric Power Industry," *Public Choice* 19 (Fall 1974):1–42.

3. For an account of the concerns about railroad pricing abuses, see Paul W. MacAvoy, *The Economic Effects of Regulation* (Cambridge, Mass.: MIT Press, 1965); Gabriel Kolko, *Railroads and Regulation, 1877–1916* (Princeton, Princeton University Press, 1965); Thomas Gale Moore, *Freight Transportation Regulation Surface Freight and the Interstate Commerce Commission* (Washington, D.C.: American Enterprise Institute, 1972).

4. A firm that was a natural monopoly at first might face competitors. But because, by definition, one firm could produce the industry output at lower cost than two or more firms, there would be strong pressures on the competing firms to merge to increase their joint profits. If there is no merger, the firm that grows most rapidly and thus has the lowest unit costs will be able to drive the other competing firms out of business. See Darius W. Gaskins, Jr., "Dynamic Limit Pricing: Optimal Pricing under Threat of Entry," *Journal of Economic Theory* 3 (September 1971):306–322. A fuller exposition covering a broader array of cases is found in Gaskins, "Optimal Pricing by Dominant Firms" (Ph.D. diss., University of Michigan, 1970).

Much of the recent literature on contestability, cited in note 5, suggests that the mere possibility of entry will restrain a monopolist from charging the short-run profit-maximizing price. The policy implication of that theory seems to be that regulation is unnecessary to restrain monopoly behavior; potential entrants will restrain monopolists without the need for regulation.

We disagree. We believe that there are firms in many industries that possess monopoly power and are not currently restrained by potential entry. That may be particularly true of firms in the transportation and telecommunications industries, which have large sunk capital investments. For example, we do not believe that existing local monopoly telephone companies operate in highly contestable markets today, and we do not believe that potential entry today adequately restrains their behavior.

We also believe, however, that public utility regulation is not the way to restrain their behavior. We recommend rules such as mandatory interconnection and the repeal of any restrictions on new entry and additional competition as ways to deal with monopoly power and to increase the contestability of the market. See Elizabeth Bailey, "Contestability and the Design of Regulatory and Antitrust Policy," *American Economic Review Papers and Proceedings* 71 (May 1981):178–183.

5. Traditional definitions and discussions of natural monopoly typically assume a single-output firm. Implicit in such analyses is the assumption that public utilities produce a single, homogeneous product or service; for example, electric utilities produce electric power and telephone companies produce telephone service. More realistically, public utilities produce a multiplicity of outputs having significantly different demand and cost characteristics, although some of the different utility services are actually the same output offered to different groups at different prices.

The recent literature on natural monopoly explicitly recognizes the multioutput attributes of modern public utilities and defines a natural monopoly in the context of a multioutput firm. In terms of this literature, an industry is a natural monopoly if a given output combination can be produced more cheaply by a single firm than by any number of individual, stand-alone entities. More technically, the cost function for the multioutput natural monopoly firm is subadditive; that is, the total cost of producing a given level of multiple outputs by a natural monopolist is less than the sum of the costs of producing the same output levels by individual firms. A basic conclusion of this literature is that economies of scale are neither necessary nor sufficient for characterizing an industry as a natural monopoly.

Important references in this emerging theoretical literature include William J. Baumol, "Contestable Markets: An Uprising in the Theory of Industrial Structure," *American Economic Review* 72 (March 1982):1–15; William J. Baumol, John C. Panzar, and Robert D. Willig, *Contestable Markets and the Theory of Industry Structure* (New York: Harcourt Brace Jovanovich, 1982); William J. Baumol, "On the Proper Cost Tests for Natural Monopoly in a Multi-product Industry," *American Economic Review* 67 (December 1977):809–822; Robert D. Willig, "Multiproduct Technology and Market Structure," *American Economic Review Papers and Proceedings* 69 (May 1979):346–351; John C. Panzar and Robert D. Willig, "Free Entry and the Sustainability of Natural Monopoly," *Bell Journal of Economics* 8 (Spring 1977):1–22; William J. Baumol, Elizabeth E. Bailey, and Robert D. Willig, "Weak Invisible Hand Theorems on the Sustainability of Multiproduct Natural Monopoly," *American Economic Review* 67 (June 1977):350–365; and Gerald R. Faulhaber, "Cross Subsidization: Pricing in Public Enterprises," *American Economic Review* 65 (December 1975):966–977.

Testing the implications of this new theory of natural monopoly presents formidable empirical difficulties. For example, testing the cost function for subadditivity may require data for nonobservable output levels. For discussion of this point as well as a brief review of the relationship of the recent natural monopoly theory to Ramsey pricing and sustainability, see Vinson Snowberger, "Sustainability Theory: Its Implications for Governmental Preservation of a Regulated Monopoly," *Quarterly Review of Economics and Business* 18 (Winter 1978):81–89. See also Martin Weitzman, "Contestable Markets: An Uprising in the Theory of Industry Structure: Comment," *American Economic Review* 73 (June 1983):486–487; and Marius Schwartz and Robert J. Reynolds, "Contestable Markets: An Uprising in the Theory of Industry Structure: Comments," *American Economic Review* 73 (June 1983):488–490. For a response, see William J. Baumol, John C. Panzar, and Robert O. Willig, "Contestable Markets: An Uprising in the Theory of Industry Structure: Reply," *American Economic Review* 73 (June 1983):491–496.

6. For more details on the definition of a public utility, see Alfred E. Kahn, *The Economics of Regulation: Principles and Institutions* (New York: John Wiley, 1970), vol. 1.

7. Courts have a great deal of trouble deciding precisely what constitutes a common carrier. One important FCC case seems to define a common carrier as a firm that engages in common carriage. See *NARUC v. FCC*, 525 F.2d 633 (Court of Appeals for the District of Columbia, 1976).

8. This is a slight oversimplification. Paul Joskow has pointed out that regulators tend to prefer price decreases to price increases, making the earned rate deviate from

44 • *Unnatural Monopolies*

the allowed rate. See Paul C. Joskow, "Pricing Decisions of Regulated Firms: A Behavioral Approach," *Bell Journal of Economics and Management Science* 4 (Spring 1973):118–140. On the other hand, when costs are decreasing, earned rates may exceed the allowed rate due to regulatory lag. See Kahn, *Economics of Regulation,* 2:48.

9. Examples of statutory references to price discrimination include the Communications Act of 1934, as amended, 47 U.S.C. 202(a); and Robinson-Patman Discrimination Act, 15 U.S.C. 13; see also F. M. Scherer, *Industrial Market Structure and Economic Performance,* 2d ed. (Chicago: Rand McNally, 1980), pp. 495–496. The literature on Ramsey pricing shows that what is often judged legally to be price discrimination might, under certain restrictive assumptions, be the best available way to price output in order to maximize overall social welfare. Frank P. Ramsey, "A Contribution to the Theory of Taxation," *Economic Journal* 37 (March 1927):47–61; and William J. Baumol and David Bradford, "Optimal Departures from Marginal Cost Pricing," *American Economic Review* 60 (June 1970):265–283. The Robinson-Patman Act literature shows that what is legally price discrimination (for example, quantity discounts) may not be economic price discrimination at all. Scherer, *Industrial Market Structure,* pp. 571–582; Robinson-Patman Act, 15 U.S.C. 13.

10. Airline deregulation has changed which airlines serve which cities and in some cases has led to the serving of small cities by more efficient small-sized airplanes. It has not led to a wholesale loss of service to those cities. See Daniel A. Graham and Daniel P. Kaplan, "Airline Deregulation Is Working," *Regulation* (May–June 1982): 26–32.

11. See note 5 above.

12. For example, the FCC required DATRAN to continue providing service even after it filed for bankruptcy.

13. The FCC has struggled unsuccessfully for years to determine correctly the costs of AT&T's various services. See Walter G. Bolter, "The FCC's Selection of a 'Proper' Costing Standard after Fifteen Years—What Can We Learn from Docket 18128?" in ed. Harry M. Trebing, *Assessing New Pricing Concepts in Public Utilities,* MSU Public Utilities Papers, (East Lansing: Michigan State University, 1978), pp. 333–372.

14. See Graham and Kaplan, "Airline Deregulation Is Working."

15. This discussion also ignores the ability of a monopoly firm to present, and the apparent willingness of a regulator to accept, noncomparable data so that adequate cross-checks and consistency checks cannot readily be made; examples are historical data for one service and forward-looking data for another service and average or fully distributed cost data for one service and incremental or marginal cost data for another service.

16. The requirements on an economic regulatory agency that tries to do its job properly according to traditional public utility regulatory concepts are not very different from the requirements on a central planning agency in a socialist or communist country.

17. Such evasion need not be illegal or even improper. Income tax laws strongly affect business and consumer decisions on questions such as whether to buy or rent—in order legally to minimize their tax liability.

18. See Harvey Averch and Leland L. Johnson, "Behavior of the Firm under Regulatory Constraint," *American Economic Review* 52 (December 1962):1052–1069; Elizabeth Bailey, *Economic Theory of Regulatory Constraint* (Lexington, Mass.: Lex-

ington Books, D.C. Heath, 1973); and Charles W. Needy, *Regulation Induced Distortions* (Lexington, Mass.: Lexington Books, D.C. Heath, 1975). See also John T. Wenders, "Peak Load Pricing in the Electric Utility Industry," *Bell Journal of Economics* 1976):232–241.

19. A relatively new kind of cost of regulation is the addition of legal costs to en-sure customer representation before regulatory bodies, paid for by either taxpayers or ratepayers. See *Office of Communications of the United Church of Christ* v. *F.C.C.,* 610 F.2d 838 (1979), FCC Docket 78-205, and Section 281 of H.R. 6121. (1980).

20. Walter G. Bolter, "Depreciation Practices: A Status Check on the Industry's Best Bet," *Telephony,* April 27, 1981, pp. 24–28; and Walter G. Bolter, "Moving around the Depreciation Barrier and into the Modern Competitive Era," *Telephony,* May 25, 1981, pp. 28–34. See also Walter G. Bolter and David A. Irwin, *Depreciation Reform: A Critical Step in Transforming Telecommunications to a Free Market* (Washington, D.C.: Bolter and Irwin, September 1980).

21. Nina W. Cornell, Michael D. Pelcovits, and Steven R. Brenner, "A Legacy of Regulatory Failure," *Regulation* (July–August 1983):37–42.

22. It is ironic that many telephone company officials now agree that they should be allowed to depreciate telephone equipment much faster than they did in the past; however, they tend to assume that current ratepayers should accept higher rates to cover the faster rate of depreciation. Generally it does not seem to occur to them that they should write off their underdepreciation so that it would become a loss to their stockholders. See, for example, Bernard G. Ragland and Robert J. Wolfenbarger, "The Capital Recovery Implications of Telecommunications Deregulation," *Public Utilities Fortnightly,* July 7, 1983, pp. 25–32.

23. For example, the FCC has found that traditional common carrier regulation of firms without significant market power imposes costs on society and the firms in-volved without offsetting benefits. See *First Report and Order in the Matter of Competitive Common Carrier Services,* CC Docket no. 79-252, 85 F.C.C. 2d 1 (1980), and *Notice of Inquiry and Proposed Rulemaking in the Matter of Competitive Common Carrier Services* in CC Docket no. 79-252, 77 F.C.C. 2d 308 (1979).

24. See Federal Communications Commission, *In the Matter of Allocation of Frequencies in Bands Above 890 Mc.,* Memorandum Opinion and Order, 29 F.C.C. 825 (1960); and *Specialized Common Carrier Decision,* 29 FCC 2d 870 (1971).

25. John S. McGee, "Predatory Price Cutting: The Standard Oil (N.J.) Case," *Journal of Law and Economics* 1 (October 1958):137–169.

26. There is a growing but unsatisfactory economic literature on ways to prevent or deal with predatory pricing behavior by firms. The problem with the literature is that to carry out any of the proposals often would require the imposition of the sort of detailed regulation that we argue should be abolished. See Phillip Areeda and Donald F. Turner, "Predatory Pricing and Related Practices under Section 2 of the Sherman Act," *Harvard Law Review* 88 (February 1975):697–733; F.M. Scherer, "Predatory Pricing and the Sherman Act: A Comment," *Harvard Law Review* 89 (March 1976): 868–903; Oliver E. Williamson, "Predatory Pricing: A Strategic and Welfare Analysis," *Yale Law Journal* 87 (December 1977):284–340; Paul L. Joskow and Alvin K. Klevor-ick, "A Framework for Analyzing Predatory Pricing Policy," *Yale Law Journal* 89 (De-cember 1979):213–270; and William J. Baumol, "Quasi-Permanence of Price Reduc-tions: A Policy for the Prevention of Predatory Pricing," *Yale Law Journal* 89 (November

1979):1–26; but see also John S. McGee, "Predatory Pricing Revisited," *Journal of Law and Economics* 23 (October 1980):289–330.

27. *Final Decision* in Docket 20828, 77 F.C.C. 2d 384 (1980); *Memorandum Opinion and Order* in Docket 18128, F.C.C. 76-886, released October 1, 1976; *Report and Order* in CC Docket 79-245, 84 F.C.C. 2d 384 (1981).

28. It is ironic that while some utility regulation has been intended to prevent certain kinds of cross-subsidies by the regulated monopoly firm, other regulation has been designed to create cross-subsidies where none might have existed in the absence of regulation. Regulation has not always been successful in either preventing unwanted cross-subsidies or forcing desired cross-subsidies. See Nina W. Cornell and Douglas W. Webbink, "Common Carrier Regulation and Technological Change: The New Competition in the Communications Industries," in U.S., Congress, Joint Economic Committee, *Special Study on Economic Change, vol. 5: Government Regulation: Achieving Social and Economic Balance,* 96th Cong., 2d sess., December 8, 1980, pp. 197–224.

29. One of the worst examples of regulatory creep was the extension of regulation from railroads to trucks and water barges.

30. One alternative to giving away exclusive franchises is to have firms bid competitively for the franchise. See Oliver E. Williamson, "Franchise Bidding for Natural Monopolies—in General and with Respect to CATV," *Bell Journal of Economics* 7 (Spring 1976):73–104. The problem with that solution is that it does not reduce the monopoly power of the franchise winner; it only transfers or redistributes some of the monopoly profits or rents from the winner to the local government agency.

31. An extremely interesting case on exclusive franchises is Mountain States Legal Foundation's suit against the city of Denver for granting Mile Hi Cablevision an exclusive franchise in Denver. See Fred Dawson, "A Kingdom under Fire," *Cablevision Plus,* December 13, 1983, pp. 5–7ff; and "Signals Checked on All-Out Cable Expansion," *Broadcasting,* November 15, 1982, pp. 35–36.

On occasion, industries such as airlines where rapid entry and exit is possible have been mistakenly assumed to have the characteristics of a natural monopoly when in fact they do not have the same kind of large and permanently sunk capital investments. See, for example, Elizabeth E. Bailey and John C. Panzar, "The Contestability of Airline Markets during the Transition to Deregulation," *Law and Contemporary Problems* 4 (Winter 1981):125–145; and Elizabeth E. Bailey, "Contestability and the Design of Regulatory and Antitrust Policy," *American Economic Review Papers and Proceedings* 71 (May 1981):178–183.

32. *Final Decision* in Docket 20828, 77 F.C.C. 2d 384 (1980); and *First Report and Order* in CC Docket no. 79-105, 85 F.C.C. 2d 818 (1981). It has also been proposed that private line service be deregulated. See Jerry B. Duvall and Michael D. Pelcovits, "Reforming Regulatory Policy for Private Line Services: Implications for Market Performance," FCC Office of Plans and Policy Working Paper No. 4 (December 1980).

33. See Leonard W. Weiss, "Antitrust in the Electric Power Industry," in *Promoting Competition in Regulated Markets,* ed. Almarin Phillips (Washington, D.C.: Brookings Institution, 1975), pp. 135–173; and Walter J. Primeaux, Jr., "A Reexamination of the Monopoly Market Structure for Electric Utilities," in Phillips, *Promoting Competition,* pp. 175–200.

34. See Darius W. Gaskins, Jr., and James M. Voytko, "Managing the Transi-tion to Deregulation," *Law and Contemporary Problems* 44 (Winter 1981):9–32; and Alfred E. Kahn, "Applications of Economics to the Imperfect World," *American Economic Review, Papers and Proceedings* 69 (May 1979):1–13. For a somewhat dif-ferent view, see Walter G. Bolter, "The Continuing Role of Federal Regulation in the Transition to Competition in Communications," in *Issues in Public Utility Regulation,* ed. Harry M. Trebing (East Lansing: Michigan State University, Graduate School of Business Administration, Division of Research, 1979), pp. 401–417. See also Daniel Kelley, "Deregulation after Divestiture: The Effect of the AT&T Settlement on Com-petition," FCC Office of Plans and Policy Working Paper No. 8 (April 1982); Jerry B. Duvall, "The Conceptual Framework of Common Carrier Policymaking at the Federal Communications Commission in Recent Years: An Economist's Perspective," *Pro-ceedings of the 1981 Rate Structure Symposium on Problems of Regulated Industries* (Columbia: University of Missouri Extension Publications 1981), pp. 351–374: and Jerry B. Duvall, "Emerging Rate Structures in Interstate Communications," (paper presented at the Fourteenth Annual Michigan State University Institute of Public Utilities Conference, Williamsburg, Va., December 14, 1982).

35. The question of defining the precise conditions of interconnection in both physical terms and payments is a nontrivial exercise. See, for example, Nina W. Cor-nell and Michael D. Pelcovits, "Access Charges, Costs, and Subsidies: The Effect of Long Distance Competition on Local Rates," in *Telecommunications Regulation To-day and Tomorrow,* ed. Eli Noam (New York: Harcourt Brace Jovanovich, 1983); and Roy L. Morris and Robert S. Preece, "Negotiating Improved Interconnection be-tween U.S. Telcos and Their Competitors," *Telecommunications Policy* (September 1982):179–198.

Mandatory interconnection was the solution adopted in the St. Louis railroad terminal case, *Terminal R.R. Assoc. of St. Louis* v. *U.S., 393* U.S. 979, 89 Sup. Ct. 447 (1968). The steps necessary to apply it to the telephone service today are elab-orated in Nina W. Cornell, Daniel Kelley, and Peter R. Greenhalgh, "Social Objectives and Competition in Common Carrier Communications: Incompatible or Inseparable?" in *Energy and Communications in Transition,* MSU Public Utilities Papers (East Lansing: Michigan State University, 1981), pp. 43–74.

36. See also Nina W. Cornell, Daniel Kelley, and Peter R. Greenhalgh, "Social Ob-jectives in Common Carrier Communications: Incomparable or Inseparable?" in *Energy and Communications in Transition.*

Comment

Leland L. Johnson

Nina Cornell and Douglas Webbink present a wholesale condemnation of rate-of-return regulation. Given the obvious ills of current practices, surely most would agree with the authors' recommendations to test for the presence of monopoly power, require interconnection, encourage intermodal competition, and use antitrust restrictions.

Going beyond these recommendations, however, I am troubled that the authors offer no positive suggestions about other mechanisms that should be substituted for rate-of-return regulation. They observe that "monopoly exists and is likely to be abused, and we believe the society is right in trying to prevent that abuse. But public utility regulation is not the way." What, then, is the way? The authors seem to be urging immediate and complete abolition of utility regulation. If it is true that under current regulation, "no consumer yet has been protected from abuses of monopoly power or ever will be" and that this form of regulation is an "unacceptable fraud on the public," a recommendation of immediate and total deregulation would logically follow.

I would be willing to accept this harsh assessment of regulation if monopoly power arose only occasionally or were a transitory phenomenon. But as the authors note, monopoly power does exist in important areas, and they offer no convincing evidence that the problem would disappear in the foreseeable future even if their four recommendations were fully implemented. For example, they reject the notion of contestability where the threat of entry may restrain monopolists. Rather, they assert that there are firms in many industries that possess monopoly power and are not currently restrained by potential entry. They go on to note that local telephone companies in particular fall into this category. If they are right, should we immediately deregulate the local telephone industry? I would feel uncomfortable in urging such a course.

The fundamental issue is whether society is better off with a defective form of regulation or with firms free to exercise whatever monopoly power they have without rate-of-return constraints. We need much more evidence, and Cornell and Webbink offer little help. Surely they overstate their case when they assert that "no consumer has yet been protected from abuses of monopoly power or ever will be." It is hard to imagine that at least some consumers have not been made better off by lower rates and better service required by regulation. The question is whether the losses to such consumers would be outweighed by gains elsewhere, if rate-of-return constraints were immediately abandoned.

Much dispassionate and careful analysis will be needed in the future to estimate the relative gains and losses in freeing particular markets from regulatory constraints. Cornell and Webbink, recapitulating familiar complaints about regulation and posing their arguments in terms only of black and white, do not carry us far.

Despite the authors' vociferous complaints, I favor continuing rate-of-return regulation in markets where monopoly exists and is likely to continue in the foreseeable future. As barriers to entry and exit fall, as a consequence of technological advance and other factors, I would favor the prompt phase-out of regulation.

The long-distance telephone market is an excellent case in point. After the American Telephone and Telegraph (AT&T) divestiture is completed and all long-distance carriers are assured of nondiscriminatory access to local telephone exchanges, AT&T's long-distance telephone services will be ripe for deregulation. The almost daily reports of new investment plans by the competing long-distance carriers suggest that this market is indeed contestable, despite AT&T's current overwhelming market share. As just one example, I have learned that a 5,000 mile fiber optic system has been planned by a joint venture of Southern New England Telephone Company and the CSX Corporation to serve the Boston, Detroit, New Orleans, and Miami areas. Such developments will hasten the day when we will enjoy the benefits of a totally deregulated long-distance telecommunications market.

The same cannot be said today for local telephone service; however, as technological developments provide economic alternatives to the conventional local loop to serve not only large business enterprises but residential subscribers as well—perhaps toward the end of the century—we can seriously entertain the notion of local telephone deregulation as well. In the meantime, we may be better off with rate-of-return regulation to provide at least partial protection from monopoly power while bending every effort to encourage development of competitive markets where they do not now exist.

3

Public Utilities: Antitrust Law and Deregulation

William H. Mellor III
Malcolm B. Allen, Jr.

C ompetition is a fundamental element of a healthy U.S. economy. Generally the free interaction of market participants yields the greatest social benefits by providing the most efficient allocation of scarce resources. Antitrust laws were passed in the hope that courts would be able to preserve the competition necessary to the operation of this economic system. Vast amounts of case law, scholarly writing, and political debate have influenced the practical application of antitrust principles, such that antitrust law has developed into a potent, yet often unpredictable, force in the operation of U.S. business.[1]

Because of its potential impact, antitrust law must be considered in any discussion of utilities deregulation. In this context, the critical question is the role that antitrust law will play in a deregulated environment. This is a difficult question due to the nature of utilities and the governmental bodies that regulate them.

All utilities, as well as cable television, currently are subject to the antitrust laws to some extent; however, electric utilities, telephone companies, and cable television each differ in their history and relationship to government. Each frequently exists as a government-created monopoly, but deregulation would leave each in a slightly different position with respect to potential antitrust liability.

No one discussion can raise, much less resolve, every issue concerning the deregulation of such vital industries. Here we examine the antitrust ramifications of deregulating public utilities and cable television.

Public Utilities and Governmental Authority

The term *public utility* invokes a variety of assumptions and judgments. Social policy and the law have merged to create quasi-governmental industries. Regulatory schemes were spawned by beliefs that utilities were natural monopolies and regulation was necessary to ensure efficient distribution of certain necessities. Although laws applicable to utilities vary among states, all public utilities firms have one common trait: they are required by law to serve a specified area, and people have the right to demand service. The devotion to public use must be such that the public generally, or that part of it served by the utility, has the legal right to demand that the service shall be conducted with efficiency and at charges deemed reasonable by the appropriate regulatory bodies.

The social concern for the availability of these utility services has given rise to regulation at all governmental levels. The authority to impose regulation is derived from sources specific to the different governing bodies. The different sources of authority are significant for application of the antitrust laws in both the present environment and under deregulation. Current types of regulation insulate utilities from some antitrust exposure and affect the central operations of utilities. Efforts at deregulation therefore must be thorough and consistent or existing utilties will be placed in the untenable position of having greater liability with reduced ability effectively to compete.

At the federal level, the power of Congress to impose regulation is granted by the Constitution, in which the commerce clause grants Congress the power to regulate commerce between the states.[2] This power is one of the broadest constitutional delegations. As long as an activity involves or affects interstate commerce, congressional regulation is constitutionally valid. The "affects" test is easily met, and virtually no activity is so local in nature that Congress may not reach it with legislation under the commerce clause.

At the state and local levels, regulation may be directed at any business "affected with a public interest," a principle derived from the early Supreme Court case of *Munn* v. *Illinois*.[3] In *Munn*, the Illinois legislature passed a statute fixing the maximum price that could be charged for grain storage. This statute was challenged as a taking of private property without just compensation in violation of the Fifth Amendment. The Court upheld the statute, pointing out that regulation is appropriate when property or its use takes on a public interest:

> When one devotes his property to a use in which the public has an interest, he, in effect, grants to the public an interest in that use, and must submit to be controlled by the public for the common good, to the extent of the interest he has thus created.[4]

States impose regulation under their police power authority to adopt laws promoting the "order, safety, health, morals and general welfare." Although a state's power to regulate has parameters, it may adopt whatever economic policy might be reasonably deemed to promote public welfare and enforce that policy by legislation adapted to its purpose.[5]

Power to impose regulation at the municipal level is derived solely from the state through its legislature.[6] That delegated power may be enlarged, abridged, or entirely withdrawn by the legislature at its pleasure. However, the state, by home rule provisions of its constitution, may vest local government with some degree of local sovereignty. Home rule provisions deprive the state legislature of the ability to revoke the delegated municipal power at whim.

Legislatures have the power to delegate to a municipality three essential legislative powers: police power, the power to tax, and eminent domain. Municipal regulation of utilities is an exercise of police power. The dependence of municipalities on delegated authority has not drastically constrained their regulatory power. One court, summarizing municipal powers, noted that "A municipality possesses and can exercise the following powers and no others: first, those granted in express words; second, those necessarily incident to the powers expressly granted; third, those absolutely essential to the declared objects and purposes of the corporation—not simply convenient, but indispensable."[7] The Supreme Court summarized the power of the municipal corporation to regulate in *Schmidinger* v. *Chicago* when it stated that municipal corporations may regulate any trade, occupation, or activity that might "injuriously affect" the public health, safety, comfort, and welfare.[8]

Under its commerce power, Congress could impose regulation on any public utility, but it has not always done so. Congress has left the regulation of purely intrastate operations of electric utilities to the states. Electric utilities are regulated pervasively at the state level, usually through a public utilities commission. But when an electric utility sells power across state lines, it becomes subject to extensive federal regulations. When a municipally owned electric utility operates solely within the city's boundaries, it is subject primarily to municipal regulation. Additionally, various operational aspects of any utility, including natural gas production and transmission, smokestack emissions, and hiring policy, may be subject to pervasive federal regulation.[9]

Cable television, the newest activity subjected to utility-type regulation, is not heavily regulated at the federal level. Although possibly subject to some of the Federal Communications Commission (FCC) regulations applicable to broadcast media, the current deregulatory efforts at the FCC have minimized federal interference in cable. Some states, however, have imposed a regulatory scheme on cable.[10] There are also attempts in other states to make cable television subject to forms of common carrier regulation.[11] Generally, however, cable television is subject to extensive regulation under municipal police power authority. Unlike traditional utilities, cable television is still experiencing an evolution in which its ultimate regulatory framework is far from certain. Because of its expanding technology, multifaceted operations, and First Amendment ramifications, cable television has great potential to challenge past assumptions used to justify utility-type regulation.

General Antitrust Concepts

In the late nineteenth century there was a growing popular belief that accumulation of virtually unlimited economic power in the hands of a few was a serious danger. Groups of traders and producers were able to expand rapidly by forming trusts. There was increasing concern that the trusts had and would use their power to oppress individuals and to injure the public. The trusts were basically designed to reduce competition, and consequent price control was feared. Responding to these fears, Congress passed the Sherman Antitrust Act in 1890 in an attempt to prevent economic concentration and to preserve competition.[12]

The substantive provisions of the Sherman Act are stated in broad language. Section 1 declares all contracts, combinations, and conspiracies in restraint of trade unlawful. The focus is on concerted action by two or more actors having anticompetitive effects on interstate commerce. Section 2 prohibits monopolization, combinations or conspiracies to monopolize, and attempts to monopolize.

Congress also enacted the Clayton Act.[13] Section 2 of the Clayton Act forbids certain discriminations in price and in services that lessen competition or tend to create a monopoly. For example, discount prices to large customers, where not economically justified, can be ruled a violation of Section 2. Section 3 outlaws tying arrangements, requirements contracts, and other exclusive arrangements. A tying arrangement arises when a seller conditions the sale of one product on the purchase of another product. Conditioning the provision of city sewer service on subscribing to the municipally owned electric system rather than a competing investor-owned electric company would be a classic tying arrangement. A requirements contract is an agreement whereby a buyer agrees to purchase all of its requirements for a particular product from a single supplier. The requirements contract arrangement becomes illegal when the seller exercises so much economic power that the purchaser is unable to refuse to enter the agreement. Section 7 prohibits mergers, stock, or asset acquisitions between corporations where the effect would be anticompetitive.

State Action Exemption

"State action" is a label applied to any conduct, private or public, that is so intimately tied to the state that courts consider it to be an act of the state as sovereign and therefore not subject to antitrust liability. The state action exemption is a judicial response to the inherent conflict between federal antitrust policy and the state's police power to regulate particular activities. Regulation such as the granting of exclusive licenses, allocation of market areas among competitors, or establishing rate charges for services have obvious anticompetitive effects and frequently result from state regulation. If such conduct is deemed to be state action, it will not be subject to scrutiny under the federal antitrust laws. Regulation of utilities by state utility commissions in many contexts creates an exemption that insulates certain activities, such as rate-of-return regulation, from liability. Deregulation could have its most profound effect in the legal arena by removing this protection.

The state action exemption, also known as the Parker doctrine, was pronounced by the U.S. Supreme Court in *Parker* v. *Brown*.[14] In *Parker*, the California Agricultural Prorate Act authorized state officials to establish marketing programs for agricultural products produced within the state in order to restrict competition among growers and maintain prices in the distribution of produce to packers. The act was challenged as a violation of the Sherman Act.

In upholding the California Agricultural Prorate Act, the Supreme Court relied on the language and the legislative history of the Sherman Act. The program "derived its authority and efficacy from the legislative command of the state."[15] Nothing in the Sherman Act or its history indicated that it was intended to be applied to activities directed by a state legislature. Such an unexpressed purpose is not lightly attributed to Congress. "The state in adopting and enforcing the prorate program made no contract or agreement and entered into no conspiracy in restraint of trade or to establish monopoly but, as sovereign, imposed the restraint as an act of government which the Sherman Act did not undertake to prohibit."[16]

Beginning in 1975 with *Goldfarb* v. *Virginia State Bar*, the Supreme Court handed down a series of decisions explaining and narrowing the state action exemption.[17] In *Goldfarb*, the bar association published a fee schedule, enforced by the state bar association, that recommended minimum prices for common legal services. Petitioner Goldfarb alleged that the minimum fee schedule was price fixing in violation of section 1 of the Sherman Act. The bar association sought protection from the Sherman Act under the state action exemption.

The Supreme Court rejected this contention: "The fact that the State Bar is a state agency for some limited purposes does not create an antitrust shield that allows it to foster anti-competitive practices."[18] The state of Virginia did not, by the Supreme Court rules, require the particular anticompetitive activity challenged in *Goldfarb*. It is not enough that the anticompetitive conduct is "prompted" by state action; anticompetitive activities must be compelled by direction of the state acting as a sovereign in order to be exempt from scrutiny under the Sherman Act. This decision set the stage for a significant examination of utility activity.

In *Cantor* v. *Detroit Edison Co.*, the Supreme Court decided the application of the state action exemption to activities of a state-regulated utility.[19] In this case, it was not the utility's status as a monopoly in the provision of electricity that came under scrutiny but rather its secondary activities. The Michigan Public Service Commission (PSC) pervasively regulated the distribution of electricity within the state. It also approved as part of Detroit Edison's rate tariff a light bulb exchange program whereby customers could exchange burned-out bulbs for new ones at no charge. This program could not be changed without PSC approval. Detroit Edison was the only electric utility regulated by the PSC that offered such a program. In its marketing area, Detroit Edison was the sole supplier of electricity and supplied consumers with almost half of the standard-sized light bulbs they most frequently used. A retail druggist selling light bulbs alleged that Detroit Edison used its monopoly power in the distribution of electricity to restrain competition in the sale of light bulbs in violation of the Sherman Act.[20]

The Supreme Court noted that while the distribution of electricity was highly regulated by the PSC, the distribution of light bulbs was unregulated. The PSC's approval of the Detroit Edison plan did not implement any statewide policy relating to light bulbs. In refusing Detroit Edison's claim to the state action exemption, the Court stated that a mere possibility of conflict between state regulation and federal antitrust policy is insufficient to imply an exemption from the Sherman Act. Such an exemption will be implied only when necessary to make the regulatory scheme work. Michigan's regulation of the distribution of electricity was unimpaired by applying the Sherman Act to the distribution of light bulbs, and therefore the state action exemption was not available.

A subsequent case analyzed another aspect of utility activity. *City of Lafayette* v. *Louisiana Power & Light Co.* involved the generation and sale of electricity by a municipality in competition with an investor-owned utility.[21] The cities were alleged to have undertaken illegal tying arrangements by conditioning city sewer and water service on connection to the city-owned electric service. It was assumed that the actions would have been illegal if taken by a private company. The cities argued that since they were a subdivision of a state and could exercise only delegated power, they were exempt from antitrust attack. Additionally the cities argued that Congress never intended to subject local governments to the antitrust laws.

The Supreme Court rejected these arguments. The Court reasoned that Congress subjected all "persons" to the antitrust laws and municipalities are "persons" subject to any number of laws, including environmental, equal opportunity, and antitrust laws. The cities' conduct in selling electric power was not part of a "clearly articulated and affirmatively expressed" state policy that was actively supervised by the state, and therefore the city was not immune from the antitrust attack.

The issue of state action exemption availability to a home rule municipality was decided in *Community Communications Co.* v. *City of Boulder.*[22] Boulder is a home rule city that had been delegated all powers held by the state of Colorado. Under that power, Boulder sought to use the police power to prohibit the expansion of cable television services while the city considered further regulation and entry of other companies. The Supreme Court held the state action exemption inapplicable. Since the delegation of home rule powers was neutral on the issue, it therefore could not constitute a clearly articulated and affirmatively expressed state policy.

In the utility context, the state action exemption provides protection from antitrust challenge only for activities that are the subject of specific state regulation. Generally the state utilities commission will approve electric service rates pursuant to legislative mandate. Since such rate regulation is part of a clear and express state policy, it would be exempt from antitrust challenge; however, as illustrated by *Cantor* v. *Detroit Edison*, the availability of the state action exemption for one activity in a regulated firm does not ensure exemption for every activity of the firm. Although rate setting is likely exempt due to legislative mandates to the public utilities commission, other activities, such as purchasing, that are not subject to public utilities commission regulation, could be subject to antitrust challenge.

The definition of what activities are protected by the state action exemption is still in flux. The concern evidenced by cities and some industries after the *City of Lafayette* and *Boulder* decisions has abated somewhat as courts appear to be reluctant to subject governmental entities to antitrust liability. Nevertheless, court decisions indicate that the range of utility activity that can be shielded from liability is being narrowed.

Immunity from Antitrust

While the state action doctrine seeks to resolve potential conflicts between state economic regulation and federal antitrust policy, the immunity doctrine seeks to resolve similar conflicts between federal regulation and federal antitrust laws. The cases seeking to resolve the conflicts posed by each doctrine are indistinguishable in many ways. The case law finding that federal regulation has immunized the regulated activity from antitrust frequently borrows from concepts developed under the state action doctrine. The ultimate question in both is whether Congress intended for the regulatory scheme to prevent antitrust review of the challenged action.

This can be illustrated by the federal regulation of electricity. In 1920 the Federal Water Power Act made provision for the licensing of hydroelectric power facilities.[23] The Federal Power Commission (FPC) was given power to award licenses and to regulate the rates, services, and accounting practices of licensees in the absence of state regulation in such matters. The Federal Power Act of 1935 extended federal regulation to interstate transmissions of electric energy and to interstate wholesale sales of electricity.[24] Private companies engaged in the interstate transmission of electric energy were subject to FPC regulation respecting interconnection of facilities; sales of facilities, mergers and stock acquisitions; issuance of securities (in the absence of state regulation); rates applicable to interstate sales of electricity for resale; service improvements; accounting methods; and interlocking directorates.

The regulation was broad. The issue of antitrust immunity under the Federal Power Act was raised in *Otter Tail Power Co.* v. *United States*.[25] Otter Tail contended its refusal to sell power to competing municipal systems was immune from prosecution because in granting the FPC the authority to compel involuntary interconnections of power systems under the act, Congress intended such action as a substitute for application of the antitrust laws. The Supreme Court emphasized that the major thrust of the Federal Power Act was to encourage voluntary arrangements:

> Congress rejected a pervasive regulatory scheme for controlling the interstate distribution of power in favor of voluntary commercial relationships. When these relationships are governed in the first instance by business judgment and not regulatory coercion, courts must be hesitant to conclude that Congress intended to override the fundamental national policies embodied in the antitrust laws.[26]

As illustrated by *Otter Tail*, despite a pervasive regulatory scheme, an intent to immunize is difficult to attribute to Congress. Only where Congress is explicit can immunity be assumed.[27]

Regulatory statutes are seldom explicit regarding the relationship of antitrust law and regulation. The establishment of a comprehensive regulatory scheme could be understood to substitute regulation for antitrust rules with respect to some or all of the regulated industry's behavior. But the creation of an agency to oversee and control an economic sector never embraces all the market decisions made by a regulated firm. The role of antitrust in an industry subject to federal regulation varies widely. Where the industry is explicitly exempted from antitrust jurisdiction or is so pervasively regulated that government oversight has replaced market forces in controlling critical management decisions, the role of antitrust is minimal.

Faced with a potential conflict between antitrust and administrative regulation, the usual judicial approach has been to follow the national commitment to competition as expressed in the federal antitrust legislation and to allow antitrust challenges. Public utilities regulated by the federal government already have their actions subject to antitrust scrutiny in the absence of an express grant of immunity or a clear possibility of conflict between the antitrust laws and the regulatory objectives. Accordingly, deregulation at the federal level would be unlikely to expose utilities to massive new antitrust liability.

Monopoly under the Sherman Act

The greatest antitrust exposure facing public utilities in a deregulated environment is monopolization. Utilities, of course, are monopolies enforced by the government, a fact that thus far has insulated them from certain types of antitrust liability.[28] The broad parameters of the monopoly offense have been established in a series of cases. Courts classify as monopolies under Section 2 of the Sherman Act those situations where a seller or group of sellers has control over market price and the economic power to exclude competitors. This monopoly power over price may result from control of a sufficiently large part of a product available in the market from control of a strategic aspect of the market. In *American Tobacco Co.* v. *United States*, the Supreme Court stated: "The material consideration in determining whether a monopoly exists is not that prices are raised and that competition actually is excluded, but that power exists to raise prices or exclude competition when it is desired to do so."[29]

Existence of Monopoly Power

To determine whether a firm's market position constitutes monopoly power or merely a strong but competitive position, the firm's power must be measured within a relevant market. Relevant market defines the area of effective competition within which the defendant operates. Market must be defined in terms of both the geographic areas within which the trade may be limited and the products that might be affected by the conduct. Identification of market turns on the patterns of trade that are followed in practice.[30]

Geographic market is a shorthand phrase to describe "the arena within which the strength of competitive forces is measured."[31] Geographic market does not necessarily mean the selling place. Consideration also must be given to industry and public recognition of the geographic area as a distinct arena of competition. In addition, consideration must be given to the cost of supplying or transporting the product to an area outside the current market. For example, the relevant geographic market for cable television could include, besides the area already served, all areas into which expansion is economically feasible.

Determination of the relevant product market depends on how different the offered products are from one another in character or use. For example, the Supreme Court, in *United States* v. *E.I. du Pont de Nemours & Co.*, closely examined the issue of defining a product market in a suit alleging monopolization of cellophane.[32] The Court adopted as the relevant product market all flexible packaging materials, including brown wrapping paper, waxed paper, and aluminum foil. For each possible use of cellophane, there are one or more alternatives not controlled by du Pont. As a result, du Pont was found not to have monopoly power. Of course, the substitutability of one product for another, called cross-elasticity of demand, will vary with the facts of each case. For example, the cross-elasticity of demand for retail electric power is low. Since present technology provides virtually no large-scale, practical substitute for retail electricity, proof of monopolization in this product market in most cases would be relatively uncomplicated. On the other hand, a frequent defense in cable television antitrust suits is that network television, full-power broadcast television, master antenna television systems, multipoint distribution service (MDS), direct broadcast satellites (DBS), movie theaters, newspapers, and magazines all are reasonable substitutes for at least some of the products offered by cable. Proof of monopolization in this product market would be lengthy, complicated, and expensive.[33] No more definite rule can be declared than that products reasonably interchangeable by consumers for the same purposes make up that part of trade or commerce, monopolization of which may be illegal.

Use of Monopoly Power

In *United States* v. *United Shoe Machinery Corp.* three tests were set forth to determine whether a firm with monopoly power has monopolized in violation of Section 2: (1) whether it has acquired or maintained a power to exclude others by using an unreasonable restraint of trade in violation of Section 1 of the Sherman Act; (2) whether the firm uses or plans to use any exclusionary practice, which might not amount technically to a restraint of trade; and (3) whether the firm has an overwhelming share of the market, in which case it illegally monopolizes merely by engaging in ordinarily permissible business practices, absent a showing by the defendant of extenuating circumstances.[34]

Although currently insulated to some degree, utilities can engage in acts that subject them to liability. For example, monopolizing behavior as distinguished from monopolistic structure was held illegal in *Otter Tail Power Co.* v. *United States.*[35] Otter Tail sold retail electric power in 465 towns in three states. The Justice Department charged Otter Tail with monopolization and attempting to monopolize. The thrust of the charges against Otter Tail focused on its methods of preventing the towns it served from establishing their own municipal systems. The practices challenged included the refusal to sell power at wholesale to municipally owned systems where Otter Tail had been selling retail power, the refusal to wheel power through its transmission lines, and litigation to delay establishment of municipal systems.

Having rejected Otter Tail's claim of immunity, the Court found that Otter Tail had used its monopoly power to foreclose competition, albeit by a nonprivate enterprise, in violation of the antitrust laws. Otter Tail existed legally as a monopoly. It was Otter Tail's predatory use of that monopoly position that violated the Sherman Act.

While the definition of monopoly is constantly being revised to address new and different situations, it clearly would apply to utilities operating under PUC permits or to cable television companies doing business under exclusive municipal franchises. Nevertheless, these businesses have not been subject to extensive antitrust liability because of their status.

Court-Created Standards to Determine Antitrust Liability

Section 1 of the Sherman Act prohibits "every" contract or combination in restraint of trade, but courts quickly realized that Congress could not have intended to forbid certain common business arrangements that as a practical matter restrict the commercial freedom of the participants. In *Board of Trade of Chicago* v. *United States,* Justice Louis Brandeis stated that "the true test of illegality is whether the restraint imposed is such as merely regulates and perhaps thereby promotes competition or whether it is such as may suppress or even destroy competition."[36] The courts have determined that only those restraints that are unreasonable are prohibited.

In determining whether an activity is illegal, the courts must first consider whether the activity falls within a category of per se offenses. A per se offense is patently anticompetitive and by definition illegal. No justification for such an agreement is recognized. These types of activities, "because of their pernicious effect on competition and lack of any redeeming virtue are conclusively presumed to be unreasonable and therefore illegal without elaborate inquiry as to the precise harm they have caused or the business excuse for their use."[37] Price fixing, territorial allocations among competitors, and group boycotts are all accorded per se treatment.[38]

If the conduct does not fall within a per se unreasonable category, the court will apply the rule of reason, "the standard traditionally applied for the majority of anti-competitive practices challenged under section 1 of the Sherman Act."[39] The rule of reason is a judicial analysis that allows a court to look beyond the activity challenged for justifications of its seemingly anticompetitive nature. The court will look at facts peculiar to the business to which the restraint is applied, its condition before and after the restraint was imposed, and the nature of the restraint and its effect.[40] Under the rule of reason, "the history of the restraint, the evil believed to exist, the reason for adopting the particular remedy, the purpose or end sought to be attained, are all relevant facts" to be considered by the court in determining whether the restraint is reasonable.[41]

Even if a regulatory scheme does not confer immunity, the fact of regulation is relevant in rule-of-reason analysis. When a regulated entity complies with its duties under the regulatory scheme, the antitrust laws do not apply to the challenged activity without regard to the requirements of the regulatory structure. If, at the time of the alleged anticompetitive conduct, the firm had a reasonable basis to conclude that the conduct was necessitated by the regulatory authority, the action does not violate the antitrust laws.[42]

The original purpose of the rule of reason was to inject a degree of rational fairness into the analysis of allegedly illegal conduct. The degree to which it has succeeded in this purpose is debatable. It does, however, provide courts with a tool for tailoring the antitrust statutes to implement the policy of competition without ignoring practical, historic realities. For example, in *Board of Trade of Chicago,* one commodity exchange rule prescribed a short period for trading a certain category of contracts and prohibited transactions outside trading hours at any price other than the closing bid. This rule was challenged as an illegal price-fixing arrangement. Although the rule clearly fixed commodities prices for the substantial part of each day, it was sustained under the rule-of-reason analysis. Among the saving circumstances considered by the court were: the form of the rule (a limitation on the hours of competitive price making rather than an explicit prescription of price); the use of a competitively established price as the price for off-hour trading; the limited scope of the rule, applying to only one narrow class of grain that competed with other classes of grain on the Chicago and other exchanges; and the effect of the rule to favor certain small traders and to encourage all traders to bid and offer during the official trading period, thus maximizing the exchange's efficiency as a competitive market.

Liability after Deregulation

At present, many business practices of utilities and cable television companies are subject to the antitrust laws. Caution must be exercised in a variety of areas.[43] The structure created for providing service must be carefully implemented to avoid the appearance of illegal joint action or improperly preferring customers. Territorial allocation agreements and subsidization of one class of service by overcharging another also risk incurring liability.[44] Activities taken to secure an exclusive permit or favorable treatment for provision of service may also expose the company, the government entity, and the individual private and public officers to liability for damages.[45]

Upon deregulation, utilities currently regulated by public service commissions would face new risks of antitrust attack. Rate structure, power grid systems, and monopolization of certain markets would be vulnerable due to the removal of state involvement necessary to create a state action exemption. Cable television companies and municipalities enjoying governmentally created monopolies are already potentially subject to antitrust actions. Telephone companies currently are in the throes of readjustment after the American Telephone and Telegraph divestiture. Accordingly it is in the established power-producing utilities that the potential disruption or unfair impact, through abrupt total deregulation or carelessly imposed piecemeal competition, is greatest.

While the primary reason for deregulation is market efficiency, this goal cannot be attained without careful thought. Many utilities currently are operating effectively, and total deregulation, done precipitously, could subject these industries to substantial antitrust liability for practices established in good faith or from government edict. Competition imposed in a piecemeal manner, on the other hand, could have the effect of crippling existing operations and at the same time creating an environment of regulated competition that creates new inefficiencies that protect or favor fledgling competitors.

It is essential to deregulate in a manner most likely to bring about the benefits intended. The antitrust laws will be a significant force in any such efforts. The rule of reason must be applied to those activities exposed to antitrust scrutiny for the first time. This will ensure that practices established in compliance with the regulatory scheme are not the cause of massive damage actions against the existing operators. The rule of reason could be used to recognize the historic development of utilities and to provide a grace period or readjustment period to ensure the desired results of deregulation. Efficient operations would not be disrupted unnecessarily. Although the rule of reason by its very nature suffers from some uncertainty in its application, it also provides flexibility that can alleviate harsh results when applied to newly deregulated utilities. Increased certainty could be achieved if Congress or state legislatures passed laws declaring specific activities to be reasonable. In the meantime, those actions already subject to the antitrust laws would remain ripe for litigation by new competitors, thus continuing judicially enforced competition in these established areas.

Notes

1. The significance of antitrust lawsuits is magnified by the fact that they are relatively easy to bring at both the federal and state levels.

2. U.S. Const., art. I, spec. 8, cl. 3.

3. 94 U.S. 113 (1887).

4. Ibid., at 26.

5. Ibid.

6. *Joslin Mfg. Co.* v. *Providence,* 262 U.S. 668 (1922).

7. *Merriam* v. *Moody's Executors,* 25 Iowa 163, 170 (1868).

8. 226 U.S. 578 (1912).

9. See, generally, Public Utilities Regulatory Policies Act of 1978, 15 U.S.C. sec. 3201 et seq.; Clean Air Act of 1955, 42 U.S.C. sec. 1857 et seq.; and Title VII of Civil Rights Act of 1964, 42 U.S.C. secs. 2000e–2000e (15).

10. Alaska, Kansas, Michigan, Missouri, Nevada, and South Dakota currently impose state regulation on cable.

11. There is proposed legislation in Arizona, Nebraska, New York, and New Jersey that would subject cable to forms of common carrier regulation.

12. 15 U.S.C. sec. 1 et seq.

13. 15 U.S.C. secs. 5–16.

14. 317 U.S. 341 (1943).

15. Ibid., at 350.

16. Ibid., at 352.
17. 421 U.S. 771 (1975).
18. Ibid., at 791.
19. 428 U.S. 579 (1876).
20. Ibid., at 581.
21. 435 U.S. 389 (1978).
22. 455 U.S. 40 (1982).
23. 41 Stat. 1063 (1920).
24. 16 U.S.C. sec. 791 et seq.
25. 410 U.S. 366 (1973). For a fuller discussion of this case, see text accompanying note 16.
26. Ibid.
27. See, for example, 7 U.S.C. secs. 291–292. For example, the Capper-Volstead Act of 1922 provides immunity from the antitrust laws for agricultural cooperatives. Recently passed by the Senate, Senate Bill 66 may well illustrate the point if it retains its present language. Although it indicates that municipal award of exclusive cable television franchises may be permitted, it does not expressly exempt cities from antitrust liability for such action.
28. See the text quoted from *Parker* v. *Brown,* indicated by notes 15 and 16.
29. 328 U.S. 781 (1946).
30. *United States* v. *United Shoe Machinery Corp.,* 110 F. Supp. 295, 303 (D. Mass. 1953), *aff'd per curiam* 347 U.S. 521 (1954).
31. P. Areeda, Antitrust Analysis ¶201, at 71 (1967).
32. 351 U.S. 377 (1956).
33. For an excellent discussion of the reasons why cable television should not be considered a natural monopoly with a narrowly defined relevant product market, see Harry M. Shooshan and Charles Jackson, "Cable Television—The Monopoly Myth and Competitive Reality" (unpublished study prepared for the National Cable Television Association).
34. 110 F. Supp. 295, 342 (D. Mass. 1953).
35. 410 U.S. 366 (1973).
36. 246 U.S. 231 (1918).
37. *Northern Pac. R.R.* v. *United States,* 356 U.S. 1, 5 (1958).
38. The aim and result of every agreement to fix prices is the elimination of one form of competition. Regarding territorial allocations, see *United States* v. *Topco Assocs.,* 405 U.S. 506 (1972). Territorial allocations among competitors can have no other effect than to destroy competition between the firms in that territory. The courts presume the restraint illegal and therefore avoid costly inquiry into the circumstances surrounding the agreement. Regarding group boycotts, see *Klor's Inc.* v. *Broadway-Hale Stores,* 359 U.S. 207 (1959). A group boycott is an agreement among firms to refuse to deal with the targeted firm with the purpose of changing the boycotted firm's conduct in the marketplace. Such an agreement runs directly counter to the philosophy that spawned the antitrust acts and therefore is presumed illegal.
39. *Continental T.V., Inc.* v. *GTE Sylvania, Inc.,* 433 U.S. 36 (1977).
40. *Board of Trade of Chicago* v. *United States,* 246 U.S. 231, 238 (1918). See also *United States* v. *Topco Assoc., Inc.,* 405 U.S. 596 (1972).

41. *Phonetele, Inc.* v. *American Tel. & Tel. Co.,* 664 F.2d 716, 738-39 (9th Cir. 1981).

42. Ibid. It should be noted, however, that AT&T has not been successful in its attempts to use this defense in recent lawsuits. See, for example, *Sound, Inc.* v. *AT&T.* 631 F.2d 1324 (8th Cir. 1980), *Essential Communications Systems, Inc.* v. *AT&T,* 610 F.2d 1114 (3d Cir. 1979).

43. We point out these areas for purposes of illustration only and are not advocating application of antitrust to this or any other activity.

44. *United States* v. *AT&T,* 552 F. Supp. 131 (D.D.C. 1982).

45. *United Mine Workers* v. *Pennington,* 381 U.S. 657 (1965); *Eastern R.R. Presidents Conference* v. *Noerr Motor Freight, Inc.* 365 U.S. 127 (1965). (Houston Cable Television Case)

Comment

Sue D. Blumenfeld

T he actual degree of protection afforded to utilities and their local regulators from antitrust exposure is not substantial. Because antitrust immunity is not easily found, the transition from regulation to deregulation suggested by William Mellor and Malcolm Allen will not be too harsh. Regulated sectors of the economy may enjoy a limited amount of protection from antitrust liability pursuant to three doctrines: (1) express repeal of the antitrust laws (where a federal regulatory statute by its literal terms displaces the antitrust laws); (2) implied repeal (where a federal regulatory statute by its operation necessitates some displacement of the antitrust statutes); and (3) state action (where a state acts to displace the antitrust laws).

Putting aside the area of express repeal—it is readily detected and not generally relevant to the industries discussed here—these comments focus on the implied repeal and the state action doctrines. The extent of utility exposure has become somewhat clearer in recent years, although federal regulation has never limited antitrust challenge to utility conduct to any great degree.[1] The state action doctrine, in contrast, may have afforded some substantial immunity in the past but in the 1970s it began to be significantly narrowed by a series of Supreme Court decisions. These decisions clearly establish that utilities regulated at local levels do not generally enjoy immunity from antitrust prosecution either. A final area to examine is the antitrust exposure of the local regulators as a result of the Supreme Court's decision in *Boulder Community Communications Co. v. Boulder.*[2]

Implied Repeal

An implied repeal of the antitrust laws is generally found only where necessary to make the regulatory scheme work.[3] *Otter Tail Power Co. v. United States* made clear that electric utilities could find little comfort in the fact that their activities are subject to federal regulation.[4] In the telecommunications field, antitrust defendants have similarly found little security. American Telephone & Telegraph (AT&T) has continually sought safe harbor in this doctrine, with rather consistent failure.[5] Arguing that its business is pervasively regulated at the federal level by the Federal Communications Commission (FCC) and at the state level by the state utility commissions, it has claimed antitrust immunity for its pricing, its refusals to interconnect with competitors, and other activities that allegedly aided its monopolization of the industry. These arguments have gained little favor in the courts.[6] The company's numerous antitrust settlements, not the least of which was the government's litigation ending in divestiture, are perhaps the most realistic indications of the narrowness of the exemption.

Some specific discussion may be helpful. In the pricing area, for example, the mere fact that tariffs are filed by a utility with a regulatory body clearly does not protect those prices from antitrust scrutiny.[7] Only where those prices are actually prescribed by the agency—that is, where the agency dictates what those rates must be—will such activity be immune.

State Action

The state action doctrine is similarly narrow. In *Parker* v. *Brown* the Supreme Court held that implementation of a state regulatory program creating a cartel for the raisin market was safe from antitrust challenge.[8] That decision is largely understood on the bases of general notions of federalism and the principle that states were not intended targets of the antitrust laws. *Parker* seemed very significant for thirty years as an insulator of utilities from antitrust prosecution, but in less than eight years the Supreme Court has reduced it to minor proportions. The so-called *Parker* doctrine has since been received with a certain amount of judicial hostility, being constantly refined and narrowed in scope. In *Goldfarb* v. *Virginia State Bar,* the Court denied immunity for minimum fee schedules promulgated by local bar associations and enforced by the state ethics rules.[9] In *Cantor* v. *Detroit Edison Co.,* approval by the state public utility commission of the utility's practice of bundling electricity service and light bulbs was found insufficient for antitrust immunity.[10] In *California Retail Liquor Dealers Assn.* v. *Midcal Aluminum, Inc.,* a state statute requiring resale price maintenance was held invalid because of its conflict with the antitrust laws.[11] In *Midcal,* the Court held that immunity had to be based on a clearly articulated, affirmatively expressed, actively supervised, state arrangement to displace competition. This is the governing formulation today.

Although these cases demonstrate a consistent hostility to claims of immunity for private conduct, other cases show a similar aversion to anticompetitive conduct by public officials. In *City of Lafayette* v. *Louisiana Power & Light Co.,* a municipal power company was deemed subject to antitrust liability for activities not authorized by the state.[12] The opinion, controversial because it was the first time cities had been held subject to antitrust scrutiny, was narrowly decided by a five-to-four decision. Although the chief justice offered a narrow justification for the ruling—that the cities should not be immune when they engage in proprietary activities—the remaining justices in the majority appeared to apply *Parker* and its progeny without regard to whether the defendant was a private party or a public official.

Community Communications Co., Inc. v. *Boulder,* the most far-reaching of these decisions, appears to confirm that local public officials and cities enjoy no greater protection than do private citizens, even when fulfilling their governmental functions.[13] The Court there held that a municipal grant of an exclusive cable franchise was subject to antitrust scrutiny. The state's home rule provision for municipalities was insufficient to find the existence of state action; the requisite state articulation of affirmative policy to displace the antitrust laws was absent.

Lower court resistance to apply the ruling in *Boulder* suggests the popular opinion that the Supreme Court has gone too far. For example, in *Gold Cross Ambulance* v. *City of Kansas,* a city ordinance providing for sole source provision of ambulance service, pursuant to state law permitting cities to regulate such service, was held to constitute state action, and thus city officials were immune from antitrust challenge.[14] Similar resistance to *Boulder* was found in *Pueblo Aircraft Service, Inc.* v. *City of Pueblo* with respect to a municipality's contracts with private parties for services rendered at a municipal airport.[15] And the U.S. Court of Appeals for the Fifth Circuit granted rehearing of its earlier decision upholding antitrust liability of a city with respect to cable franchising activity.[16]

Whatever comfort the cities and their officials may take here, private companies must not. Regulated companies' conduct raising antitrust concerns should not be similarly sheltered from investigation.

Because neither federal nor state statutes regulating private conduct have afforded substantial antitrust immunity, markets that are deregulated will not necessarily undergo traumatic transitions. In other words, no sudden antitrust exposure would occur because that exposure, in the main, has always existed. As Judge Harold Greene ruled:

> In the absence of a determination that the regulatory scheme confers antitrust immunity, the practical effect of regulation will therefore be considered by the Court "simply as another fact of market life."[17]

Notes

1. See, e.g., *Otter Tail Power Co.* v. *United States,* 410 U.S. 366 (1973); *United States* v. *Terminal R.R. Ass'n,* 224 U.S. 383 (1912).

2. 455 U.S. 40 (1982).

3. *Silver* v. *N.Y. Stock Exchange,* 373 U.S. 341 (1963).

4. 410 U.S. 366 (1973).

5. See, e.g., *Sound, Inc.* v. *AT&T,* 631 F.2d 1324 (8th Cir. 1980); *Essential Communications Systems, Inc.* v. *AT&T,* 610 F.2d 1114 (3d Cir. 1979).

6. See, e.g., *United States* v. *AT&T,* 461 F. Supp 1314 (D.D.C. 1978).

7. *MCI* v. *AT&T,* 462 F. Supp 1972 (N.D. Ill.) aff'd sub nom., *AT&T* v. *Grady,* 594 F.2d 594 (7th Cir. 1978), cert. denied, 440 U.S. 971 (1979).

8. 317 U.S. 341 (1943).

9. 421 U.S. 773 (1975).

10. 428 U.S. 579 (1976).

11. 445 U.S. 97 (1980).

12. 435 U.S. 389 (1978).

13. 455 U.S. 40 (1982).

14. 538 F. Supp 956 (W.D. Mo. 1982), aff'd, 705 F.2d 1005 (8th Cir. 1983).

15. 679 F.2d 805 (10th Cir. 1982), cert. denied, 103 S. Ct. 762 (1983).

16. *Affiliated Capital Corp.* v. *City of Houston,* 700 F.2d 226, (5th Cir. 1983) rehearing granted, 1983-1 Trade Case. ¶65,597.

17. *U.S.* v. *AT&T,* 524 F. Supp 1336, 1347 (D.D.C. 1981), quoting *ITT* v. *GTE,* 518 F.2d 913, 935-36 (9th Cir. 1975).

4

Private Contracting versus Public Regulation as a Solution to the Natural Monopoly Problem

Thomas Hazlett

T he central importance of the possibilities, limits, and costs of private contracting in understanding just what encompasses the natural monopoly problem was first recognized in the modern literature by Harold Demsetz. In his pathbreaking "Why Regulate Utilities?" (1968) Demsetz disabled the naive, scale economies view of natural monopoly by pointing out "that the asserted relationship between market concentration and competition cannot be derived from existing theoretical considerations and . . . is based largely on an incorrect understanding of the concept of competition or rivalry."[1] This conclusion was based on two major findings. First, in a zero transactions cost world, all gains from trade may be exploited by efficient dealings between monopolist and consumers or between consumers and some rival supplier (including consumers themselves in the case of vertical integration). This zero transactions cost case is trivial in an empirical sense but not in a theoretical one; indeed such an assumption repeatedly had been implicitly employed to produce a regulatory solution deductively superior to unregulated private markets. Second, there is no theoretical reason why competition for the market is necessarily less effective than competition within the market. Moreover, supposing monopoly profits are a predictable consequence of monopoly, there is no theory explaining why the initial rivalry to gain a property right to a future monopolistic income stream fails to transfer the present value of those gains to consumers in an efficient, consumer-welfare-maximizing way.

Demsetz's argument suggests frustration in dealing with questions of market power in a framework that takes market structure as given. In such a paradigm, with market forces implicitly ruled out of consideration, there is no means of constraining the market power of an incumbent "natural monopolist." The questions Demsetz raises lead automatically to an examination of the global nature of competitive forces. Franklin Giddings suggested a century ago that "limitation of the range through which the series of competitive acts may extend but increases the amount of normal competition, since by preventing the wasting of capital it increases one of the chief competitive forces."[2] Today we might be interested to search for those competitive forces that disappear from the naked eye but not from the economic world when one firm dominates a given geographical market.

A Model of Contract

As a first approximation assume that a particular service, say door-to-door cable television transmission, will be (efficiently) supplied by only one firm throughout a given community. Assume also that the public authorities make no attempt to regulate this market in any way other than through enforcement of the traditional civil and criminal statutes. What emerges under this laissez-faire regime is one cable provider, exhibiting substantial economies of scale relative to the size of the market and charging rates not only above marginal cost but above average cost, thus earning monopoly rent. (This single firm cable provider could be the result of one firm's beating everyone to the punch or of an efficiency mandated merger of rival cable producers.)

The existence of such monopoly returns would invite entry. We assume that potential suppliers other than the incumbent have access to the same technology and cost curves as the incumbent.[3] Money traded in capital markets at competitive rates of return would be drawn to the cable monopoly market where an appreciably larger return is to be gained. Yet two factors are said to prevent entry. First, the existing (incumbent) firm could resort to predatory behavior to forestall the entrant (here, predatory may mean a price below average cost and above marginal cost; in the natural monopoly market this would suffice to preclude entry). Second, the available rate of return to a second cable provider serving, say, a 50 percent market share will be less than the monopoly returns currently enjoyed by the cable monopolist and may even be less than the competitive rate of return. (Social costs also would be high to build a second system for reasons quite evident in this stereotypical natural monopoly case.)

Either problem by itself may be of sufficient magnitude to deter entry, yet neither is insoluble to the potential entrant. In fact, the single impediment to competition in the case of natural monopoly (which prevents the flow of capital to its most highly valued employment) is the problem entailed in entering into long-term contracts with the consumers of such services prior to entry. First, it may be difficult to identify customers of a particular product years ahead of delivery dates. Second, it may be costly to enforce a long-term agreement after major capital investment has been undertaken.

Fortuitously, public utilities like cable witness a ready solution to both of these problems. Consumers of cable services will be just those residents of a particular geographic region now and in the future. Identification is no problem, for all owners of real estate will capitalize the gains (or losses from being guaranteed a long-run solution—or no solution) to the monopoly utility pricing problem. And enforcement of long-term contracts need not be costly, particularly if local governments or the courts allow and reliably enforce contracts with cable customers that attach to landownership so that the agreement remains in force when title is passed.

In this way, a potential entrant into cable services could solicit subscribers prior to the actual construction of such a system. These contracts would guarantee a price and quality package approximating the competitive level because the outside competitor has no market power. It is presumed that such contracts would leave considerable leeway for the customer to choose among various services provided by the cable operator and even allow the choice of no service at all. It would, however, grant the cable entrant an exclusive dealing arrangement with the occupant(s) of a particular address over a fixed period of time (perhaps ten to twenty years to allow the entrant to depreciate specific capital, which is the motivation for expending effort on such contracts in the first place) in exchange for the cable operator's assurance of competitively priced cable services.

Assuming that the costs of marketing preentry exclusive dealing contracts are a modest portion of the natural monopolist's capital investment and assuming that the incumbent monopolist does not itself offer matching, competitively priced long-term contracts, it is in the interest of each consumer to commit contractually to deal exclusively with the entrant. Prior to sinking the physical capital infrastructure, a competitor has now appropriated the incumbent's market, and consumers have achieved a market solution consistent with welfare maximization.

The question may arise as to why the incumbent has not locked up the market with monopolistically priced long-term contracts. Clearly it is not in any consumer's interest to sign such an agreement, for it offers no protection; the worst a nonsigner can be penalized is infliction of noncontract monopoly prices. If charging an optimal monopoly price, the monopolist cannot additionally expect consumers to sign away their flexibility to choose a rival firm should one present itself over the life of the monopolist's investment. The entrant trades competitive price assurance for consumer exclusivity, a viable, positive sum exchange.

Wasteful Duplication?

Once the competitive entrant has enlisted contractual obligations from some threshold proportion of the community's residents, say 90 percent,[4] it will become clear that the entrant has a viable business proposition.[5] Since the entrant solicited customers based on the prospect that revenues would at least compensate for long-run total costs, it is now profitable to build a second cable system in the community. Yet this would lead to social losses due to duplication. The availability of the original monopolist's cable system, all of it, we assume, nonsalvageable in some alternative market, mitigates against this. Since the competitor entered into contracts guaranteeing service at a time when the prospect of having to build its own cable system was very real, it is now financially capable and legally obligated to do so or purchase some substitute.[6] Since the construction would render the capital value of the existing monopolist's investment close to zero, the incoming competitor is in an advantageous bargaining position relative to the existing capital structure; that is, the entrant can expropriate the incumbent's quasi-rents but not vice versa.[7]

While a bilateral monopoly situation exists, the incentives for both parties to come to terms at some price are quite high, given the large amount of nonsalvageable capital (that is, not salvageable except by agreement between the once and future monopolists) at stake. The entering competitor now stands to capture rents by using its considerable market power over the incumbent monopolist to purchase the existing system of capital infrastructure for less than its replacement cost. If new customers were solicited for long-term exclusive dealing contracts at competitive prices equal to long-run average cost, then the entrant realizes rents as soon as it locks up by contract that percentage of the consuming public that makes the established monopolist's sunk investment worth more to the entrant than to the incumbent.

This result is so powerful that it shifts the entire question; not only does the established monopolist lack the ability to exact monopoly returns, it may not have the ability to exact competitive returns.[8] The large-scale investment of what immediately becomes a sunk cost looms as a ripe source for exploitation to an incoming cable operator. Under these circumstances, we will have to explain why any firm would enter a market under a regime of free entry, even if the opportunity to establish a position as natural monopolist were available, unless protected by long-term contractual guarantees.

It is commonly argued for certain monopolies—cable television being a prime example—that the municipal government must guarantee a monopoly franchise (erect legal barriers to entry), or else no investment will be forthcoming. Yet in several communities, cable systems have been constructed by private firms without monopoly franchises; there is entry even under a free entry policy. Without such legal protections (obtained either politically or by private contract), firms may adjust their willingness to sink nonsalvageable capital accordingly. Not only would outside competitors of equal cost efficiency lurk to raid their market, but a change in technology could make the utility's services competitively obsolete. The possibility of this negative windfall is foreseen by the monopolist when the initial investment is made. It may thus protect itself by contract from expropriation (or will enter without such protection only when the expected present value of losses from expropriation is sufficiently less than the expected present value of the gains from entering the market so as to compensate for the risk of loss). Conversely, consumers will not, without payment, sign agreements that make them hostages of the cable firm. Should new technologies become available, consumers should like the flexibility to take advantage of them.

Here the trade-off is apparent. Without guaranteeing the monopolist's investment, the consumers may receive much less service than they would like to pay for. But if consumers tie themselves to the monopolist for a lengthy period unconditionally, they may well be giving away future windfalls to the monopolist.[9]

This is not a unique consumer welfare problem. The flexibility-inflexibility trade-off may be dealt with in a rivalrous market context, either by firms simply risking it (as when General Motors commits $2 billion to a new and uncertain car design), by consumers simply risking it (as investing in a personal computer), or by firms competing to offer consumers the optimal (competitive) level of flexibility by contract. Periodic adjustments in the contract could be made by an explicit arrangement involving some institution of private arbitration. Since no firm has market power when all are competing for the market, a zero profit condition holds even under natural monopoly, and the competitive outcome for consumer flexibility obtains.

Under the predominantly employed institution governing cable television provision, a publicly let monopoly franchise, consumer options are signed away in long-term exclusive dealing contracts negotiated in the political sphere. Victor Goldberg argues that the primary purpose of such contracts is to forestall the introduction of technological innovation that would make the incumbent monopolist's capital obsolete. This agreement to forgo future pro-consumer technology will invite the monopolist to invest more in specific capital infrastructure and hence improve its ability to satisfy additional consumer demands in the short run, a period that may last several years. Goldberg's conclusion is that political suppression of innovation may increase the present value of the stream of demands satisfied. But as Robert Ekelund and Richard Higgins have shown, to obtain this efficient result one must assume a high degree of consumer risk aversion.[10] More fundamentally, it ignores alternative institutional arrangements where consumers contract directly on this flexibility-inflexibility trade-off. Nor does Goldberg's model explain why political agents will know what level of risk aversion to choose for the consumers, nor why, knowing this, they would seek to maximize their constituents' private interests. The important theoretical conclusion is that private contracting, in the abstract, is fully capable of encompassing any gains to risk-averse consumers from precluding future innovation.

Parameters of Competition under Private Contracting

Even where only one firm survives in a market, competition among an elastic supply of potential competitors may serve to constrain market power. This constraint will be tighter as the costs of marketing competitive systems are reduced. Obviously if these costs were zero, market power would be zero. This case is not without analytical significance because the assumption of zero transactions costs is implicit or explicit, depending on the expense undertaken by the expositor in the model of perfect competition, and it is to this ideal that monopolistic output restrictions are contrasted in welfare economics. Even more to the point of this discussion is the fact that nonzero transactions costs between consumers and political agents are excluded by assumption in Goldberg's plausible efficiency case for regulation. This is all the more anomalous given that Goldberg's intention is to create a transactions costs explanation for regulation of long-term arrangements.

As a practical matter, it may be feared that the high cost of persuading a sizable majority of the community to sign long-term exclusive dealing commitments will in fact render the constraining power of this competition impotent. Richard Posner dismisses private long-term contracting in natural monopoly markets because "the buying side may be too fragmented to bargain effectively (as is true of telephone subscribers, for example)."[11]

Goldberg, interestingly, raises the possibility that "the alternative to regulation need not be a publicly let franchise contract; it could simply be private individual contracts made under the jurisdiction of the public law of contract."[12] Goldberg proceeds to discount the practicality of this solution not on appeal to a transactions costs problem but on consideration of the implications of the antitrust laws. In Goldberg's framework, then, regulation by government is called for to shield certain proconsumer exclusive dealing arrangements from civil and criminal liability. Additionally Goldberg relies on political agents' administering public utility regulation to solve a market failure that is itself created by political agents' inflicting antitrust regulation against the consumer's interest.

But here I sidestep arguments involving antitrust law and focus on the empirical question concerning the cost of contracting privately to eliminate the natural monopoly consumer welfare problem. This question has not been carefully addressed either logically, save by Posner, whose writing has been largely ignored on this issue, or empirically.[13] This is curious since the entire structure of natural monopoly theory rests on the assumption that these costs are overwhelming. Here I shall evaluate the logic of the private contracting solution before considering empirical evidence in the cable television industry.

First, it may be argued that consumers would be reluctant to enter exclusive dealing contracts for extended periods based on apprehension over forgoing flexibility in consumption. Yet the inevitability of a long-term relationship with one particular provider of the public utility is established by the economics of the market. Tying up one's options is not what one does in choosing to sign a long-term contract. The consumer's options have already been delimited to but one firm by existing cost conditions. By contracting with one firm versus another, consumers are allowed to expand their options by selecting the natural monopolist of choice.

Under monopoly franchising, such choices are made on behalf of consumers (at least nominally on their behalf) by political bodies. Competition for political selection naturally leads firms to supply politically demanded cable services.[14] Allowing open entry into the cable or other utility business by abolishing monopoly franchising would shift the price-quality offering so as to appeal to a different set of demanders. This consumer-oriented competition would serve to end the cross-subsidization of interest groups inherent in politically awarded cable television monopolies.[15]

Numerous court actions in the cable television market currently have been brought by cities and franchise holders against outside suppliers underpricing incumbent firms, thus cream skimming the market. (Entire markets have also been stolen from incumbents, of course, eliminating the cream-skimming allegation altogether.) This may be simply a case of a discriminatory pricing scheme being broken by competitive forces and not a case of what economists describe as inefficient cream skimming.[16]

Competition to gain customers directly rather than by political franchise competition could utilize various institutional arrangements to lower marketing costs. A potential entrant could solicit long-term contracts by gathering the endorsement of community leaders, consumer advocates, and respected local business leaders, who themselves have a financial stake in competitively priced utility services.

Additionally, brand name competition among vying cable companies could reduce information to consumers. The argument that brand name information is of little value due to the infrequency with which consumers make purchases, that is, sign long-term commitments, is without standing. Nationally integrated firms, operating in dozens of localities, would be in a situation, at any one time, of facing several pending renewals. Their quality performance, then, would be constrained by the effects on their brand name to the extent that information travels across localities, which one suspects it does quite freely.

Large developers, apartment building owners, home-owners' associations, and other community groups would lower marketing costs for their individual members or inhabitants and also reduce informational costs for community residents and property owners outside such institutions who could simply free ride on the endorsement of those groups selecting the best competitor. (Of course, those consumer groups investing in a search for the best utility provider and whose search is costlessly taken advantage of by others as free riders also have more to say in selecting the winning monopolist. In that sense they are remunerated for their effort.)

In the average city, the great bulk of the population figures to be incorporated either in multifamily housing or associations with relatively low-cost ways of researching alternatives and disseminating information as to the individual's self-interest. The endorsement of a city's apartment owners' association alone could prove decisive in determining the winning franchise. Moreover, as an unregulated monopolist raised prices above competitive levels, such neighborhood businesses, organizations, or large-scale landowners and developers would likely initiate a competitive challenge to the established monopolist.

In considering the private contracting solution, Maurius Schwartz and Robert Reynolds argue: "Such long-term contracts are likely to be infeasible because of the cost of monitoring and enforcing quality and performance. . . . Long-term contracts are particularly unlikely where new entrants are involved since the quality and cost of their product is relatively unknown."[17] While national brand name competition is a relevant consideration, the primary response to this point is that there will be a long-term contract, either implied or explicit, because of the technological and economic nature of the relationship.[18] The long-term contract is a given; the question revolves around whether the state is the only institution equipped to administer such a contract efficiently. I suggest that it is possible to conceptualize and empirically observe alternatives.

As for entrants being unable to compete where long-term contracts are involved, brand name competition may proceed apace, the newness of a firm's involvement in one particular community (or one particular industry, as conglomerate integration is a predictable market response to the problem raised by Schwartz and Reynolds) notwithstanding. But this franchise problem is clearly symmetric: political selection of franchise monopolies, regulated or unregulated, must rely on some assessment of quality assurance just as a private contractual arrangement does.

Three Problems

There remain at least three problems regarding long-term competition for private customers. First, are the transactions costs prohibitively expensive? Second, if several firms sign customers to contracts but only one firm survives, by what process will the customers who signed with nonsurvivors obtain service? Third, there is a price discrimination problem.

Transactions Cost Problem

What is the transactions costs problem in individually soliciting every community resident for utility service? Viewed from one perspective, the problem appears insurmountable: dozens of firms taking a shot at the franchise, each ringing doorbells, sending mailers, clogging the local television and radio airwaves. Yet such expensive monopoly-seeking activities are unprofitable beyond a limited scale in search of privately acquired monopoly. Such costs are constrained by the potential entry of more appealing competitors.

Since information is costly for consumers to obtain to distinguish the competitively priced options open to them, the price offered by the winning monopolist will be above long-run average cost but not by more than the cost of informing consumers about lower-priced alternatives. Since the winning firm will have to incur selling costs equal to this amount to beat out its rivals, there are no above-normal returns. Moreover, there is no welfare loss, for such informational costs are real costs (properly understood as the price of discovering consumer choice in a world where such discovery is not costlessly available to the market or the government). And since expenditure on such is constrained by potential competition that faces no entry barriers, the investment in selling costs to provide consumer information on alternative sources of supply will tend to the optimal level, that is, the amount consumers as a class are willing and able to pay for in the face of their ignorance concerning market opportunities.

Because of uncertainty among firms as to which product consumers will select, firms contending for monopoly markets might enter in direct competition during this solicitation stage. It is unlikely, however, that large numbers will do so in any one market, for the expected gains necessary to sustain multiple entry can be justified only by prices that will remove the firm charging them from contention for the monopoly. (In fact, multiple entry—that is, any more than one firm engaging in the marketing of long-term contracts—can be explained only by asymmetric expectations concerning consumer preference or relaxation of the natural monopoly assumption.) Here the market imposes a discipline by threat far more efficiently than by the wholesale waste of resources that would flow from numerous firms' all pursuing the same competitive returns. Yet that waste would be inexplicable in a world in which such costs are internalized. Contrarily the transactions costs problem that arises from the private pursuit of publicly protected, above-normal returns will likely constitute a social cost problem far in excess of any alleged transaction efficiencies realized from public auctioning or regulation of natural monopoly firms.

Consumer Risk

The second problem concerns the seeming incompatibility between competitive marketing before the investment is made and natural monopoly once it is built. How are consumers who sign up with a "losing" rival for the monopoly to be served? This is actually a two-stage problem. In the early stage of competition for the monopoly, mergers between firms would simply change the name on the long-term contract in the consumer's possession. In the latter stage of competition, when it has become apparent which the dominant firm will be, mergers will no longer be possible because the beaten competitors will have nothing to sell. Only this last stage problem raises a question of consumer welfare because it points out a seeming externalities dilemma: if a competitor ties up consumers but does not become part of the eventual monopolist survivor, consumers who did commit to a long-term relationship will then be at the mercy of the survivor, which will have every incentive to charge them monopoly prices.

This situation can be prevented by a procedure wherein each competitive bidder for the community's franchise posts a performance bond guaranteeing the consumer who signs up the package of services, prices, and quality listed in the contract. Nor need the municipal government require such a bond, since consumers' risk aversion would push competitive firms to offer this as part of their private long-term contract (without consumer risk aversion, this entire question becomes moot). Such bonds would ensure that, should a firm fail to gather sufficient customers to build its system, it would contract with the winning monopolist to do so. Since the winning monopolist could charge monopoly prices to the outcompeted rival's customers without entering into such a contract, the performance bond must be capable of paying off the present value of the difference between competitive and monopoly prices per customer signed. This alone will act as a powerful deterrent for firms attempting to enter markets frivolously. If the results obtained in the earlier discussion hold and actual entry is limited to one firm in each regional market, this problem evaporates.

But a further question may be raised: why will consumers care about signing up with one particular firm if they are compensated by their cable company should another emerge victorious? Why don't they just sign up with any bonded firm, given the fact that this single decision will not be decisive in determining which their cable company will be?

This model looks like a private voting model. But different incentives can easily be included within the model to improve on this: the indemnification of customers of nonsurviving firms could (and probably would) contain some slippage so that the customers bore some cost if they enlisted with a losing firm; and the possibility that two or more providers may indeed offer service in the same neighborhood (a relaxation of the natural monopoly assumption is a practical consideration of importance because the consumer will not in general know whether the service will end up as a natural monopoly when it is initially offered, and even with this knowledge will not know what geographical boundaries each franchise will assume).

Linda Cohen has pointed out that the introduction of bondings in the private contracting solution approaches a regulatory solution in its own right and brings forth some of the same agency problems of the public sector regulatory solution that this alternative seeks to improve upon.[19] She is quite right. Two advantages appear to emerge with the private contracting alternative, however, that may mitigate much of this similarity. First, the area of public regulation involved with private bonding is delimited to a far narrower range of issues when a private constitution relies on legal enforcement of some problematic issues, unresolvable by the private parties themselves, than does government regulation, which delegates all decision making, especially of price and service quality, to the legal-political sphere. Second, competition for private consumers will not be independent of this adjudication problem but will encompass it, such that consumers may select firms with relatively agreeable dispute-settling institutions and track records.[20]

Price Discrimination

The last problem, price discrimination, is most interesting. It concerns not those customers who sign up with the nonsurviving firm(s) during the pre-building competition phase for the monopoly but those who fail to sign up at all. Because the competition for the long-run monopoly position entails no market power, competitive prices must be charged (indeed, guaranteed) during the time a firm is bidding to become the long-run monopolist. Yet once the dominant firm has emerged, this survivor can then be viewed as having considerable market power over those consumers not protected by long-term contract. The survivor could mop up the market by charging its last customers monopoly prices.

If, however, it is recognized that such an opportunity exists for the eventual winner when the rivalry begins, then it is evident that competitive firms would lower their prices in the competitive stage of the contracting process even below average cost. By securing exclusive dealing privileges with a sufficient proportion of the utility's possible clients, the firm precludes other providers from operating at sufficient scale to threaten its ability to exact monopoly returns from some residual of the general consumer population. Competition for this monopoly return will in turn suppress prices in the initial competitive stage below costs. In fact, all the monopoly returns available from price discrimination against late signers of long-term contracts will be competed away in the struggle to exploit them. The beneficiaries of this price discrimination scheme, then, will not be the cable monopolists but the consumers who commit themselves early on to a particular cable provider. In essence, they will receive a premium for incurring the burden of risk in deciding on a particular cable company before additional information (such as which firm seems to be winning) becomes available.[21]

The existence of price discrimination against late signers facilitates a private contracting solution without undue delay in the marketing phase and offers a handy remedy for any possible hold-out problem. In this model, there is no gain, but a substantial loss, to be incurred by refusing to cooperate with a competitively priced entrant. The hold-out problem is thus cleanly disposed of.

Political Regulation and Public Contracting

Barry Mitnick concedes that Harold Demsetz has "demonstrated with his market-like solution, the traditional decreasing-costs explanation [of natural monopoly] is insufficient."[22] An attack on Demsetz's approach by Harry Trebing, Oliver Williamson, and Victor Goldberg, however, has led to an analysis of the costs of long-term contracting that provides "a potential rationale for natural monopoly regulation (or, at least a framework for examining that rationale)."[23]

For both Williamson and Goldberg, it is the inherently risky character of investment in specific (nonsalvageable) capital that a natural monopolist engages in that prompts government regulation. This argument gives regulation an efficiency motivation (where efficiency is measured from the perspective of the consuming public). Williamson argues:

> At the risk of oversimplification, regulation may be described contractually as a highly incomplete form of long-term contracting in which (1) the regulatee is assured an overall fair rate of return, in exchange for which (2) adaptations to changing circumstances are successively introduced without the costly haggling that attends such changes when parties to the contract enjoy greater autonomy.[24]

Goldberg develops this theory further. He sees the essence of natural monopoly as a marriage between firm and consumer wherein a divorce would be exceedingly costly for both sides. In that both parties are thus stuck with each other, the natural response is to spell out the terms on which the long-lived relationship will proceed. Unhappily imperfect information and the possibility of opportunistic behavior severely limit our ability to make such specifications (once we step beyond the zero transactions costs world and into our own). "While the parties might want to go into considerable detail at the formation stage concerning the rights and obligations of each party given various contingencies," writes Goldberg, "it will prove too costly to specify the precise terms of the contract and it will be desirable instead to use rough formulae for mutual agreement to adjust the contract to current situations."[25] This brings a demand for some sort of constitution to regulate the relationship.

Goldberg asserts that regulation of natural monopoly may be an efficiency-motivated attempt to provide such a constitution but offers no more than a plausible case for some constitution. His only reference to the alternative of natural monopoly regulated by private long-term contract is his footnote citing legal contract difficulties that create problems "well beyond the scope of this essay." Elsewhere Goldberg equates private decision making with the "discrete transaction" model that, he claims, is "the paradigmatic contract of economic theory."[26] He states that intertemporal contracting and information costs raise a case for government regulation:

> Unless we are willing to bestow the individual with extraordinary analytical powers, there is substantial room for rational but limited, individuals to develop alternative institutional arrangements—such as regulation or governmentally imposed standards on contractual terms—that will be superior to the private contract, free choice alternative. The explicit recognition of the relational aspects of many transactions not only leads to a broader feasible role of government (in an allocative efficiency framework), but also suggests a very different set of criteria against which to judge efficiency.[27]

The most basic criticism of this view is that Goldberg has not explained why, if such regulation is in the consumer's individual interest, the government must be called on to impose it. The model outlined features a private competition for consumers wherein individual purchasers would be offered an array of product choices, including choices as to a relational constitution. A firm could privately contract directly with the city council, a panel of judges, an agency of the local government, or even the elections board to arrange for voter selection of officers to compose a special oversight body or to establish private voting mechanisms as has been done within corporations or with thousands of home-owners' associations.[28] Thus, private competition dominates the efficiency-motivated explanation of regulation.

Goldberg deems regulation a "way consumers, in effect *delegate* to the agent" in order to achieve efficiency.[29] One is immediately struck by the lasting veracity of Joseph Schumpeter's maxim: "The theory which construes taxes on the analogy of club dues or of the purchase of the services of, say, a doctor only proves how far removed this part of the social sciences is from scientific habits of mind."[30] It is eminently proper to suggest "a very different set of criteria against which to judge efficiency," when previous analyses criticized long-term relationships of any character (as the current state of antitrust law would clearly attest). Why private market mechanisms would fail this expanded test of efficiency remains unexplained.

What appears straightforward, rather, is that the agents charged in Goldberg's model with creating the efficient arrangements—local politicians and regulators—will not be selflessly moved to provide them. Instead the politicians-as-entrepreneur will seize the possibility of natural monopoly as a profit-maximization opportunity. Goldberg postulates a "benevolent agent" to carry out the task of creating competitively priced long-term contracts. This "agent will, in effect, be called upon to manufacture group preferences."[31]

But if we include the political actor as subject to the normal rationality assumptions, we may hypothesize that the actor will maximize the consumer surplus of those constituents over whom he or she may lay political credit.[32] That is, a politician who seeks to improve (lessen) the client's welfare has some probabilistic expectation that he or she may take the credit (get the blame) for such welfare increases (decreases). This individual is interested in maximizing net consumer surplus weighted by the probability that such surplus will be associated by constituents with his or her political action. (This is only a slight restatement of Sam Peltzman's maximizing function for the political agent.)[33]

This behavioral assumption instantly biases the politician's actions toward monopolistic restrictions in that competitively priced services will be received by consumers who will in general thank only the firm providing such services. Even then, they will not overwhelmingly express their gratitude because the consumer remains rationally ignorant as to the potential costs of monopoly. Rival politicians could attempt to inform consumers as to the costs of monopoly once it is imposed, but (as Goldberg has convincingly argued) much of the purpose of such regulation is to tie up long-term commitments not subject to election year whims. Communication of the benefits of free trade and competition during the election year preceding the awarding of a monopoly contract additionally runs into free rider, information cost, and multiple issues problems discussed in so much of the public choice literature.

Empirically we observe municipal governments creating regulatory solutions where none, by Goldberg's standard, are necessary; regulated municipal refuse removal, for example, involves supervised monopoly of a business in which no long-term investment in highly specific capital is required. From the political maximization assumption, one should expect that the internalized benefits to political agents of government-sponsored monopoly are nearly always greater than the benefits from government-permitted private monopoly, even where the latter secures the proconsumer allocational effects of real and potential competition. (By definition, the cross-elasticity of demand from one community to the next is very low for natural monopolies, which is why politicians would fail if they attempted to turn services that were not naturally monopolistic or geographically specific into government-sponsored monopolies.)

As an example, a privately derived natural monopolist in cable would offer maximum consumer surplus under the model of competition developed but would also leave zero surplus for politicians to extract except as they themselves are consumers of cable television services. On the other hand, should the city council choose the cable monopolist, it is free to select a product package and franchise stock plan distributing surplus (consumers' and producers') to targeted constituents, thus protecting the politician's property right to the surplus.[34]

Moreover, the politicians' benefits are positively correlated with the inflexibility of any long-term agreement reached. Cross-subsidies steer benefits to politically elastic demanders and tax (with monopoly prices) politically inelastic demanders.[35] Thus the present value of benefits to favored interests increases as the probability that the agreement is rigid and long lasting rises. Robert Michaels develops this rationale in explaining the existence of inert bureaucracy. Whereas William Niskanen tries to explain the behavior of bureaucrats who maximize their utility, Michaels seeks to understand why legislators create and set into motion maximizing bureaucrats. Michaels asserts, "The politician-as-entrepreneur will often have good reasons to establish an 'uncontrollable' bureaucracy which acts like Niskanen's. Only if he can do so can he sell durable legislation to interest groups."[36]

This more realistic view of the political process is extremely damaging to Goldberg's efficiency defense of regulation because Goldberg argues that regulation can provide just the proper amount of flexibility, when natural monopoly economies compel some trade-off between short-term liquidity and long-term maximization. What Goldberg sees as a solution to the trade-off is to promise a long-term (inflexible) relationship governed by a (flexible) governing body. Flexible pricing rules, such as rate-of-return regulation, are the prime example. But the pursuit of self-interest by political agents is shown to undermine such flexibility in regulation in practice. Pricing rules are likely to be devised by civil service employees or captured bureaucrats, neither a reliable representative of consumers' interests but hired for a distinct purpose altogether: "A bureaucracy independent of the enacting legislature may be desirable to both parties to a political bargain because of its role as enforcer."[37]

In this respect, we should not be surprised to find politicians creating monopoly barriers for reasons other than consumer welfare maximization. The virtually universal cartel licensing of taxicabs, where specific investment is confined to a city medallion, leaps to mind because regulation rules out such flexible approaches as jitney service and part-time drivers. Thus, it may be shown that the transactions costs associated with obtaining a government-let (and -regulated) franchise monopoly will equal the present value of the supranormal profits available from obtaining the exclusive dealing arrangement. This can be derived from Posner's familiar argument regarding the costliness of competition for a monopoly.[38] Even if a publicly issued franchise creates some transactional efficiencies, these would necessarily be competed away on elaborate campaigns to gain the more lucrative award. It is in the interests of political agents to encourage this wasteful competition, given institutional impediments to conducting straightforward exchanges for political favors. While it may be valueless to consumers in general, it is a rivalry that reveals the most desirable political package from the standpoint of political agents. It is just this sort of competition that such agents erect monopoly barriers to encourage. And since the privately gained natural monopoly could not be so lucrative to the private supplier, with its competitive price structure constrained by potential entry, no rent-seeking investment would be advanced to obtain it. Any alleged transaction efficiency created by government auctioning or regulation of natural monopoly must be weighed against this output-restricting incentive on the part of the regulators and the social costs expended to obtain the monopoly. The question as to the more efficient form of control, potential competition versus government regulation, becomes an empirical matter.

Finally, we cannot fail to note what may be the most disappointing aspect of Goldberg's model: its failure to deal with the informational problem of regulators. How are these agents to know which products consumers are willing and able to pay for? And how best to provide them? Under what quality conditions? What is the optimal shape and scope of the relational constitution? Rather than answer or even raise such questions, Goldberg chooses to analogize market institutions into governmental ones and to postulate that there really may not be much of a difference after all. When speaking of contracts entered into "voluntarily" versus those "imposed" by rule of law, he states that "the line between private and public rules (restrictions) is blurred . . . a complex admixture of public and private jurisdictions."[39] When the lines start to become too blurry, we must remain alert to the fundamental differences when consumer preference is revealed through actual choice making by individual consumers as opposed to the central directioning conducted by regulators who do not bear the costs or consume the benefits of their choice making.[40]

Franchise Bidding versus Public Regulation: Their Convergence

In his path-breaking 1968 discussion of franchise bidding versus public regulation, Harold Demsetz's essential point was that the existence of high and asymmetric transactions costs was necessary for the presence of monopoly returns and that this criterion is not deducible a priori but is rather an empirical presumption. This chapter progresses precisely in the direction he indicated. Confusion seems to have developed in the literature concerning an abstract formulation that was put forth as simply a theoretical construct: Demsetz's consideration of a publicly held auction. The Demsetz solution to the natural monopoly problem, in fact, has come to be known as replacing direct government regulation with a municipal auction among competitive private firms. Once the natural monopoly is defined by a local governmental agency, an auction for such a franchise could be held. Firms would be asked to submit price schedules as opposed to lump sum payments, and the city officials could select the lowest price bid. In an open, noncollusive bidding process involving an elastic supply of potential suppliers, this winning bid would just equal the competitive price (that is, either a price equal to long-run average cost or a multipart tariff yielding a marginal price equal to marginal cost).[41]

Certain assumptions must be employed in the Demsetz model, such as the restriction of competition among firms to the price-quantity dimension (there are no quality differences), price schedules of competitors can be unambiguously ranked, the good is known by the municipal government to be a natural monopoly, and so on. There is much that is troubling about employing the public auctioning model in a real world policy framework. Perhaps if Demsetz had been aiming at such a practical use, he would have taken pains to state more than two important assumptions (that there be no market power over inputs and that competitive bidders be unable to collude).

The heterogeneity problem arises quickly in cable franchising. A municipal government issues a request for proposals (RFP) and proceeds to hold hearings to evaluate rival firms' offerings. Each presents a distinct menu, differing in a number of dimensions: channels, programming, physical plant, disruptions to local streets, public access and local origination facilities, reliability, composition of firm ownership, and so on.

In selecting its (sole) cable franchise, Scottsdale, Arizona, for example, faced the contenders shown in table 4–1. The variance in price bids is large, and the choice among firms is still nontrivial. Telecable, the lowest nominally priced cable service by a comfortable margin, did not receive the city's award. Third-ranked (by nominal price) United did. The city's report announcing the award did not even mention United's rate structure as a consideration, dwelling instead on the listed criteria: "Management . . . the Future . . . Community Programming . . . Other Innovative Commitments."[42] Appar-

Table 4–1
Scottsdale Cable Television Price Bids

Bidding Firm	Average Monthly Cost per Subscriber
Telecable	$22.96
Sammons	29.47
United	32.26[a]
Cross Country	34.35
Teleprompter	35.44
Scottsdale Cablevision	39.10
Capital Cities	45.82
Camelback Cablevision	54.39

Source: "Cable Television Final Report" (City of Scottsdale, November 1981).
[a]Winning bid.

ently most impressive was the creation of a nine-member management committee, of whom four would be appointed by council members themselves, and a $25 million investment in community programming over the fifteen-year life of the franchise (in comparison to a $19.3 million capital cost to be incurred in the first seventeen months of the franchise).

The simple task of choosing the firms with the lowest rate structure, this example demonstrates, quickly ceases to be simple. As Donald Sizemore observes of cable franchising battles in general:

> Few public servants, elected or appointed, have the time or background to understand fully what cable television will mean to their communities. Local government frequently calls in consultants to develop "needs assessments" and to evaluate the responses to the request for proposals for a cable system. But frequently local governments get standardized packages that scarcely reflect a community's make-up or service needs. And it is not unusual for cable companies to be able to orient their proposals toward specific consultants whose evaluation systems have been studied. Thus, what looks good on paper may well bear no relationship to reality. . . . Apparently there is considerable difference in perception among the cable companies, local government, and the consumers as to the services cable television should provide.[43]

Such inherent deficiencies with the public auctioning solution have long been noted. Delos Wilcox reports that one bidder for a franchise in Boston around 1900 agreed to pay the city 100 percent of gross revenues for the life of the franchise.[44] This behavior telegraphs some sort of opportunistic behavior. Charges of corruption were widespread in the early days of this municipal function in the United States. Often it was observed that political agents were engaged in franchising actions in blatant contempt of consumer welfare maximization. One particularly amusing episode, also in Wilcox's detailed survey, occurred in Oregon. State legislators there passed a measure requiring that any firm, to receive a street railway franchise, would have to provide free passes to legislators and other public officials. This law was quickly overturned by popular referendum.[45]

These obvious shortcomings of a system of publicly let franchises are introduced here to establish the equality, not inferiority, of public auctioning versus public regulation. In the public auction, regulation is present; it simply occurs at an instant in time as opposed to Goldberg's elongated regulation over time. The essential terms of public utility performance are spelled out by the political agents auctioning and/or regulating the franchise (in the real world, the two are often combined). In general, the difficulties with political regulation of economic activity have to do with the informational and incentive problems of the regulatees and regulators and have little to do with the temporal aspects of the regulatory scheme specifically selected.

To the extent that more flexibility is preferred to less, all else equal, Goldberg's model may have something to recommend itself; it allows regulators to impose Demsetz's special case, fixing prices and the service menu at the moment of franchise letting while also encompassing the option to impose a more liquid arrangement calling for price and service adjustments according to some regulatory regime. Of course, where all else is not equal, inflexibility may be preferred (as a means of securing certain investments, for example), as Goldberg is thorough in noting.

The public auction model retains political agents as the final arbiters of price-output variables. It may be reasonable to suppose that consumers themselves would desire a more flexible arrangement with a public utility operator than the fixed-point solution offered in the municipal auction. In this respect, the auction must either be expanded to include such long-run regulatory contracts or sink to nonoptimality. On the other hand, should such flexibility not be desired by consumers, political agents in Goldberg's regulatory framework could, as true consumer representatives, simply adopt the Demsetz auction solution.

Further, Demsetz did show what this auctioning example was introduced to show: that under the assumption of perfect information on the part of government regulators, there is no reason for them to regulate; they are able to enact a solution approximating perfect competition in resource allocation to begin with. But the regulatory problem must, to be fruitful analytically and interesting for public policy, deal with the informational and incentive realities of alternative institutions.

Goldberg has recognized this, but he has looked at only half the picture: private transactions costs. Public-sector transactions costs and agency problems must be equally considered in developing a general theory of natural monopoly regulation. Goldberg's model does not presume prescience on the part of political agents. Indeed Goldberg perceives regulation as a flexible, real world response to changing conditions of demand and technology. Yet he does appear to assume that, given the disruptions of the private marketplace, political agents passively adjust so as to pursue selflessly and with full information the interests of their constituents: welfare-maximizing regulation. If a symmetric view of private omniscient agents faithfully resisting opportunistic behavior were hypothesized, there would be no long-term contracting problems for regulators to adjudicate.

In practical terms there is little to differentiate between the Demsetz solution and the Goldberg propositions. Since both models vest political agents with the responsibility of choosing the optimal solution, the precise contractual shape of the regulatory form selected would appear endogenous to both systems. It remains an interesting economic question as to why political agents overwhelmingly prefer rate-of-return regulation for the electric utility industry and essentially franchise auctioning to regulate cable television. But the logical and empirical implications of either solution appear to converge, when contrasted with the private contracting (laissez-faire) alternative. If political agents choose to use their monopsony power as the consumers' buying agent or benevolent regulatory administrator, then there should appear some visible advantage to consumers in the form of lower prices, better service, or both. The primary critique to both approaches is identical in that consumers have a critical agency problem in delegating their choice making to regulators that may or may not act in their interests.

I have presented three distinct explanations for why administrative public regulation has evolved in naturally monopolistic markets. The oldest and still most commonly held theory states that regulation was necessary to prevent a two-stage consumer dilemma: an initial phase of overinvestment, ruinous rate wars, and wasteful duplication of capital, followed by a second stage of consolidation, monopoly, and exorbitant pricing. This I shall call the traditional rationale for regulation.

Victor Goldberg rejects this approach, arguing that declining-cost industries cannot be judged monopolistic on technological cost conditions alone. He sees the natural monopoly problem as the riskiness associated with long-term dealing through an uncertain future. His efficiency defense of regulation explains public agency as a transactions cost economizing device, where long-term contracts are beyond the ability of private market transactors to achieve (at least in a cost-effective manner). I call this second explanation the Goldberg hypothesis and assume that it encompasses the public auctioning solution, for reasons already given.

Third, I have discussed the view that models government regulation as a political response by maximizing political agents. In its first approximation, this capture theory sees regulators as created and controlled by the industries they regulate.[46] In its more sophisticated rendition, it views legislators and bureaucrats as brokers in a complex market for political favors.[47]

Cable Television: A Case Study of Natural Monopoly and Its Regulation

The emerging industry of cable television (sometimes misdefined as the CATV, or community antennae television industry) market provides a fascinating laboratory in which to study these competing hypotheses concerning the natural monopoly problem. The industry is in the infant stage where the legal limitations on competitive activity have not existed so long that there is little hope of separating monopolistic factors imposed by economic conditions from those imposed by state intervention. Moreover, the industry, thousands of individual systems (over 5,800 in 1982), has a number of varying institutional arrangements in force, each a distinct attempt to deal with the peculiar relationship in an industry characterized by large elements of "natural monopoly."[48] State regulation by commission occurs in eleven states: Alaska, Connecticut, Delaware, Hawaii, Massachusetts, Minnesota, Nevada, New Jersey, New York, Rhode Island, and Vermont.[49] The primary level of regulation, even in these state commission jurisdictions, is administered through the franchising process at the local government level. Generally the city council issues such a franchise. The typical procedure is for the council to grant a "nonexclusive" award—but to issue only one. According to conflicting accounts, this is done either to deflect possible antitrust litigation or to give the municipality some continuing market power over the incumbent once the grant is issued (that is, the threat of entry).

The vast majority of municipalities limit their franchise grants to one per region. Larger cities usually divide themselves into franchise segments, issuing multiple, nonoverlapping awards. But we are fortuitous in having a small sample of cities that have invited duplicative cable competition; several of these have engaged in what the industry calls overbuilding. This relatively small list of duopolistic cable markets is rapidly increasing, however, due to the innovation of a technology making direct contracting for cable services by developers and others far less costly than before. Because this "private cable" market gives us head-to-head competition within allegedly naturally monopolistic markets and is the source of a large amount of ongoing litigation concerning the meaning of a franchise monopoly in cable, this promises to be an excellent submarket for study. Before moving to study these competitive situations, it should be noted that a broader analysis of the cable television industry would include discussion of municipal ownership, subscriber owned (co-op) systems,[50] and, most important, jurisdiction of free entry, where no franchise is attempted by the local authorities.[51]

Private Contracting

A straightforward test of the efficient contract explanation of regulation could be constructed by examining utility arrangements in large-scale privately owned housing developments, where privately owned refers to one firm's owning the entire development (examples are Leisure World, Sun City, and Epcot Center). The owner of such a development would desire to provide the efficient solution from the individual resident's point of view so as to capture all such efficiency gains in the capital value of the development's properties. Wherever developers of such communities specifically defy the arrangements provided by local authorities for a particular mode of utility provision, expending significant legal costs in the process, we are led to suspect either a cross-subsidy regulatory scheme in which the development's residents would be forced to suffer net negative returns or a cream-skimming incident that may arguably be inefficient to allow (it is important to note that Goldberg does not use this argument as justification for public agency).[52] I will consider the former implication after having first dismissed the latter as a plausible explanation in the case of cable television distribution.

The efficiency argument against cream skimming maintains that some investments may provide net consumer benefits but be sustainable only under a regime of price discrimination against consumers with a relatively high demand price. The problem occurs when an entrant lures away these high-demand-price customers by offering them a slightly lower-priced alternative.

This scenario is suspect as a general theoretical proposition in that it is so sensitive to highly restrictive assumptions that it is clearly inappropriate in describing the economics with respect to the specific test of cable television. As for the general case, if the net gains to consumers are being diminished because one class of customers has reduced its contribution to the fixed costs entailed in the efficient solution, there will always exist some subsidy that could be paid to deserting consumers out of the gains of the remaining consumers. The two-part tariff arrangement can be redesigned to achieve the necessary consumer compliance, wherein alternative technologies are underpriced so as to keep consumers' contributions to the fixed-cost efficient solution. If such an arrangement is not logically possible, it can only be because alternative technologies offer greater consumer surplus than the initial fixed-cost solution. Moreover, if the costliness of separating markets is introduced to explain why such a logically possible price discrimination scheme is not obtainable in practice, this reasoning begs the entire issue of cream skimming: well-defined submarkets are being targeted and absconded with by entrants with relatively high marginal costs. Identification and separation of these submarkets are precisely what the problem entrant is charged with doing in the first place.

With respect to the specifics of cable television, the cream skimming in evidence differs from that posed in the economic efficiency argument.[53] That is, monopoly, single-part tariff arrangements discriminate against consumers in high-density, low-cost-of-service locations (such as apartments, condominiums, hotels, hospitals, and trailer parks) and discriminate in favor of low-density, high-cost suburban home owners. The monopoly franchise incumbent truly views the multifamily unit as cream and is understandably upset whenever rivals attempt to underprice this lucrative submarket with competing technologies or economic arrangements. But this is a transparent case of cross-subsidy for political efficiencies and has no resemblance to the economic efficiency argument against cream skimming. This instance offers a classic illustration of Alfred Kahn's observation that "there is a general presumption in favor of *true* cream-skimming; it tends to *eliminate* unjustified price discrimination."[54]

Let me return to the issue of single-owner developments that attempt to evade the publicly imposed cable television monopoly. Some have argued that a developer might seek to contract with an independent (nonfranchise) firm in order to take the monopoly rents inherent in cable television for his own. This argument runs afoul of the double-counting fallacy. If a developer imposes a monopoly solution on potential customers, the demand for the developer's property will adjust downward, lowering its value by just the amount of the monopoly overcharge. The developer has no power to charge a profit-maximizing monopoly price for its property and tie in a monopolistically priced utility service. Indeed the only reason the developer does not simply distribute cable free of charge to home owners or tenants is due to the variation in consumer preference for cable. If no heterogeneity among buyers were evident, there would be no reason to incur the accounting expense of monthly billing. (Some developments apparently do distribute cable television in this way. Tucson Estates Cable Co., for example, charges $30 installation but no monthly fee. This suggests a homogeneous community with respect to cable television demand.)[55]

Competition for the Cable Television Monopoly:
Illustrative Cases

Vista, California. One clear instance of private contracting for cable television occurred recently in Vista, California (near San Diego). A large Canadian developer, Daon Corporation, was constructing a 4,500-home planned community in the late 1970s. Subsequent to its market research, the firm approached an independent supplier of local cable television services, Billy Daniels and Company, to consider servicing its development. The cable company, a national firm, agreed to take the franchise and to pay the legal costs that Times-Mirror Cable Company, the city of Vista's sole franchise holder since 1966, was expected to impose. (The Times-Mirror management made it expressly known that they would bring suit against any entrant for violation of what they perceived to be an exclusive franchise monopoly. Times-Mirror did, in fact, sue. It lost, however. In January 1981 the Vista City Council, under a California court order, issued a second cable franchise to a Billy Daniels and Company subsidiary, Pala Mesa Cablevision.)

The motivation for Daon's opting out of the city-designated franchise monopoly is fairly clear-cut in this case: Times-Mirror offered twelve to fourteen channels of programming, whereas Billy Daniels's system delivered thirty-five (prices were approximately equal). But even where such factors are less obvious, the developer's choice in this sort of situation should be trusted as welfare maximizing for consumers. Any inefficiency imposed by the developer on potential customers will simply lower the value of property (that is, the monopoly exploitation will come out of the developer's own hide). This constrains the developer to act in the consumers' interests.[56]

The long-term commitment between Daon (developer) and Billy Daniels (cable supplier) was in the form of a franchise agreement issued by the city of Vista (nonexclusive, for Times-Mirror was already operating under its own agreement with the city). This leads, perhaps, to the Goldberg argument that government may be efficient at adjudicating complicated long-term agreements between consumers and producers, particularly when large uncertainties are present (as, for example, technology in the cable television industry). Three points are relevant here, however.

First, whether the city is a truly efficient regulator is not actually at issue because contracting parties are not bearing the cost of whatever service the city is providing. It is possible that Daon and Billy Daniels are simply free riding on city-provided legal services that would be purchased at less than taxpayer cost should the subsidy be withdrawn.

Second, the actual regulation called for in the contract is extremely loose in form. Installation fees and monthly charges for basic cable are listed; no mention is made of prices or qualities of other premium offerings, nor is there a listing of what services constitute the basic program package (the Federal Communications Commission does not allow local governments to regulate the price of premium services). Nor is any review mechanism included to have such prices and services regulated by city officials. City regulation becomes effective only if the operator seeks to raise rates for basic cable service. These tariff hikes must be approved by the city council; their action is entirely passive. The cable operator is solely responsible for updating the cable programming menu in accordance with new technology, and so on. This hardly makes the city a close analogy to the flexible regulatory constitution hypothesized in the Goldberg model. To be consistent with the regulatory contract model of regulation, the entry of Billy Daniels and Co. into a nonexclusive franchise territory should have resulted in higher effective prices owing to an absence of government-imposed constraints on monopoly pricing (assuming that cable television is a natural monopoly; if it is not, the Goldberg model has an additional informational-agency problem because it is regulated as if it is). Yet here we observe that the entrant was invited in by the developer because of its lower effective prices. This is clearly anomalous to the efficiency view of public agency over natural monopoly, and the resulting legal skirmishes lend support to the cross-subsidy (capture) hypothesis of regulation. More pointed evidence contradictory to Goldberg's explanation of regulation is the fact that it was the new entrant that was invited in because of its commitment to a heavier specific capital investment, laying more expensive cables to bring in more than twice as many channels.

Co-Op City, the Bronx. Co-op City is a 300 acre, thirty-five-building apartment complex of some 15,000 units, privately owned and operated by the Riverdale Corporation. Riverdale conducted its own franchise bidding procedure entirely analogous in form to those held by municipal governments, right down to the pro forma RFP. It issued "a detailed Request for Proposals to the entire SMATV [satellite master antennae television] industry to solicit bids for a contract with Co-Op City. . . . Eight bidders responded. . . . the Board selected the one which appeared to offer it the best deal and we began a long and complex negotiation which has led to a proposed contract [since consummated]."[57] This winning firm was Satellite Television of New York Associates (STONYA). Its private contractual arrangement with Co-Op City differs from those between New York City and its exclusive cable franchises in the following respects:[58]

1. The apartment owner receives 10 percent of all cable television revenue (as opposed to the 3 percent cities normally receive) because the FCC cap does not apply to private developers.
2. Should the franchise be sold, Co-Op City receives 10 percent of the capital gain.
3. Cable operator provides television cameras in all sixty-five building lobbies and closed circuit lines to each apartment so residents can monitor their building's entryway for security and convenience in identifying incoming guests. This lobby channel is provided to all tenants without fee.
4. Cable service provided at "marginally lower rates" obtained through competitive bidding between potential cable suppliers. (Rates may not be raised without Co-Op City's approval.)
5. Little local origination or public access programming is called for beyond the security channel.
6. The agreement contains a "finest state-of-the-art service package," delivering 104 channels, which must continue to offer a program menu commensurate with, at rates no higher than, those offered by the city's franchisees.

Regarding the developer's kickback (items 1 and 2), it must be reiterated that this vertical contract integration will, in a competitive housing market, be dissipated in rivalry for consumers in the form of lower rental fees and home prices (although a price discrimination element may remain). As the development's attorney has boasted, "The implications of such a state-of-the arts TV system are obvious and all positive. It will increase security and make apartments more valuable and marketable while enhancing the viability of the community."[59] Co-Op City has no market power over cable services. Thus the inclusion of this service with the housing package with a rebate back to Co-Op City can be understood only as a price-discriminating arrangement available to all of Co-Op City's housing market rivals, which will constrain any excess returns (from the rebate scheme) to zero.

The proconsumer aspects of this arrangement, particularly the private security channel provided to noncable subscribers and the modern 104-channel system, which represents a top-of-the-line investment in specific capital without municipal monopoly guarantees, cast doubt on the need for such guarantees to obtain such benefits. More to the point, the city and state of New York have filed suit against this arrangement. That the New York governments are tenaciously pursuing a lawsuit against the Co-Op City management may involve the issue of simple wealth distribution: because the Co-Op City development is entirely on private property, the contract cable firm has not applied for a city permit (the legal justification for local franchising and/or regulation and/or taxing of cable being that city streets, rights-of-way, and utility lines are being utilized) and hence pays no city fees on cable receipts. Still, the Goldberg-alleged inefficiency associated with unregulated private monopoly should at least poke through this arrangement into the price-quality package offered consumers, particularly as a higher rate of "taxation" is levied by the private SMATV-Co-Op City agreement than in the government-franchised alternatives (10 percent on gross revenues versus 3 percent on gross revenues). Moreover, the argument that regulation is needed to raise tax revenues should do more to embarrass the efficiency defense of regulation than to further it.

Indeed, the government's entire case smacks of Posner's regulation by taxation. The primary charge, made by several city and state regulators and made here by the city's chief of cable franchising, Leonard Cohen, is that competition from SMATV will make it impossible to bring service to all Bronx residents because it "creams off . . . a highly desirable area."[60] In fact, the city of New York received only one bidder, Cablevision, for the Bronx franchise; the franchisee accepted only on condition that it would thereby gain the right to wire some more lucrative neighborhoods outside the Bronx. Now that STONYA is serving Co-Op City (which has 2 percent of the borough's population), Cablevision says it will no longer exercise its franchise (although it has been invited by Co-Op City to compete head to head with STONYA).

This leads one rather irresistibly to the conclusion that significant cross-subsidization takes place in ordering cable franchises to serve all comers (takers, really), at rates unadjusted for cost differentials. Where heterogeneity in the consumer product market leads firms to expect widely varying subscriber-to-plant-mile ratios, price-to-marginal-cost ratios will vary widely. This discriminatory pricing scheme is just what monopoly franchises serve to protect.

It would be dangerous to conclude that a discriminatory one-price policy is designed to subsidize service in poorer parts of town such as apparently is the case in the Bronx franchise. Subscriber-to-plant-mile ratios may be lower in poor neighborhoods due to an income effect holding penetration levels down; yet this would appear much less a factor in most environs than the offsetting fact that affluent suburban homes are set on spacious home sites. Since the poor tend to dwell in high-density neighborhoods, even a low penetration would be expected to yield a higher density of subscribers than where wealthy suburbanites live two families to the acre. If this reasoning is incorrect, it is wrong by its assumption of natural monopoly cost conditions; proponents of regulated monopoly franchising are well advised to leave this distributional argument aside.

Private Cable. In the instance of Co-Op City we were introduced to an interesting new technological competition, SMATV, to traditional cable in the form of community antennae television.[61] This means of distribution can bring CATV-quality (or better) reception to homes in high-density clusters by utilizing much more modest capital investment than that required for its more established rival. The problem with SMATV is that it generally is equipped to transmit just 12 to 20 signals (channels) compared with CATV's 54 to 108 channel capacity. Furthermore, lines cannot take the SMATV signal several miles away, as can the CATV cable. Both of these problems, however, can be remedied by installation of multiple SMATV receivers. Co-Op City's 35 highrise apartment buildings and 256 townhouses are being delivered 104 channels. The advantage of SMATV is that for high-density areas of at least 250 units, it is significantly cheaper than CATV.

As of 1982, an estimated 500,000 subscribers were being served by SMATV operators nationally, specifically catering to real estate developments.[62] This subindustry has shown rapid growth in that the FCC allowed SMATV only beginning in 1981. Now the only federal requirement is that the FCC be sent a notice informing it of the operator's existence; no permit is necessary. At least forty firms offer SMATV services to customers.

The real estate industry has been enthusiastic about the emergence of this competitor to CATV. Indeed it has allied politically with private cable, as it is called, to lobby against CATV-industry-sponsored legislation in state capitals and Congress and entered lawsuits jointly. The primary advantages for the developer's contracting with SMATV, according to industry sources, are the following:

1. Whereas cable franchise monopolies in previous years have been accustomed to hook-up fees of $100 to $150 from a developer to wire cable to each housing unit, SMATV firms offer free hook-ups and pay the developer a percentage of receipts.
2. SMATV operators sell their service as nondisruptive; developer complaints as to broken windows, trampled shrubs, and other problems, have plagued CATV installation procedures in the past.
3. SMATV operators sell customized service more easily to a planned housing development than do franchise monopolies (city governments will

issue such franchises only to CATV firms). Special services, such as a security television channel in the Co-Op City instance, can be readily adapted to the developer's specifications.

Numerous lawsuits are now in the courts pitting developers and SMATV operators, on one side, against city governments and franchise cable monopolists, on the other. Hence legal action to escape regulation appears widespread. A veritable litany of lawsuits, wherein natural monopolists trek to court to fend off irrationally eager entrants, is now in evidence.[63] It is worth noting that incumbent monopolists are always, in the cases I reviewed, allied with the local political franchise-granting entity.

So far most courts have sided against exclusive franchise arrangements. Moreover, the FCC has taken an aggressively pro-SMATV stance. "There are a lot of new technologies coming on stream now," says FCC official James McKinney. "Regulating them locally like cable-TV systems could have a chilling effect on those new technologies and keep them from developing, so we're flatly prohibiting that."[64] Why the FCC should take a more procompetitive stance than local governments is an interesting public choice topic. An avenue of approach might be to focus on the cartelistic relationship between local politicians and cable suppliers; this is a cartel arrangement that can be expanded to include the federal regulator only at great cost, and disruption to the cartel itself. Interesting, too, is the fact that Governor Hugh Carey's office took an early stand loudly in favor of free entry, endorsing Co-Op City's plan to bring in SMATV, which he called "a model system," while endorsing "a competitive and open marketplace for telecommunications."[65] If regulators can be reliably trusted to promote efficient outcomes, it is perplexing that the local regulators are pursuing a diametrically contradictory course from that of the federal regulators. Which "efficient" regulators does the efficiency defense of regulation choose to file its brief on behalf of?

The hostility with which local regulators greeted the FCC decision putting "state and local governments . . . on notice that regulatory overreaching will not be tolerated" is revealing.[66] William Finneran, chairman of the New York State Commission on Cable Television, claimed the ruling would be "devastating" to the "orderly growth of cable" and to "the hopes of poor and marginal income families." Most important, he scored the private developers: "Assertions that SMATV fosters a 'free competitive marketplace' are a blatant untruth," because landlords would be certain to choose SMATV operators over cable operators just to wriggle out of local government taxation of franchised CATV firms and to split such revenues together.[67]

Since, however, the vast majority of cable suppliers are taxed just 3 percent of gross receipts, this implies that no more than this modest margin can be credited with shifting landlords to private cable. If this slight differential would be sure to deliver all the developers to the currently available alternative technology, as Finneran strongly warns, then the efficiency loss must be slim indeed.

An additional issue of interest that emerges in these lawsuits is challenging to Goldberg's contention that government agents may be required to create long-term dealing arrangements that give investors the right incentives to sink specific capital. It is plain that, at least in the cable industry, the "benevolent government agent" sometimes attacks just the sort of exclusive dealing contractual relationship that Goldberg holds out as the plausible rationale for government-imposed entry barriers and the like. A January 1984 state court decision struck down an exclusive dealing arrangement between the 400 unit Robert Mills Apartments in Maple Shade, New Jersey, and ACS Enterprises, a Pennsylvania-based SMATV-operator involved in over 200 systems nationwide.

In exchange for a twenty-year exclusive franchise to serve the apartment building, ACS sunk $40,000 ($100 per unit) in wiring the complex in 1978 and agreed to pay the landlord a commission on each subscription. This arrangement was attacked by the local cable franchise monopolist, Maple Shade Cable, serving some 4,500 subscribers. When the landlord denied Maple Shade Cable the privilege of wiring the apartments for cable based on his previous commitment to ACS, the cable company sued and won, on the grounds that such exclusive dealing was restraining trade.[68]

Similarly the Florida courts have upheld a state law giving cable franchise monopolies the right to install their systems on private property, even when the property owners wish not to deal with them. This rules out the possibility of exclusive dealing with any but the municipally chosen monopolist.[69] Additionally, legislation pending in Congress in 1984 (H.R. 4103 and S. 66) would make cable monopoly access to private dwellings mandatory by federal statute. A lobbyist for the SMATV trade association warns that the law "gives the cable company a tremendous competitive advantage over SMATV. It allows large cable companies to overbuild SMATV and put SMATV out of business."[70]

This appears to point out just the sort of circumstance Goldberg believes justifies entry barriers. As the price of attracting specific investment capital in a state-of-the-art technology, it may be optimal to sign away future options even where those options possibly will prove of greater consumer satisfaction. SMATV, quickly and courteously installed and offering a medium-sized array of pay services, may yield a higher present value to consumers than the option of waiting for high-cost, larger-sized CATV offerings. How regulators will realize this subtle rationale, where judges and legislators are busy working to subvert it, is unexplained. (Federal courts have upheld exclusive dealings between apartment owners and SMATV operators when challenged by another SMATV operator as being anticompetitive.)[71]

Some may argue that this discussion of city governments and franchise monopolists fending off entrants is valid empirically but incorrect in the aspersions I allege they cast on the transactions theory of regulation. That is, it may be argued that after an initial investment in nonsalvageable capital is made by some franchise monopolist, it is reasonable to expect, given a human propensity for opportunistic behavior, that some initial beneficiary of the sunk investment will now find it in his or her interest to renege on the exclusive dealing arrangement with the introduction into the marketplace of new, preferred possibilities. In this light, the litany of lawsuits over cable competition would represent good-faith city governments and cable franchise holders protecting their long-term commitments against opportunistic free riders. Sadly, this argument has great difficulty in logically explaining the circumstances of the cases I have discussed, which mostly involve competition for scratch (that is, no sunk investment by the monopolist was at issue).

First, the argument that a property developed later in time can efficiently be coerced into entering an exclusive dealing arrangement must make some highly unrealistic assumptions (pertaining to current technologies somehow vanishing from the marketplace in future periods) because the land has no value to capitalize by giving up its future options. In that it receives no service during the period in which the exclusive award is granted, it is trading away future options for no gain in current service. Hence, it is impossible to view this as an exchange; we are led to infer a cross-subsidy explanation, wherein current demanders may receive lower rates and better service in return for the business of soon-to-arrive community residents, as the most favorable Goldbergian interpretation.

Second, this argument does not fit the facts of the cases observed: Who is free riding on sunk investment? Each situation involved an extension of service to residents not initially served by the franchise monopolist. This gives us an open market for long-term agreements; the divergence between the market's estimation of efficiency under these terms and the local government regulators points to an agency problem of nontrivial proportions.

Subscriber-Owned Cable. As another constraint on monopoly market power, we have the interesting institutional structure known as the cooperative, or subscriber-owned, cable. Approximately seventy-five such systems exist in the United States, mostly small in size, serving rural communities, and old (sixty are estimated to have been built prior to 1955).[72] Yet Davis, California, awarded in 1982 its municipal franchise to a cooperative, making it the largest U.S. subscriber-owned cable system as ranked by franchise area (15,000 homes). (Cable Regina in Saskatchewan, Canada, was incorporated as a subscriber-owned system in 1974 and today serves over 40,000 subscribers.)

This institution may be most informative to consider as a source of potential entry. Any opportunistic behavior by a regulated or unregulated monopolist could be dealt with by threat of subscriber-owned entry. Should the incumbent monopolist be disciplined by this threat, then entry need not occur. Should this threat suffice to constrain monopoly power, then the members of the community (specifically, cable subscribers) would themselves benefit in the form of lower prices: they internalize the benefits from threats of entry (which may be costly to make in a credible fashion).

Duplicative Municipal Franchising. Perhaps the most serious and nagging anomaly confronting the natural monopoly premise and regulatory conclusion in the cable television market is the persistence of overbuilds. Given the wasteful duplication view, the existence of physical (as opposed to potential) duopoly is inexplicable; given the regulation as a long-term contract theory, the result must surely be suboptimal underinvestment. Yet the overbuild phenomenon appears to be growing. Households served by two or more cable operators rose in number from some 100,000 homes at the start of 1979, whereas in mid-1981 there were at least eight overbuilds representing some 500,000 homes.[73]

Allentown, Pennsylvania, has had a decade and a half experience with head-to-head competition. Service Electric Cable began service in 1951; Twin County Cable entered the market against the entrenched natural monopolist in the 1960s. Combined penetration in the hilly region with low-quality off-air reception is 95 percent. Three-fourths of the city is open to either rival; Service Electric has 59,000 subscribers, Twin County 57,000. Rates are comparable to the national average. In 1982, Service Electric (Allentown) was charging $7.50 for monthly basic service, and Town County (Northampton) $7.65, against a national average of $8.46. While their combined basic-plus-Home Box Office (HBO) rates were nearly identical to nationwide averages, this is because of higher-than-average premium (HBO) rates, and these rates are unregulated by any municipal government. Both systems have recently upgraded to thirty-five channels; nonexclusive franchising rights do not appear to have limited their net incentive to invest in nonsalvageable capital. I refer to a net incentive because although the existence of a cofranchisee reduces the expected return from specific capital by introducing the possibility of loss through new technology employed by the rival, better marketing effort by the rival, or a business misfortune, it increases the investment incentive through competitive rivalry and elimination of X-inefficiency.[74] This trade-off appears to reveal a proconsumer tilt toward competition because both Allentown firms offer full service, state-of-the-art program menus at average prices without excessive guarantees or "undue damage to the bottom line."[75] Moreover, in the face of regulation by competition, consumers are not subjected to a loss of options by regulation by regulators. Should a technological breakthrough or entrepreneurial innovation offer to improve welfare, residents will not be tied to obsolete technologies by regulators committed to sunk investments. As Goldberg argues that this privilege may be an important right to sign away, so as to encourage heavier specific investment in the current period, we should prize a rival institutional setting in which a comparable level of nonsalvageable investment is secured without any such loss of consumer flexibility.

A more recent entrant into the overbuild subset is the 9,000-home cable market in Paramus/Hillsdale, New Jersey. Most interesting here, perhaps, is the existence of preentry long-term contracting: "Both companies offered incentives to initial subscribers, with UA-Columbia providing free installation and the first month free and Cablevision offering free installation and a 10 percent rate reduction to those who committed to at least six months of service. Cablevision also offered premiums, such as small appliances and radios, for early subscriptions."[76] Such informal long-term agreements may be sufficient, given appropriate costs of contract, to induce the optimal level of investment. Apparently consumers in this market are none the worse for lack of an explicitly regulatory constitution. Jim Kofalt, top executive of Cablevision, believes that "the competition between the two companies resulted in a higher penetration than would have otherwise occurred." This is just the efficiency criterion we are looking for.

The price, size, and basic penetration data shown in table 4–2 will help in analyzing the effect of municipal franchising-regulation by comparing prices and penetration ratios in duplicative franchise localities with national averages. First, I shall underscore the problems in analyzing these data. Most fundamentally, if our desire is to see the effect of head-to-head combat on prices, quality, and output, there exist no data specific to these overbuild situations. Franchises operated in oligopolistic markets are usually involved in a mixture of monopoly and nonmonopoly franchise areas. (Exceptions, where entire systems exist in a duplicate franchise area, include Phoenix, Arizona; Columbus, Ohio; Slidell, Louisiana; Paradise Valley, Arizona; and Manatee County, Florida.) Data from any one system include data from both types of jurisdictions.

Also troubling is the existence in Columbus, Ohio, of gentlemen's agreements to respect an informal quadrant division of the city. However, the lack of a legally enforceable barrier to cross-competition should serve to lessen specific capital investments under the regulatory contract explanation and should be unworkable (leading to wasteful duplication) under the traditional efficiency defense. (Curiously, the phenomenon may be a brief for collusion.) Therefore, although we get less information on the costliness of the duplication question than we would like, these data still bear directly on either efficiency defense of regulation. Most important, in any jurisdiction with directly competitive franchise awards, whatever monopsonistic power the government could employ on behalf of consumers is significantly lessened. This is the primary motivation in examining this duplicative franchise situation.

Along these lines, it is important to state that a city with two or more franchise holders does not present the threat to incumbent behavior present

Table 4–2
Duplicative Franchise Competition in CATV

System	Subs	P basic	P prem	Basic pen	Ratio
National Average	n.a.	8.46	9.58	55.0	1.00
Columbus, Ohio	54,848	10.95	7.95	56.6	1.08
Columbus, Ohio–ATC	32,225	8.95	9.45	45.0	1.05
Columbus, Ohio–KBLE	10,000	8.50	6.50	35.1	.86
Columbus, Ohio–Qube	59,100	9.00	9.95	42.5	1.08
Slidell, La.	6,205	8.50	8.95	33.1	.97
Slidell, La.–WOM	4,778	7.50	7.95	55.5	.86
Paradise Valley, Ariz.	2,005	10.50	10.00	44.8	1.09
Paradise Valley, Ariz.	500	7.50	9.50	13.2	.90
Phoenix, Ariz.	27,613	8.50	9.95	31.3	.98
Phoenix, Ariz.–Storer	8,735	8.00	8.50	25.6	.87
Allentown, Pa.	36,800	7.50	9.00	40.9	.97
Northampton, Pa.	55,000	7.65	10.00	55.0	1.04
Bergen Co., N.J.	29,468	7.00	10.75	47.0	1.01
Wayne, N.J.	115,160	8.50	10.50	41.3	1.08
Huntington, N.Y.–TVC	19,000	8.50	6.00	40.4	.80
Huntington, N.Y.–CBLVN	n.a.	4.25[a]	16.98	n.a.	1.17
Troy, N.Y.	34,338	9.50	9.00	66.7	1.02
Delaware Co., Pa.	22,925	7.50	6.95	34.9	.85
Chester, Pa.	10,000	9.21[b]	6.54	n.a.	.85
Bryan, Texas–Mid	12,500	4.00[c]	8.00	78.1	.66
Bryan, Texas–CollegeSta	8,500	4.00[c]	9.95	73.9	.77
Florence, Ala.	21,454	9.00	10.95	74.8	1.08
Manatee Co., Fla.	21,587	8.25	9.00	54.5	.96
Manatee Co., Fla.–CVC	4,200	8.95[a]	8.49	42.5	.97
Sample Average					.96

Source: Paul Kagan Census, December 31, 1982. Data for some franchises unavailable. A listing of duplicative franchise cities was compiled from a review of news publications and the trade press.

Notes: Subs = number of subscribers to basic service; P basic = price of basic service; P prem = price of premium channel (usually HBO); Basic pen = proportion of subscribers per homes passed; Ratio = P basic + P prem / state avg P basic + Nat'l Avg P prem (state averages for premium services were unavailable).

[a]Price data were obtained by contacting the cable company directly and obtaining current (June 1984) prices. These data were deflated by 1.06 to adjust to real prices as of December 31, 1982. Huntington Cablevision, which has a very low basic price and a very high HBO price, bundles its premium channel with several other satellite entertainment networks, and so this may well be misleading.

[b]Data were obtainable only through Television Factbook as of April 29, 1981. These data were inflated by 1.09 to bring to real December 31, 1982, prices.

[c]Lowest in state.

in a scheme of absolute free entry where potential competitive forces lurk undeterred. In a duplicative franchise city, entry is still proscribed. Yet it seems plain that to the extent that the municipality does use its bargaining position on behalf of consumers (which is the proposition we seek to test), the admission of multiple franchisees will reduce that bargaining ability. There should be no mistake about the direction of influence; a multifranchise community relies more on economic market constraints and less on political ones.

However tentative should my conclusions be regarding data unadjusted for cost or demand shifts among communities, these numbers are suggestive. They indicate that overlapping franchise cities do not appear prohibitively expensive, which may be why we see them. If the duplication of facilities problem is in evidence, it will take a more subtle analysis to find it.[77]

In Bryan, Texas, a city of long-standing overbuild, we see prices for basic cable service that are the lowest in the state. Overall the combined price of basic and HBO monthly service is 4 percent lower in the multiple franchise cities. Moreover, it is clear that the threat of cable competition can motivate incumbent behavior. In a city not in my survey, Presque Isle, Maine, the city government has issued duplicative franchises. An incumbent firm, now owned by Group W, was providing only twelve channels of service. In the early 1980s, the city issued a second franchise. The incumbent quickly announced plans to upgrade to a fifty-four-channel service menu, complete with the modern complement of satellite stations. This was put into operation in February 1983. The second firm decided not to enter an already established fifty-four-channel system.[78] The real competitive significance of the multiple franchise cities, then, is that their existence signals the possibility of direct competition, making the second entry threats of outside firms or municipal governments that choose to use this bargaining chip credible.

Conclusions

> The essence of the regulatory approach . . . is the acceptance of a single company (or group of existing companies) as society's *chosen instruments* for performing the service in question. It vests in that chosen instrument, by license, explicit responsibility for providing good and economical service to all comers; it imposes obligations on it that go far beyond obligations imposed on private companies in the economy generally; and it subjects it to all sorts of controls. In return, it protects it from competition. In brief, it places society's principal reliance on conscious and explicit planning, by monopolists or a limited number of selected companies on the one hand and regulatory commissions on the other.[79]

As developed, refined, and received, our current theory explaining why regulation is called for in naturally monopolistic industries is based on information problems in a complex environment. Faced with a complicated world and complex long-term relationships in that world, regulators are seen as a low-cost mechanism for imposing rules on monopolists. Yet by the very same problem, that of limited information, we are led to question the ability of regulators to know what rules efficiency dictates or, divining such wisdom, their altruism in implementing such to the detriment of more profitable opportunities. William K. Jones, in a demonstration of the dimensions of our faith in administrative directioning of economic outcomes, writes that from an optimal regulatory standpoint, "it may be preferable to reform the operating practices or pricing policies of the incumbent rather than to approve new entry."[80] The trick is that were we to know what to tell the incumbent to do, we would never have reason to call on or allow the rampant confusion, chaos, anarchy, and duplication that characterize competitive enterprise. There appears all too little room in our models of the world, and particularly those we impose on our vision of naturally monopolistic markets, to give the discovery process of the market its fair due. While economists since before Adam Smith have spoken of competition's virtues explicitly, there is small enthusiasm to attempt the far more demanding task of inserting the competitive process implicitly into our theories of the market.

How ironic that a theory based on bounded rationality would serve to justify what Kahn has so aptly labeled a system of "explicit planning." That many of the pitfalls of long-term relationships, such as the occasional need for employment of exclusive dealing, are inherent in either private or public schemes of contract is not to be denied. What must be seriously questioned, however, is how such arrangements may rationally be imposed by a process that first liberates decision makers from the discipline of competitive market forces. The transactions costs theory of regulation begins by pointing out the complicated world in which decisions are made and then retreats to a world run by a decision maker who makes no complicated decisions—indeed one who faces no choices but simply adjudicates as a wise and omniscient construct.

Certainly Goldberg succeeds in creating a plausible case for government regulation of natural monopoly, yet plausibility may be overrated. What we are truly interested in are arguments that are both logically possible and convincing explanations of fact for a set of relevant circumstances. Yet the actual course of circumstances makes proconsumer regulation little more than a plausible theoretical exercise.

This critique of natural monopoly theory has taken the hard case; it has dealt with public utility regulation over an established market and settled for comparing existing firms under rival regulatory frameworks. It is assuredly the dynamic cost of regulation, the substitution of bureaucratic inertia for the competitive struggle of the marketplace, that so concerns the astute analyst. The economic system's success in creating wholly new markets and organizations has assuredly the greatest impact on consumer welfare over the long haul. In this regard Posner ominously warns:

> The most pernicious feature of regulation would appear to be precisely its impact on change—its tendency to retard the growth of competition that

would erode the power of regulated monopolists. To embrace regulation because an industry is today a natural monopoly and seems likely to remain so is to gamble dangerously with the future. To impose regulation on the basis of a prophecy that the industry will remain monopolistic forever may be to make the prophecy self-fulfilling.[81]

It is this long-run dynamic that looms as the most tragic casualty of the regulatory reflex. Even economists who are ready to concede some steady-state advantages of monopoly licensing and government regulation still strongly oppose the concept in policy terms due the dominating costs such a scheme imposes in the dynamic context. The easiest case for the regulator to make is the static argument for effective price reductions for consumers from known methods over a given technology. The most fundamental, and damning, criticism of the public agency method is not that it condemns consumers to inefficient output restrictions or deprives consumers of clearly superior alternatives but that regulators armed with the power to restrict entry will prevent whole industries from arising altogether. Virtually every contemporary analyst, confronted by the histories of bureaucratic behavior in the Interstate Commerce Commission, the Civil Aeronautics Board, or the Federal Communications Commission, is perplexed by this dilemma. William Jones accepts regulation's premise that "the purpose of such a restriction upon entry is to prevent wasteful duplication of facilities and the kind of costly competition consequent upon nonrivalrous behavior of multiple firms in natural-monopoly markets." Yet he is struck by this maxim's obvious abuse:

> The danger is that regulatory restrictions upon entry will be employed to bar entry into markets which lack natural-monopoly characteristics and in which competition would be beneficial. (Restrictions upon entry into trucking and air transportation are examples of misplaced entry controls; these markets do not exhibit natural-monopoly characteristics, and the regulatory programs in these industries lack any other discernible rational foundation.)[82]

Yet the industries Jones cites as mistakenly monopolistic were certainly once viewed by regulators and economists alike as prime candidates for the regulatory solution. While hindsight is useful and history is fun, the policy discussion cannot be furthered by explanations as to yesterday's regulatory failing. These mistakes are endogenous to the solution. As economist Thomas Sowell is able to discern from the regulatory situation in telecommunications, wherein the FCC's first response to the advent of cable technology was to stifle it for a solid decade, public agency comes as a package deal:

> Cable television made possible an unlimited transmission of stations to any given point, unlike broadcasting through the air. The whole structure of the industry—networks, affiliates, advertising patterns—could have been un-

dermined or destroyed by the new technological possibilities. So too would have been the existing regulatory apparatus, which was no longer needed after the industry was no longer inherently monopolistic. But as in transportation after alternative modes (autos, airplanes) eliminated the railroad monopoly on which the I.C.C. was based, so in communications the response to the elimination of the initial rationale for regulation was to *extend* the regulation to encumber and contain the new threatening technology.[83]

It is hoped that this discussion has contributed to the theoretical and policy debate surrounding the question of natural monopoly. Perhaps it rages hottest today on the timely matter of cable television regulation, on which this chapter has focused. As an emergent technology, cable offers great promise to consumers and producers alike. Yet it is, as Sowell suggests, too vulnerable to the excesses of restrictive and reactionary regulation. A recent study coauthored by Alfred Kahn concludes that "cable systems lack the economic and legal attributes of a natural monopoly and that all major markets and submarkets in which cable competes (or is likely to compete) are workably competitive with a number of alternative suppliers."[84]

Perhaps it is too late for the railroad customer of 1920, the trucking shipper of 1940, or the airline passenger of 1960. But it is not too late for today's cable television consumer to ask simply: if Alfred Kahn cannot see elusive and shadowy gains from a speculative policy of municipally mandated exclusive dealing, are we to give our blessing to the Oxnard City Council's quest for government-crafted efficiency?

Notes

1. Harold Demsetz,, "Why Regulate Utilities?" in *Journal of Law and Economics* 2 (April 1968):55.
2. Franklin Giddings, "The Persistence of Competition," in *Political Science Quarterly* 2 (March 1887):78.
3. In a fuller model of market power such an assumption would not be necessary, because anything "available" to an incumbent is, by virtue of the notion of exchange, available to an entrant. See Harold Demsetz, "Barriers to Entry," *American Economic Review* 72 (March 1982).
4. Is this feasible? Such contracts would certainly carry a penalty clause for failure to sign up early (or, equivalently, some bonus for early signing), and this penalty would be significant if monopoly rates were well above competitive rates (and if they are not, we may not have a problem). Since such contracts are attached to real property, this penalty becomes capitalized in the value of the property. It would certainly take somewhat less than a 90 percent market share to decide which natural monopolist will stay and which will exit. Customers who end up paying above competitive rates because of their refusal to enter into long-term competitively priced contracts are simply seen to be purchasing some flexibility.

5. It is not feasible for the incumbent, but soon to be extinct, monopolist to buy out the entrant at this point or any other. Although the gains from keeping an unregulated monopoly are higher than the competitive returns soon to be realized by the entrant, there are no barriers to exclude unlimited entrants that could hold up the incumbent with threats of entry. In fact, the community's citizens would be in a perfect position, one suspects, to incorporate a succession of cable competitors, sign up and sell out, thus appropriating all of the monopolist's rents and quasi-rents.

6. The performance of the legal obligation could be "insured" at competitive rates either explicitly or implicitly by brand name competition on the reliability frontier.

7. Depending on operating costs, the sunk capital would not necesarily become worthless because the old firm would stand to gain a share of the market by servicing the customers not committed to long-term contracts with the competitor and with the rival's customers after their long-term commitments ran out. Because it is conceivable this firm could stay operational, the entrant must deflect opportunistic behavior by consumers who might be tempted to deal with the former monopolist, which, on facing successful competition, has incurred a substantial reduction in the opportunity cost of its capital.

8. See Victor Goldberg, "Toward an Expanded Theory of Contract," *Journal of Economic Issues* 10 (March 1976), and, "Regulation and Administered Contracts," *Bell Journal of Economics* 7 (Autumn 1976).

9. Notice that the symmetric nature of this problem, which Victor Goldberg seems to miss, may mitigate its effect somewhat or entirely. That is, the firm that enters a market first, aggressively establishing its product, customer relations, capital structure, and brand name, may be in store for positive windfalls at the hands of new technology, which may make its old investment not obsolete but increasingly valuable. Cable television is just such an industry where it appears that positive windfalls have been enjoyed by established cable systems as new programming and services have come on line. Undeniably competing technologies have, conversely, been discovered to undermine cable's market. To the extent that these countervailing effects balance, the problem of windfalls is lessened.

10. Robert Ekelund and Richard Higgins, "Capital Fixity, Innovations, and Long-Term Contracting: An Intertemporal Economic Theory of Regulation," *American Economic Review* 72 (March 1982).

11. Richard Posner, "Natural Monopoly and Its Regulation," *Stanford Law Review* 21 (1969):562.

12. Goldberg, "Regulation and Administered Contracts," p. 444.

13. Within the industrial organization literature, Judge Richard Posner is the only analyst to take up the private contracting solution to the natural monopoly problem considered here. See Posner, "Cable Television: The Problem of Local Monopoly," Rand Memorandum RM-6309-FF (May 1970), and Posner, "The Appropriate Scope of Regulation in the Cable Television Industry," *Bell Journal of Economics and Management Science* 3 (Spring 1972):98–129. His analysis is both interesting and compatible with my own. Just two major disagreements arise: Posner's treatment of the turnover from one monopolist to another, as when a contract period with a utility supplier has run out, and the poll-like character of revealed consumer preference in selecting the monopolist of choice. Regarding turnover, there can be no predictable future advantage in being an incumbent that will not be reflected in better terms for

consumers in the initial franchising period. Posner suggests that future monopoly returns are predictable, thus implying irrational behavior on the part of initial period competitors for the monopoly gain. As for his second disagreement, the fact is that, since no single consumer will determine the supplier that the community selects as natural monopolist, we do emerge with some of the same problems that plague voting institutions in revealing consumer demand. See Thomas Hazlett, "Three Essays on Monopoly" (Ph.D. diss., University of California, Los Angeles, 1984).

14. Speaking to the suggestion that diversity be mandated in cable television by public renewal hearings of an exclusive franchisee's license, Eli Noam writes: "It is in the public interest to have communications media that need not quake before government officials. If frequent non-renewals of franchises were to occur, the result may be self-censorship and extreme caution in programming, thus perpetuating the present climate of franchise battles in which cable companies have to cater to local politicians, and where political and financial deals are often alleged to take place." See Noam, "Towards an Integrated Communications Market: Overcoming the Local Monopoly of Cable Television," *Federal Communications Law Review* 34 (1982):230–31. The reason current franchisees "cater to local politicans," however, is not because of frequent renewal hearings (the typical franchise in cable runs fifteen years) but because of the high monopoly rents thereby obtainable. All else equal, the more infrequent the hearings, and the longer the franchise grants, the more cable executives would be expected to quake during the hearings. The parameters of this competition for political marketing in cable are reported in Thomas Hazlett, "The Viewer is the Loser," *Reason* 14 (July 1982), Donald Sizemore, "The New Politics of Cable Television," *California Journal* (August 1982), and Josh Getlin, "Council Besieged by Cable TV Lobbyists," *Los Angeles Times*, August 3, 1982.

15. Posner's argument that the available monopoly returns created by a government licensing barrier will approximate the sum exhausted by firms competing for the monopoly franchise allows us to pinpoint the social savings here. Firms would, in the absence of monopoly franchising, devote resources to identifying and satisfying consumer demand. Any above-normal profit available would accrue only to those firms that had established lower cost curves (or, for a given cost curve, a higher demand curve). This model therefore pushes the competitive behavior to the efficiency frontier (as evaluated by the community's consumers) and eliminates the dissipation of resources inherent in the monopoly regulation situation.

16. See Alfred Kahn, *The Economics of Regulation* (New York: John Wiley, 1971), 2:220–246.

17. Maurius Schwartz and Robert Reynolds, "Contestable Markets, an Uprising in the Theory of Industry Structure: Comment," *American Economic Review* 73 (June 1983):490.

18. On this issue, Goldberg is quite correct: "The paradigmatic contract of economic theory (and of law) is a discrete transaction conveying a well-defined object (the ever-popular widget) in exchange for cash. . . . This discrete transactional mold is apt to be inappropriate for representing relations that are apt to take place over a long period of time and in which the parties will have to deal with each other regularly over a wide range of issues (many of them unknown in advance)." See Goldberg, "Regulation and Administered Contracts," pp. 426–427.

19. See Linda Cohen, "Comment," in this book.

20. A firm noted for buying off judges for their narrow financial gain would be at a disadvantage in soliciting customers for a new or revised franchise. This information, too, would be readily produced and disseminated by the firm's rivals. Given the multiple issues at stake in any city council race, it may be far more cost-effective to explore any one set of political agents as being anticonsumer in their regulatory powers. When the hidden, unresponsive positions of actual regulatory bureaucracies are put into the analysis, the private-public divergence becomes even clearer. Robert Michaels believes that regulatory bureaucracies are created unresponsive to consumers just so they might cooperate with certain regulatees without inflicting high costs on incumbent politicians.

21. See Hazlett, "Three Essays on Monopoly," for the size of this premium, which is calculated for the general case in appendix 1.

22. Barry Mitnick, *The Political Economy of Regulation* (New York: Columbia University Press, 1980), p. 305.

23. See Harry Trebing, "The Chicago School versus Public Regulation," *Journal of Economic Issues* 10 (March 1976); Oliver Williamson, "Francise Bidding for Natural Monopolies—In General and with Respect to CATV," *Bell Journal of Economics* 7 (Spring 1976); Goldberg, "Toward an Expanded Economic Theory of Contract"; and Mitnick, *Political Economy of Regulation*.

24. Williamson, "Franchise Bidding for Natural Monopolies," p. 91.

25. Goldberg, "Regulation and Administered Contracts," p. 428.

26. Ibid., p. 426.

27. Goldberg, "Toward an Expanded Economic Theory of Contract," p. 54.

28. It is worth remembering that no hold-out problem is evidenced in this solution. A natural price discrimination will penalize late signers. There are only negative returns to hold out for.

29. Goldberg, "Regulation and Administered Contracts," p. 445 (emphasis added).

30. Joseph Schumpeter, *Capitalism, Socialism and Democracy* (New York: Harper and Row, 1942), p. 198.

31. Goldberg, "Regulation and Administered Contracts," p. 432.

32. In a very real sense we have already violated normal rationality assumptions by endowing the political agent with omniscience over consumer preferences throughout the community.

33. Sam Peltzman, "Towards a General Theory of Regulation," *Journal of Law and Economics* 19 (August 1976):214.

34. The political agent cannot costlessly gain support in this manner; how far the trade-off will take this person in the directing of imposing monopolistic restrictions is an empirical question.

35. Where political elasticity $= (dV/dW)W/V)$ and $V =$ net political support (votes, contributions, and other) $W =$ net dollar value of the wealth transfer imposed by government.

36. Robert J. Michaels, "Long-Term Political Agreements and the Origins of Bureaucratic Power," *Public Choice* (1978):37.

37. Ibid., p. 47.

38. Richard Posner, *Antitrust Law: An Economic Perspective* (Chicago: University of Chicago Press, 1976).

39. Goldberg, "Toward an Expanded Economic Theory of Contract," p. 53.

40. See F.A. Hayek, "Economics and Knowledge," *Economica* 4 (1937); and Oliver Williamson, *Markets and Hierarchies: Analysis and Antitrust Implications* (New York: Free Press, 1975).

41. Harold Demsetz, "On the Regulation of Industry: A Reply," *Journal of Political Economy* 79 (March–April 1971).

42. City of Scottsdale, "The Final Report of the Scottsdale Citizens' Ad Hoc Advisory Committee on Cable Television" (Scottsdale, Ariz., City of Scottsdale, November 1981), pp. 16–17.

43. Donald Sizemore, "The New Politics of Cable Television," *California Journal* (August 1982):298.

44. Delos Wilcox, *Municipal Franchise* (New York: McGraw-Hill, 1910), 1:40.

45. Ibid., p. 107.

46. George Stigler, "The Theory of Economic Regulation," *Bell Journal of Economics and Management Science* 2 (Spring 1971).

47. See Peltzman, "Towards a General Theory of Regulation."

48. See Paul Kagan, *The Kagan Census of Cable and Pay TV*, 2 vols. (Carmel, Calif.: Paul Kagan and Associates, December 31, 1982).

49. Robert Entman, "Ain't Misbehavin'? Cable Television Franchising and the Case for Local Deregulation" (Durham, N.C.: Institute of Policy Sciences and Public Affairs, Duke University, 1983), p. 12.

50. See Hazlett, "Three Essays on Monopoly," chap. 3.

51. Importantly, entry is witnessed in jurisdictions where no franchises are issued (unincorporated areas of San Diego County, California, Pima County, Arizona, and Prince William County, Virginia). This is problematic to the Goldberg efficiency defense of state-imposed monopoly barriers as inducements to private investment, especially as these laissez-faire jurisdictions experience no obvious short-run higher prices as a result of "underinvestment" versus monopoly-franchised localities.

52. Care must be taken, however, in counting private developers that go along with politically chosen utilities as evidence in favor of the efficient regulation thesis because the development may be of insufficient scale to justify the sunk cost investment (even though the entire community, if allowed to choose individually, would select a means of provision other than that chosen by the authorities); and the expected legal cost (including the probability that the developer will lose a court challenge altogether) may outweigh the efficiency gains, even where the latter are positive and substantial. The per unit legal costs for smaller developments would be, we suspect, quite high.

53. The cream-skimming inefficiency argument assumes significant scale economies, dictating that fixed investment must be spread over a large, predetermined number of customers. Interestingly, while economies of density are apparent in empirical work by Bruce Owen and Peter Greenhalgh (that is, there exist savings from eliminating duplication equal to about 18 percent of total cost), there are no evident economies of scale; small systems appear to have per unit costs equal to large systems. This, again, is problematic to the natural monopoly explanation of monopoly franchising in the cable television industry; supermarkets, gas stations, dry cleaners— nearly every service business imaginable—experience economies of density but are not recommended for monopoly franchising. For further discussion, see Hazlett, "Three Essays on Monopoly," chap. 3.

54. Kahn, *Economics of Regulation* 2:225–226.

55. While evidence of significant and costly attempts by private developers to sneak out from under legally awarded monopoly grants would contradict the Goldberg thesis, it would fail to make a strong general case for the private contract solution to natural monopoly discussed earlier. If the objection to this model is that the high cost of individual contracting makes potential competition a nonbinding constraint on market power, the willingness of one developer to contract out of a monopoly franchise on behalf of 10,000 customers hardly represents itself as an interesting general demonstration of the case being argued. If, however, the opposing regulation-is-efficient argument is reduced to making its case on the basis of start-up transactions costs, this is a significant departure from the main body of that argument, which deals with a much wider, more general range of contracting problems. This would have dramatic policy implications as well, as it would shift the applicability of the pro-regulation rationale into a smaller class of plausible institutional settings.

56. We should note three alternative explanations for developer behavior in this matter distinct from the assertion that the developer was seeking to escape from a regulatory constitution that did not, on net, benefit the potential consumers of his development compared to some available alternative. First, there is the cream-skimming argument. Whatever general applicability it may possess, it has little bearing on the cable television example being discussed. Second, there exists the rationale that the developer was simply attempting to evade city taxes. (In the Vista example, the charge is wholly without substance because both the incumbent and the entrant must pay 3 percent of their gross revenues to the city.) This might conceivably lead some developers to contract out of efficient, government-regulated monopolies if the lower (zero) tax rate thereby secured more than offset the inefficiency thereby incurred. If so, some consumer welfare loss should be perceptible in the form of higher prices and/or lower quality, whenever such outside contracting does occur, and welfare losses should be bounded by the amount of tax. (In cable television, the FCC has capped local government taxation such that few franchises tax at a rate above 3 percent of gross revenues. If a corporation opts out of efficiently regulated monopoly just to escape the tax, the firm itself will have to pay taxes on any revenues it gains from such an action, so the tax bound should be multiplied by the corporation's incremental state and federal tax rate on whatever local tax savings it realized.) Third, it may be alleged that the developer is merely attempting to replace the city government as monopoly rentier, seeking to exact supranormal gains for its own benefit. But this is clearly a case for the double-counting fallacy: a developer has only one reservoir of market power. If he attempts to extract a monopoly price for cable *and* a monopoly price for his housing, he will not behave optimally. To argue otherwise is to say that the developer would profit by setting a monopoly price for the housing unit, another monopoly price for the draperies, another for the dishwasher, and so on. Cable television may be rationally priced above costs by the developer, however, as a price discrimination scheme wherein inelastic demanders are charged higher effective prices relative to elastic demanders. This, though, simply distributes the developer's fixed cost contributions among home buyers and does not lead to monopoly profits. (It is not even necessary here to assume a perfectly elastic supply of developers; should a developer have market power, he will possess such without a cable television distribution system. Any consumer loyalty, and, hence, market power, that the developer gains as a result of some uniquely preferred

cable system is a return to the developer's entrepreneurship and not a supranormal profit returned by virtue of any natural monopoly cost condition.)

57. Matthew Lifflander, "A Lawyer's View of SMATV in the Summer of '82" (New York: Moore, Benson, Lifflander & Mewhinney, August 7, 1982), pp. 4–9.

58. Since this contract is not registered with any public agency and could not be obtained on request, this discussion relies on news reports and my discussion with Matt Lifflander (particularly September 14, 1983), legal counsel for Co-Op City.

59. *Co-Op City Times*, November 20, 1982.

60. *Variety*, December 8, 1982, p. 88.

61. Owing to the recent nature of SMATV innovation, information for this subsection was obtained primarily in personal interviews with and unpublished materials provided by John Mansell (lawyer and editor, *SMATV News*, published by Paul Kagan and Associates), on September 7, 1983; attorney John Phillips of Robert MacNeil and Co., real estate syndicators who contract with SMATV firms, on October 3, 1983; and David Hanson, former cable industry executive, who now represents firms contracting with SMATV suppliers, on October 13, 1983.

62. Lifflander, "A Lawyer's View of SMATV," p. 14.

63. Other cases of relevance that have been litigated in this industry include: *Omega Satellite Products* v. *Indianapolis; Mid-America Satellite* v. *Maskata, Minnesota; Video International Productions (VIP)* v. *Dallas, Texas; Earth Satellite Communications, Inc.* v. *East Orange, New Jersey*; and *Satellink and Telstar* v. *Chicago*.

64. *Wall Street Journal*, November 9, 1983, p. 60.

65. *City News*, April 8, 1982, p. 1.

66. *Cablevision*, November 28, 1983, p. 92.

67. Ibid., November 21, 1983, p. 62.

68. *Multichannel News*, January 16, 1984, p. 6.

69. Ibid.

70. *Cablevision*, November 28, 1983, p. 52.

71. *Multichannel News*, October 24, 1983, p. 16.

72. See Bruce D. Jacobs, Marsha D. Krassner, and Cheryl R. Suchors, *Own Your Own Cable System: A Manual on Cable Cooperative Business* (Washington, D.C.: National Consumer Cooperative Bank, 1983).

73. Fred Dawson, "How Safe Is Cable's 'Natural Monopoly'?" *Cablevision*, June 1, 1981, p. 340.

74. See Harvey Leibenstein, "Allocative Efficiency vs. 'X-Efficiency,' " *American Economic Review* 56 (June 1966).

75. See Dawson, "How Safe Is Cable's 'Natural Monopoly'?" p. 334; Chuck Mazokis, "Co-Franchising: Boon or Bane?" *TVC*, December 1, 1981, p. 72; and Richard Coorsch, "Cable Could Compete," *Consumer's Research* (October 1982):24.

76. This quotation and those that follow are from Dawson, "How Safe Is Cable's 'Natural Monopoly'?" p. 340.

77. Regression analysis, where these data are adjusted for supplier shifts (local cost differences), demand shifts (such as income differences), and quality variables (number of channels included in basic package), also fails to reveal any consumer advantage from monopoly franchising. In fact, prices in directly competitive cities are significantly lower priced (with a 7-statistic of 2.07). See Hazlett, "Three Essays on Monopoly."

78. Cablevision Communications Center (P.O. Box 344, Carlsbad, CA. 92008) and Paul Kagan, *The Kagan Census of Cable and Pay TV*.

79. Kahn, *Economics of Regulation*, pp. 114–115.

80. William K. Jones, "Deregulation and Regulatory Reform in Natural Monopoly Markets," in *Deregulating American Industry*, ed. Donald L. Martin (Lexington, Mass.: Lexington Books, D.C. Heath and Co., 1977), p. 48.

81. Posner, "Natural Monopoly and Its Regulation," p. 638.

82. Jones, "Deregulation and Regulatory Reform," p. 48.

83. Thomas Sowell, *Knowledge and Decisions* (New York: Basic Books, 1980), p. 188.

84. Harry Shooshan, Charles Jackson, and Alfred Kahn, "Cable Television: The Monopoly Myth and the Competitive Reality," unpublished manuscript.

Comment

Linda Cohen

Thomas Hazlett explores the potential of private contracting for avoiding the need for monopoly regulation of cable franchises. Starting with Harold Demsetz's argument that competition for a market theoretically can be as effective an inhibitor of monopoly outcomes as competition within a market, Hazlett proposes that the only barrier to the former for the cable franchise business is limits on private contracting.[1] Hazlett further investigates the problems with private contracting, concluding, in brief, that they are easily surmountable and that a private contracting scheme is a desirable substitute for regulation of cable franchises.

The proposal is exciting and intriguing. First, government regulation inevitably seems to have unpleasant side effects of resource misallocation and enforcement difficulties, which are exacerbated in the case of developing technologies. Second, previous proposals, in particular the simple auction scheme sketched out by Harold Demsetz,[2] have been shown to fail when faced with all the complications of cable franchising, as Oliver Williamson discusses convincingly.[3] Finally, Victor Goldberg paints a rather gloomy picture about the success of any scheme at avoiding regulatory imperative for a technology like cable networking.[4] In this comment, these problems are briefly developed; then Hazlett's proposal is considered in the context of Goldberg's critique. It is concluded that problems remain outstanding. In particular, it is not clear that something very much like regulation will not be needed to arbitrate penalty or bond payments. If this is the case, then the regulation problem has been transferred from one area (price setting) to another (penalty arbitration) but not avoided. Whether any advantage is achieved in terms of avoiding classic regulatory inefficiencies is an issue that needs further consideration.

Problems with Classic Regulation

The classic regulatory institution for a declining-cost common carrier industry is an exclusive geographic franchise to the company, with regulators controlling subsequent rates and guaranteeing a minimum profit level. The problems with this approach have been well documented. Binding profit constraints based on some subset of production inputs result in input biases and resource misallocations—the Averch-Johnson issues. Information requirements for regulation are typically so severe, especially for industries that are subject to cost and performance uncertainty, that the range of principal-agent problems typically crops up. In addition to poor control of monopoly prices and outcomes, further investment misallocations that take advantage of the principal-agent relationship in a regulated industry can be anticipated. Finally, and perhaps of greatest importance, biases can be expected to the extent that the regulators are motivated by political considerations.

Williamson discusses some of these problems in his analysis of the Oakland cable auction experiment: the apparent impossibility in holding fair reauctions and a desire to negotiate with current franchise holders. Furthermore, because regulators respond, at least in part, to political rewards that differ systematically from private profit-maximizing rewards, they may well encourage different rates of innovation and the development of a different set of technical options. If regulators bear the performance risks from investment, political considerations may bias their preferences toward low-risk alternatives. In a developing industry, we would expect to see too rapid diffusion of early succcessful applications and a lower ultimate rate of innovation.[5]

High fixed investment (high entry costs), low marginal service costs, and uncertainty combine to make a cable industry unsuitable for a traditional competitive market structure. Hazlett, agreeing on this point with Goldberg and earlier analyses of the industry, maintains that the industry requires the presence of long-term contracts that have flexible provisions regarding future rates and service packages. Demsetz made early inroads on the need for classic regulation with his proposal to auction franchises; however, as Williamson established, in practice the proposal required a panoply of regulations, and performed poorly when compared to classic natural monopoly regulation. Hazlett has sketched out a far more radical scheme. At issue here is whether his proposal avoids the Goldberg regulation look-alike trap.

Hazlett Proposal

In brief, Hazlett proposes the following:

1. Cable suppliers and subscribers sign long-term contracts for a quality-price bundle. The contracts can be adjustable. Using Goldberg's terminology, Hazlett says that presence of competition will make them "optimally flexible."
2. Firms solicit subscribers in advance of construction, commencing construction once they have accumulated a viable clientele. All costs may

not be covered at that point, as firms may anticipate picking up additional subscribers after service begins.
3. Contracts are enforceable by penalties against subscribers who quit the service and bonds posted by suppliers against not providing the services promised at the stated price or contract terms.
4. Firms that do not gather sufficient subscribers to enter construction can merge with other firms or otherwise negotiate to provide services on behalf of their subscribers. Bonds cover failure to provide contracted services.

The idea, then, is straightforward: service is provided in the declining-cost industry because of the long-term contracts. Innovation and uncertainty risks are shared depending on the size of the bonds and penalties and the conditions for payment (the flexible provisions in the contract). Monopoly is avoided (at least in part) because of continuous competition for subscribers.[6] The reauction feasibility issue is avoided because auctions are unnecessary.

It is not apparent that the proposal avoids the regulation trap discussed by Goldberg. In particular, arbitrators of the bond and penalty provisions play a significant role in making the proposal work. For instance, consider the firm that initially receives inadequate subscriptions or the firm that wins the first round but faces actual uncertainty over performance. The package of services ultimately delivered to subscribers may differ from that contracted for. At some point, an ex post evaluation of the value of components of the service package and changed economic conditions and a decision regarding the contributions of uncertainty and strategic behavior by companies (or company mismanagement) are required in order to determine bond payments (to subscribers who stay with cable) and penalties (from subscribers who quit). Informational requirements and cable company expertise suggest that the arbitrator is at the same principal-agent disadvantage of the regulator. Facing the identical problem, he is likely to institute the types of regulatory solutions (for example, cost of capital regulation) that are known to be inefficient.

This result, developed in detail by Goldberg, is irrespective of who the arbitrator is. As long as the arbitrator relies on the company for information and needs that information to allocate bonds or penalties, the result is obtained. Consequently, in order to evaluate the usefulness of this proposal, we need greater detail about how flexible contracts are and how much ex post analysis is required.

Even if the proposal succumbs to Averch-Johnson considerations, it still may avoid some of the problems of political control of investment decisions. This would be a tremendous advantage. Innovation risks, in Hazlett's framework, are shared between companies and suppliers depending on the size of bonds and penalties and the conditions under which they are to be paid. Here as well, however, the arbitrator appears crucial. By specifying conditions for payment in a way that requires an ex post evaluation and reduces informational requirements for arbitrators, investment incentives may well be biased. Further development in two areas appears necessary in order to determine the advantage of the scheme in this regard. First, to what extent must the arbitrator approve or disapprove a risky strategy? Consideration of the probable guidelines and the information required for decision making will help in determining whether ex post approval is in fact a problem. Second, how is the arbitrator chosen? If this person is elected or appointed by elected officials, then he or she will be motivated to act (set up guidelines and so on) like a regulator. If the arbitrator is chosen in some other way, other problems may accrue, such as industry domination. A discussion of specific proposals for choosing the arbitrator would be useful in this regard.

Finally, notice that the problems here derive from two assumptions: that the industry is subject to significant technical change over the time period of the projected long-term contract, whose results are uncertain in the beginning, and that contracts are flexible so that risk is shared between parties and ex post evaluations of outcomes are required. If regulatory problems can be thereby reduced, limiting contract flexibility below the apparent optimal level in a world of social-welfare-maximizing regulators may be desirable.

Conclusions

An appropriate comparison for Hazlett's proposal is not whether it approximates a competitive market but rather whether it performs better than a regulated monopoly. Although it appears that some form of ex post company evaluation may be required to enforce contracts, the proposal differs in significant ways from classic regulation. First, the choice of the initial cable would be chosen essentially by direct majority rule rather than through a legislative filter. While requiring initially more information gathering and consideration by consumers, it also avoids potential legislative distortions. The net welfare result is unclear; as Goldberg discusses, delegation can be a welfare-maximizing solution. Second, some competition may in fact be obtained, which would ease the job of the arbitrator in the ex post evaluation of performance. Third, the arbitrator need not, in theory, be in the position of supporting the initial company that builds a cable. Fourth, innovation risks are shared in a unique fashion in this proposal.

The issues I raise are similar to those in Goldberg's analysis. The uncertain nature of the industry suggests that some regulation will be required. Consequently the major advantage of the proposal may be in the extent to which some of the political biases in regulation, such as risk avoidance and support of the status quo, are avoided.

Notes

1. See Harold Demsetz, "Why Regulate Utilities?" *Journal of Law and Economics* 11 (April 1968).

2. Ibid.

3. See Oliver Williamson, "Franchise Bidding for Natural Monopolies—in General and with Respect to CATV," *Bell Journal of Economics* 7 (Spring 1976).

4. Victor Goldberg, "Regulation and Administered Contracts," *Bell Journal of Economics* 7 (Autumn 1976).

5. See Linda Cohen and Roger Noll, "The Electoral Connection to Intertemporal Policy Evaluation by a Legislator," working paper (Stanford: Stanford University, Department of Economics, 1984).

6. Subscribers who enter the market after the initial round may be subject to exploitation; however, rents will accrue to the original subscribers rather than the cable companies.

5
Total Deregulation of Electric Utilities: A Viable Policy Choice

Walter J. Primeaux, Jr.

P rofound dissatisfaction with existing regulatory arrangements for controlling firms historically given public utility status in this country is commonplace today. It is rare to read an article about firms in these protected industries without encountering numerous serious concerns about the regulatory process and radical proposals for changes. Many analysts of public utility regulation fear that the existing regulatory process is simply not working. Some have asked whether rate-of-return regulation constitutes a form of cost-plus pricing in which the consumer pays a higher price because of the absence of a competitive mechanism. Recent attempts in the publications of an electric utility trade association to inform its membership of research presenting proposals for structural changes of the industry highlight the seriousness of the deregulation debate.[1]

Regulation, in all of its variations, has been unable to provide a solution that all parties to the process find acceptable. The utility firms assert that their returns are inadequate; consumers argue that prices are both too high and too frequently increased. Some academic economists have argued that utility firms are inefficient and lack an incentive to be efficient and that this condition explains the general problem of high prices.[2] This condition could, of course, simultaneously account for inadequate profits accompanying the high prices. Clearly there prevails a widespread feeling that regulation of utility firms is not working very well.

These dissatisfactions have generated pressure on the ratemaking process and have helped stir movements for regulatory reform in various parts of the country.[3] Public utility firms have become aware of the impending reforms, and some utility executives, including, for example, William Berry of Virginia Electric Power, have endorsed deregulation of electric utility firms as one means of eliminating problems within the industry.[4]

This unsettled state characterizes all regulated industries. This chapter, however, focuses attention on the electric utility industry. Perhaps the regulatory reform mentioned most often in that industry calls for deregulating only the generation function with transmission and distribution remaining a monopoly. Although this approach toward regulatory reform may have some merit, this type of change would fail fully to capture available benefits from deregulating the entire system.[5]

Substantial benefit could be gained if generation, transmission, and distribution were deregulated. Since deregulation implies the admission of competition, the overall argument is that direct competition would yield substantial additional benefit to electric utility consumers. Natural monopoly theory in general is questionable; it no longer stands unchallenged by students of the electric utility industry.[6] The industry will certainly be changed. Indeed the process is underway.

Suggestions for Change

As Burton Behling explains, criticism of the U.S. system of electric utility regulation has existed for a long time.[7] In the past fifteen years, however, interest in regulatory reform has reawakened, and several new proposals have been presented to improve the performance of firms in the business.

Deregulation of Generation Only

One of the most common suggestions for regulatory reform is the deregulation of generation only, with the present monopoly continuing in transmission and distribution.[8] This is the reform advocated by William Berry. Proponents argue that this approach would add some competitive vigor to the business without a loss of the scale economies that come from distribution and transmission. Essentially the procedure hopes to capture some market benefits from deregulating generation because that phase of the business would become competitive, with ensuing gains in efficiency caused by market forces. At the same time, the change would not cause a loss in precious economies of scale in transmission and distribution, which are the main focus of the natural monopoly theory in electric utilities. This suggested change acknowledges the benefits of the market mechanism. It also argues that economies of scale in transmission and distribution are too valuable to trade for the gain in efficiency from the change.

Another proposal argues for a regional distribution corporation (RDC) that would own all of the transmission lines in a particular area.[9] The RDCs might be regulated by the Federal Energy Regulatory Commission because of the interstate business they conduct. The RDCs would lease generating capacity from independent producers and transmit electricity to local distributing companies. These distributing companies could also own the generating units; however, they would not control the transmission network. Under this arrangement, the transmission lines would act as common carriers. Essentially this is a modified proposal to deregulate generation only.

John Landon and David Huettner also present a case for deregulation of the generating sector of the electric utility industry.[10] Under their plan, industrial customers would have more opportunity to buy power in wholesale markets or from alternative distribution companies. Under this arrangement, industrial rates would still be regulated, either by a state commission or the Department of Energy. Landon and Huettner predict that their proposed change would lower industrial rates in the long run since the marginal cost of generation should be lower and large industrial customers would be able to purchase power at prices based on marginal costs.

Edward Berlin, Charles Chicchetti, and William Gillen also support the idea that competition should be injected into the generation segment of the industry.[11] They argue, however, that competition is not a substitute for regulation and do not favor total deregulation of the generation function.

Neil Mather concludes that public ownership of the distribution system is a viable alternative for mitigating some of the present discontent with utility regulation.[12] Mather presents this alternative, along with the basic notion of competition in the generation sector of the industry, as suggested by Leonard Weiss.[13]

Spot Prices for Electricity

Linda Cohen examines the workings of the Florida Energy Broker, an hourly spot market for electricity at the wholesale level.[14] The Florida Energy Broker represents an actual attempt to make the wholesale sector of the industry more competitive. This arrangement represents an experiment for testing the possibility of greater competition in the electric power industry; however, the experiment has not provided competition at the retail level.

Cohen claims that substantial problems arise in the Florida spot market arrangement, explaining that "so long as bid and offer prices accurately reflect marginal costs, such a spot market will tend to work as well as one that generates only one price for all exchanges."[15] Cohen notes that in practice, bid and offer prices need not reflect marginal costs and under certain circumstances are unlikely to do so. The split-the-savings characteristic (whereby savings generated from the system are shared by the buyer and the seller) that the system employs lends itself to strategic manipulation by market participants. Although Cohen notes that manipulation did not seem to be a problem in the Florida market, the arrangement does create an incentive for market participants to use bids and offers to affect the exchange price. Cohen points out that two policy questions emerge from the price manipulation possibility. First, to what extent is the market distorted because inappropriate exchanges are encouraged and cost-saving exchanges are prevented by the strategic bidding? Second, what are the effects of a system in which it is impossible to determine savings from a spot market when bids do not necessarily reflect underlying costs?

Cohen mentions two other problems experienced by the Florida Energy Broker. The more serious is that caused by inconsistencies between the institutional arrangements "envisioned under the broker" and those that actually developed. This is illustrated by the example of small firms with little generating capacity. These firms have partial requirements and have contracts to buy power from other generators at the average system cost of the seller. After joining the broker, these firms could sell electricity back to their suppliers "at a price between the supplier's average and marginal system costs."[16] Although this practice has been stopped, these firms can still sell power to utilities that do not participate in the broker arrangement, thus injecting inefficiency into the system. The author suggests that this problem could be solved by eliminating partial requirements contracts negotiated under traditional rate regulations.

A second potential problem posed by Cohen is that current regulation does not provide for free participation in the market because transmission facilities are controlled by certain utilities who can limit or inhibit access. Cohen points out that the Florida Energy Broker provides a spot market for current production by current utilities, which is the first element necessary to increase competition in electricity production. However, it is unclear what role competition (under the Florida Energy Broker arrangement) can play with respect to some other important functions, including:

1. provisions for reliable supply of reserve energy;

2. contribution of the appropriate mix of baseload, cycling, and peaking capacities in the grid as a whole through planning, financing, and construction of new units;

3. maintenance of competition among plants by recontracting among owners of equity shares in existing plants.

Cohen concludes that the Florida system does not adequately provide for coordination of these grid functions: "Important strides must be made beyond an energy broker to provide these functions in a deregulated grid."[17]

Three additional papers dealing with spot pricing of electricity merit consideration here because they represent work by researchers who have strongly advocated the use of spot-market pricing to inject competition into the electric utility business.

Roger Bohn, Michael Caramanis, and Fred Schweppe discuss coordinating functions necessary to introduce the concept of spot pricing.[18] They also attempt to show how spot pricing can be used to perform some of the coordination functions. The authors note that, in theory, optimal spot prices change continually; in practice they explain that this is unnecessary and that today a one-hour interval is used. This situation exists in the Florida power broker system. Bohn, Caramanis, and Schweppe argue that spot pricing can be helpful under various partial deregulation scenarios. They further claim that limited versions of spot pricing could help some deregulation plans if applied to a few large participants. This deregulation plan includes fringe competition by independent generators, deregulation of all generators, wheeling within and between utilities, as well as deregulation of sales to large customers. Bohn, Caramanis, and Schweppe argue that their proposal could lead to a system in which all generation is deregulated and electricity prices are based on spot prices. Yet they outline some problems that could prevent the achievement of all of the coordinating functions they describe that exist under the present regulatory system. They believe that "optimal spot pricing helps to solve many problems associated with some approaches to deregulation."[19]

Roger E. Bohn, Richard Tabors, Bennett Golub, and Fred Schweppe also advocate the use of spot pricing to solve present difficulties in the electric utility industry.[20] In "Deregulating the Electric Utility Industry," they ask what decisions need to be made in a deregulated system and then examine how these decisions can be made most efficiently. They conclude that spot markets must be used; there is no other way. The authors stop short of advocating deregulation because they perceive too many unanswered questions for them to take a firm position on one side or the other. Instead they advocate the use of field experimentation to uncover real world problems that are always overlooked in theoretical studies.

Bohn, Caramanis, and Schweppe also discuss various applications of spot pricing and spatial network pricing problems, including calculating transmission charges, the efficient integration of decentralized generators into a power system, and various proposals to deregulate electric power systems. They again conclude that spot pricing alone is inadequate to allow for total deregulation of utility companies.[21]

Although these two studies are interesting, they mainly consider the price effects on the producers' side and changes that might apply to very large buyers of electricity. Benefits typical of retail markets, to the extent that they would occur, would originate from spot pricing on the supply side. In addition to price effects, the authors are concerned that service reliability be preserved in any alternative regulatory arrangements or structural changes.

Some Cost Studies of the Effect of Competition

Several authors have assessed the price effects of admitting direct electric utility competition in distribution only. B.F. Hobbs analyzed the deregulation of electricity generation, using linear programming methods.[22] Another study by Hobbs and R.E. Schuler employed simulation techniques to study the same effects.[23] Both studies focused attention on price levels that would occur if competition were allowed in the electric utility industry in upstate

New York. There are at least two difficulties in attempting to generalize their findings to other parts of the country. First, their samples do not include any firms that actually face competition. Consequently the efficiency benefits of competition are ignored. That is, although these effects are acknowledged by the authors, they do not assess them because of the nature of the data used.

A second difficulty that limits a general conclusion regarding the effects of direct electric utility competition from this research is the fact that cost levels play an important role in the way prices are established in their models. Although this condition exists in any statistical model, their models are regional in nature and reflect regional cost differences that may not exist in other parts of the country. Nevertheless, this research is important, providing a serious attempt to assess what deregulation would accomplish in terms of affecting electric utility price levels.

Some Other Proposals for Changes in the Industry

Electric Power Reform: The Alternatives for Michigan, edited by W.H. Shaker and W. Steffy, presents a lengthy examination of electric power reform.[24] Although the title may lead one to conclude that the essays are concerned with regulatory reform in Michigan, this is not the case. The papers apply generally to the issue of regulatory reform, as well as other possible ways of solving problems that currently exist within the electric utility industry.

Although all of the studies presented in the Shaker and Steffy book cannot be discussed because of space restrictions, one study is particularly noteworthy because of the novel insight it brings to problems of the electric utility industry. E.J. Mitchell advocates the development of private industry—electric power linkage.[25] This proposal is based on the fact that both manufacturing and power generating facilities require large quantities of steam. Of course, they require the steam for different purposes. This joint need, according to Mitchell, could lead to the establishment of energy industrial centers that could take advantage of the fact that potential for generating electricity exists whenever industrial steam is generated: "It has been known for many years that the additional fuel consumed in this process would be as little as half of that required to produce the same amount of power at the most efficient central station power plant."[26] Mitchell points out that substantial economies could be realized by using energy industrial centers, but the present regulatory burden discourages this type of arrangement. Thus, changing regulatory arrangements clearly would be necessary in order to utilize the system Mitchell proposed.

Conclusions Concerning Past Research

Several facts emerge from the preceding discussion. First, numerous economists have examined problems with electric utility regulation and have proposed alternatives to alleviate some of the difficulties in existing institutions. Second, although intricate proposals have been developed, they are not without problems or limitations; indeed each author accompanies the presentation of an alternative system with a discussion of possible difficulties and complications. Third, reform of the regulatory system or a modified structure for the industry is imminent. The old shield of natural monopoly no longer shelters either the firms in the industry or the regulatory commissions from criticism or pressure for change or reform. Deregulation is an idea whose time has come. Only the form of the changes and how drastic they will be remains to be determined.

Natural Monopolies and Cost Levels

None of the remedies proposed in earlier research to address the problems surrounding utility regulation in this country discusses direct electric utility competition at the retail level as a possible remedy to the dissatisfaction with the general conditions of the industry. Yet such a remedy may be desirable.

There are many attributes of natural monopoly, and these characteristics are said to make direct electric utility competition wasteful and inefficient. Of all of the natural monopoly postulates, perhaps its pronouncements on costs are the most important. The theory unequivocally declares that when two electric utility firms exist in a given city, costs will be higher than if a monopoly served the city. This attribute of natural monopoly is perhaps responsible for most objections to any policy prescription calling for direct electric utility competition.[27]

To assess the merits of these objections, two key questions must be examined. First, do economies of scale exist in the electric utility industry? Second, how are cost levels affected by direct retail competition between rival firms in a single market? In investigating these questions, I have used data from real markets with two electric utility firms competing for the same customers; consequently the conclusions are based on facts and not speculation.

The Theory

It has long been argued that rivalry in the electric utility industry would cause costs to be higher than if a monopoly existed.[28] This belief is based on the assumption that utility firms operate at maximum efficiency and incentives to operate inefficiently do not exist. If, instead, firms in the monopoly market structure operate at a cost level that is not optimum, then the assertion that electric utility competition provokes higher costs would be unsupported.

The X-efficiency theory, developed only recently by Harvey Leibenstein, was not even considered during the development of the theory of natural monopoly in the mid-1800s and early 1900s.[29] The essence of the X-efficiency theory is presented in the following discussion. In a monopoly market structure, firms are not forced or encouraged to be efficient. The discipline of the market is absent. If firms are able to cover their full costs and perhaps earn some economic profit, they may not feel the pressure to minimize costs in order to increase the rate of return earned from operations. In contrast, if firms operate in an environment of rivalry, they may not earn a satisfactory return on investment unless they are efficient and minimize costs. The reason for this possibility is quite clear. Firms facing rivalry face a more elastic demand for their product or service; consequently they must be sensitive to the presence of rivals. If they are X-inefficient, cost levels would rise and could reduce profits below levels considered to be acceptable. In contrast to a monopolist, competitive firms face more active consumer resistance if they attempt to raise prices to higher levels to compensate for the higher costs caused by the X-inefficiency factor; consequently competitive firms are induced to operate at lower costs than would be the case in a monopoly market structure. X-efficiency would originate from variable performance with a given level of inputs.[30]

For our purposes, X-efficiency means that if it does exist, competition could lead to lower costs than a monopoly in any business by improving incentives to operate efficiently. Moreover, to the extent that inefficiency exists in a monopoly electric utility firm, the inefficiency may be so large as to overcome or offset any economies of scale gained from monopoly.

Cost Examination

Although generally overlooked by economists, electric utility competition does exist. As of January 1, 1966, competition existed in forty-nine cities.[31] In these cities, supply conditions were such that consumers had a choice between being served by one firm or the other. In the Texas and Missouri cities, a customer could switch from one firm to the other at will. In Portland, Oregon, new customers could choose to take service from either company, but after choosing, they could not switch.[32] This contrast is made so that the competitive conditions in these cities will not be confused with those existing in a city where territories are allocated and duplication of facilities does not actually exist. In New Orleans, Louisiana, for example, two electric firms serve allocated territories but do not directly compete with one another. Cities such as New Orleans are of no interest to this study.

The number of competing electric firms declined to approximately twenty-seven cases as of the spring of 1981.[33] This demise of direct competition was caused by hostility of the regulatory commissions toward the existence of this kind of rivalry.[34]

Costs in the markets with the direct competition were examined to determine whether electric utility competition actually caused average costs to be higher, as the theory of natural monopoly would expect. Table 5–1 presents all of the cities in which duplicate electric facilities existed in 1966. As the table indicates, the typical ownership arrangement in the competitive cities is one in which a municipal firm competes with a privately owned firm.

Examination of data sources of the Federal Power Commission (FPC) revealed that privately owned firms filed reports with that agency, which reported cost data. Unfortunately for purposes of this study, the cost data presented in those reports or in reports published from them are not useful. Privately owned firms in the cities with competing electric companies generally operate in more than one city. Therefore cost comparisons within a particular city would require some sort of cost allocations to the competitive city and for each city in which the firm operated. The FPC reports did not require cost allocations to individual cities. Consequently it was not possible to determine cost levels for the privately owned firms in those cities with direct electric utility competition. Because of these difficulties, there was no practical way of obtaining data for privately owned firms operating in those cities with electric duopolies. Requests for operating data from the individual firms were ruled out because previous correspondence and questionnaires had received a response rate of only approximately 52 percent.[35] Therefore it was considered desirable to develop a research design that would eliminate the need for data from privately owned firms yet permit a test of the hypothesis of the cost effects of natural monopoly.

Since publicly owned firms operated in only one city, costs were easily identifiable for firms filing the appropriate reports to the FPC. Because of data limitations for privately owned firms, the sample was restricted to publicly owned firms.

Both the method and procedure of this study were affected by the nature of the available data. The potential firms were limited to the universe set out in table 5–1. The competitive subsample, however, was limited to municipally owned firms that actually filed reports from which the FPC operating data were published. Data for firms not filing these reports were unavailable.

Data from the competitive subset of firms would indicate cost levels of electric utility firms operating in a competitive environment. For purposes of comparison, another subset of firms was selected from firms not facing competition. Instead of merely comparing the two subsets on the basis of the competing-noncompeting dichotomy, it was decided that the subset of noncompeting municipally owned firms would possess certain characteristics. Generally a matched firm without competition was selected for every firm with competition.

Both the competitive and monopoly sample subsets contained some firms that generated and distributed power, as well as some firms that only distributed power. The analysis here did not make any distinction based on these differences.

Table 5-1
Communities in Which Electric Utilities Directly Compete, as of January 1, 1966

State and City	Type of Competitive Firm[a]	State and City	Type of Competitive Firm[a]
Alabama		Ohio	
Bessemer	MP	Brooklyn	MP
Tarrant City	MP	Cleveland	MP
Troy	MC	Columbus	MP
		East Cleveland	MP
Alaska		Hamilton	MP
Anchorage	MC	Newton Falls	MP
Spenard	MC	Piqua	MP
		Pomeroy	PP
Illinois			
Bushnell	MP	Oklahoma	
Jacksonville	MP	Duncan	MP
Indiana		Oregon	
Fort Wayne	MP	Keizer	CP
		Portland	PP
Iowa		Salem[c]	CP
Maquoketa	MP	Springfield	MP
		The Dalles	MP
Kentucky			
Paris	MP	Pennsylvania	
		East Stroudsburg	PP
Maryland		Stroudsburg	PP
Hagerstown[b]	MP		
		South Carolina	
Michigan		Greer	MP
Allegan	MP		
Bay City	MP	South Dakota	
Bessemer	MP	Sioux Falls	MP
Dowagiac	MP		
Ferrysburg	MP	Texas	
Traverse City	MP	Commerce	MP
Zeeland	MP	Electra	MP
		Floydada	MP
Missouri		Garland	MP
Poplar Bluff	MP	Lubbock	MP
Sikestown	MP	Seymour	MP
Trenton	MP	Sonora	MP
Kennett	MP	Vernon	MP
		Winters	MP

Source: Federal Power Commission, letter from F. Steward Brown, Chief of Power, July 29, 1969.

[a]M = municipally owned; P = privately owned; C = cooperative ownership. As indicated in Federal Power Commission *Typical Electric Bills* (January 1966).

[b]According to Case No. 5996 before the Public Service Commission of Baltimore, filed September 13, 1967, Commission Order No. 56860 provided that present customers of either utility should not be accepted by the other utility. Guidelines were then drawn up to terminate a long existing dispute and duplication of facilities.

[c]Correspondence from the Portland General Electric Company, dated August 10, 1970, revealed that Salem Electric Cooperative and that firm had entered into an agreement to eliminate duplication of facilities in Salem. A ten-year program, agreed to in 1968, will eliminate duplication.

The characteristics used to select the matched monopoly firm are as follows. First, to the extent possible, the matched firm was from the same state as the firm with which it was paired. Second, the matched firm was approximately the same size as the firm with which it was paired; if no such firm existed in the relevant state, a larger firm was deemed acceptable. In no case, however, was a competitive firm matched with a smaller firm. Third, to the extent possible, types of power sources were identical for both the matched firm and for the competitive firm. These steps were taken in an attempt to avoid several potential statistical problems that could have been incurred in their absence.[36] The monopoly and competitive firms included in the sample are presented in table 5-2.

The sample consisted of the firms set out in table 5-2 for the years 1963 through 1968. The statistical analyses were performed by combining the data in an aggregate type of analysis. More recent data were not included for several reasons. First, the energy crisis and subsequent inflation seriously affected firms in this industry. Excluding data of the 1970s helped to make the earlier data more consistent with the latter. Second, the market structure has changed through time in some cities. Including more years would have reduced the number of usable firms in the sample in the more recent years. Since the data were limited, preservation of the data points was considered important. The appropriate statistical tests were made to determine the validity of pooling the data; the tests confirmed that pooling was permissible.

The Variables

The variables thought to be important in affecting costs of the electric utility firms in the sample included scale of operation, capacity utilization, steam electric fuel costs, hydroelectric fuel costs, internal combustion fuel costs, distribution among customer classifications, consumption per commercial and industrial customer, consumption per residential consumer, market density, cost of purchased power, state differences, and a market structure variable to isolate the competitive effects on costs.

Public finance factors, tax payments, and tax-equivalent payments were ignored in the analysis. They would have made it impossible to make valid cost comparisons since these matters are not managed on a consistent basis for accounting purposes within municipally owned firms.[37]

Statistical Analysis

Using standard statistical techniques (multiple regression analysis), I developed the cost curves of both competitive and monopoly electric firms included in the sample. The results of the analysis revealed that the competitive electric utility firms achieved lower average cost levels than the monopoly firms included in the sample. The cost difference amounted to 1.5155 mills per million kilowatt hours (kwh). The cost advantage continued for the competitive

Table 5-2
Cities with Monopoly or Duopoly Municipally Owned Electric Utilities,
by Kilowatt-hours Sold, Fiscal Year 1968
(in thousands)

Cities with Competition	Kilowatt-hour Sales	Matched Cities without Competition	Kilowatt-hour Sales
Bessemer, Alabama	108,838	Florence, Alabama	447,181
Tarrant City, Alabama	56,573	Scottsboro, Alabama	98,280
Anchorage, Alaska[a]	189,357		
Fort Wayne, Indiana	330,383	Richmond, Indiana	390,824
Maquoketa, Iowa	17,528	Algona, Iowa	28,186
Hagerstown, Maryland	106,089	Bristol, Virginia	211,763
Allegan, Michigan	15,775[c]	Niles, Michigan	56,974
Bay City, Michigan	95,484	Wyandotte, Michigan	126,265
Dowagiac, Michigan[d]	21,090	Hillsdale, Michigan	64,971
Ferrysburg, Michigan	128,774	Lansing, Michigan	1,300,318
Traverse City, Michigan	67,299	Sturgis, Michigan	73,527
Zeeland, Michigan	26,952	Petoskey, Michigan	30,612
		Carthage, Missouri	55,181
Kennett, Missouri	34,915	Rolla, Missouri	52,427
Poplar Bluff, Missouri	67,197	Columbia, Missouri	189,737
Trenton, Missouri	25,451	Marshall, Missouri	36,730
Lincoln, Nebraska	124,026[e]	Omaha, Nebraska	2,343,826
Cleveland, Ohio	546,707	Springfield, Illinois[b]	692,543
Columbus, Ohio	166,771	Anderson, Indiana[b]	318,606
Piqua, Ohio	119,715	Logansport, Indiana[b]	130,236
Springfield, Oregon	166,707	Eugene, Oregon	1,185,032
Greer, South Carolina	47,727	Greenwood, S.C.	77,747
Sioux Falls, S.D.	23,526	Watertown, S.D.	57,659
		Springfield, Missouri	585,954
Garland, Texas	337,562	San Antonio, Texas	3,325,771

Sources: Federal Power Commission, *Statistics of Publicly Owned Electric Utilities in the United States,* 1968 (1969), 1965 (1967), 1967 (1969) issues.

Note: This table, which presents data for 1968 except where noted, shows the relative size of the firms used in the regression model discussed in this chapter. In the model, data were used for the five-year period 1964–1968, except in the cases of Maquoketa and Algona, Iowa, for which 1964 data were not available; Greer, South Carolina, for which 1964–1965 data were not available; Allegan, Michigan, for which 1964–1967 data were used, because there was no competition in 1968; and Lincoln, Nebraska, which had competition in 1964 and 1965 only. The fiscal year varies among the firms, generally ending either June 30 or December 31.

[a]No suitable matched city could be found in Alaska.

[b]Matched cities could not be found within the competitive firm's state. Some cost adjustments were made to compensate for state differences.

[c]1967 data; competition did not exist in 1968.

[d]This city is served by both the city of Grand Haven Board of Light and Power and the Consumers Power Company.

[e]1965 data; competition did not exist in 1966–1968.

firms until an output level of 222 million kwh was achieved. After that level of output, the competitive firms apparently would have higher costs because the effects of economies of scale overwhelm the effects of efficiency that competition seems to instill within an electric utility firm.[38]

It is important to remember that many electric utility systems have annual sales well below the 222 million kilowatt level. The FPC published data that are useful for comparison purposes. The following discussion relates to those data. In 1962, 3,190 systems had annual sales of 100 million kwh or less. Furthermore, many of the 427 systems with annual sales of over 100 million kwh must still have been below the 222 million mark, although that information was not provided in the published source. Looking at the relative sizes of systems allows the distortion caused by the present policy of restricting entry to be estimated.

Approximately 92 percent of the publicly owned systems are too small to reap the scale benefits of monopoly; these firms, if subjected to competition, would operate at lower average costs. Similarly, the data show that approximately 60 percent of the investor-owned systems had annual output of less than 100 million kwh and therefore would also operate at lower costs if subjected to competition. These percentages are very conservative estimates, even allowing for growth in electric systems since the data were compiled. It must be pointed out, however, that while the number of firms small enough to be favorably affected by cost economies of competition is large, the size of these firms with respect to the total amount of electricity sold per year is less impressive; they account for only about 15 percent of total nationwide retail sales of electricity.

To some extent the 222 million kwh mentioned above was affected by the fact that only three of the twenty-three competitive cities analyzed had power outputs exceeding 200,000 kwh. That means that the 222 million kwh cutoff was based on limited data. If more large cities had competition, much stronger evidence might be developed in general support of competition, particularly for larger cities.

The mean average cost level for firms in the study was 14,097 mills. Therefore the 1.5155 mill decrease in average cost amounted to a decrease of 10.75 percent, at the mean, because of competition. This reflects a quantitative value of the presence of X-efficiency gained through competition or an estimate of the loss caused by the absence of competition in a regulated environment.[39]

The data showed that the X-efficiency effects were more significant for small firms in the sample. To the extent that smaller electric firms face competition from larger rivals, their relative lack of power due to size forces them to operate more efficiently than they would in the absence of competition. In the case of larger firms, their size provides them with a relatively secure position compared with their smaller rivals, so there is less necessity to be efficient. These overall results are consistent with a 1948 study by the Twentieth Century Fund.[40] As the firms become larger, the beneficial X-efficiency effect finally would be neutralized, and the unfavorable effects of costs of competition will ultimately overwhelm the X-efficiency effects so that competitive firms end up operating at higher costs than monopolists.

The statistical analyses show that economies of scale do exist; however, the most significant fact is that circumstances appear to occur that cause competitive electric utility firms to produce at lower average costs than monopolies in spite of the loss of scale economies whenever competition exists.[41] These results are subject to some qualification; at outputs over 222 million kwh per year, monopoly firms in this sample operated at lower costs. Even so, public policy has been designed to discourage competition and foster monopoly under all circumstances.

Costs of Distribution

Proponents of deregulation of only the generation function argue that distribution is a natural monopoly and should not be subjected to competition; they allege, without statistical data, that direct competition would result in higher distribution costs. Since the analysis discussed earlier used a mixed sample of firms (firms that generated and distributed, as well as firms that only distributed), additional analyses were considered useful.[42]

The research procedure was similar to that discussed earlier, with one essential difference: the sample for this study was refined further into two additional subsets: one subset of competing electric firms that only distribute electricity and another subset of monopoly firms that only distribute electricity. A comparison of the average cost levels between these two subsets of firms would reveal whether distribution costs would be higher under competition, as proponents of natural monopoly suggest.[43]

The first step toward answering the question was to develop equations for the firms remaining after the two subsets were removed. The objective here was to determine whether further segmentation of the sample affected the outcome of the earlier results. The conclusion was that the earlier results were unaffected by the change.

The next step was to develop average cost equations for the newly identified sample subsets. The results do not support the natural monopoly theory in electric distribution. Actually average costs in competitive market structures for firms that only distribute were essentially equal to those in monopoly market structures for firms that only distribute. Consequently the concerns expressed by those who advocate deregulating the generation function but not the distribution function because of important losses in economies of scale seem to be unfounded. Although monopoly distribution firms may be capable of operating at lower costs than competitive distribution firms, that result was not achieved. X-inefficiency sets in in a monopoly market structure, which offsets the technical losses caused by the direct competition.[44]

Some Conclusions Concerning Costs

The results show that the natural monopoly theory is incorrect in its assertion that competition cannot take place between electric utility firms in a single city. Moreover, the theory also errs in stating that any such competition would result in higher costs than under a monopoly market structure.

These results are not restricted to generation only, and the conclusions apply to all functions of a utility system. Therefore if lower costs result from competition and consumers do enjoy substantial benefit from the rivalry in terms of better service and lower prices, the logical conclusion would seem to be one calling for total competition, not just competition in the generating function of the business.

Price Effects of Direct Electric Utility Competition

The discussion has shown that competitive electric utility firms operate at lower costs than monopoly firms. Although these results are interesting, they would lose significance for public policy purposes if the lower costs did not lead to lower consumer prices. The theory of natural monopoly forecasts higher prices with competition, but do the facts sustain this proposition?

The nature of the competitive situations, the firms involved, and most other characteristics of my research designed to assess the natural monopoly theory are nearly identical to those presented in the previous section, so they will not be repeated. Only a few important differences between this research and that presented in the previous section will be briefly discussed here.[45]

Statistical Analysis

Price effects of competition were examined through four different individual dependent variables in the multiple regression analysis. The following prices were used: the average price (total sales revenue divided by quantity sold); the marginal price between 250 kwh and 500 kwh; the marginal price between the 500 kwh rate and the 750 kwh rate; and the marginal price between the 750 kwh rate and the 1,000 kwh rate. Because of the problems in obtaining published industrial and commercial data for small communities, the analysis was restricted to residential sales. The use of unpublished data would have resulted in rate categories that were not uniform, making valid comparisons impossible.

The independent variables used were mean county estimated buying income per household; average natural gas price for the state; number of customers per square mile; ratio of total residential sales to total commercial and industrial sales; operating and maintenance expense per kwh; cost per kwh generated and purchased; three regional climatic variables to isolate the effect of climate; and a market structure variable to isolate the effect of competition.

This analysis was limited to examining data for 1967 only for the same reasons that more current data were not used in the research presented previously. In particular, 1967 data were used because an earlier study by Patrick Mann and John Mikesell explained that 1967 data represented a stable year for making comparisons.[46] Stability within the industry was considered to be important, and the energy crisis in the 1970s injected instability and uncertainty into the industry.

The results of the statistical analyses reveal that consumers obtained substantial price benefits from the direct electric utility competition. The marginal price of moving from the 250 kwh block to the 500 kwh block is statistically insignificant, so no difference actually exists at this low sales volume; however, the marginal price of moving from the 500 kwh block to the 750 kwh block is lowered by $1.34 because of competition, and the marginal price of moving from the 750 kwh block to the 1,000 kwh block is lowered by $2.25. The average price is lowered by $6.313 per 1,000 kwh because of competition. At mean prices for the sample, these reductions amount to 16 percent and 19 percent, respectively, for the marginal prices, and the average price is lowered by 33 percent. Since prices were reduced by a larger percentage than the cost reductions described previously, some portion of the price reductions probably came from a reduction in economic profits earned by the firms. Because economic profits are profits above a fair return on investment, this is a favorable change.

Some Conclusions Concerning Prices

The research reported here clearly indicates substantial favorable price effects from the direct electric utility competition. These benefits, of course, are the ultimate ones expected from competition; that is, buyers are able to purchase the service at much lower prices so consumer welfare benefits. Furthermore, these results apply to situations where firms distributed and generated electricity.[47] In other words, the distribution function was part of both the competitive and monopoly firms' costs; consequently this is another indication that distribution can be subjected to effective competition.

Direct Competition and Regulation

State statutes provide broad limits to the possibility of entry into the utility industries, but the individual state commissions largely enforce the law. Thus, both the written statutes and the commission's attitude and philosophy concerning direct competition affect the regulatory mechanism of a state. The commission's influence is substantial; indeed it is probably the major factor determining entry in this business. The public utility commissions, through their procedures and orders, forge public policy toward competition and monopoly.[48]

Although a public utility commission may exist within a given state, it may not have absolute power to affect entry of a utility firm into competition with an existing monopolist. The important variable affecting the entry of a new utility firm into competition with an existing monopolist is whether the state public utility commission has jurisdiction over the firm intending to enter. In some cases, a commission has jurisdiction only over privately owned firms within a state and is powerless over municipally owned firms. Whenever these conditions exist, it should be possible for a municipally owned firm to enter into competition with an existing privately owned monopoly firm, even if the public utility commission has a policy of restricting or prohibiting competition (table 5–3). Of course, even in the absence of absolute power to control entry, the regulatory commission's attitude toward direct competition can be important; it may exert influence to affect the outcome of an entry attempt.

Historically, regulation probably has discouraged competition in most cases. Generally policymakers have shown confidence in regulation, with the result that competition has been viewed less favorably than might otherwise have been the case.[49]

The case against competition rests on assumptions that regulation can be effective in setting customer rates that are not excessive and do not allow the public utility to earn an economic profit.[50] Irston Barnes notes that if rates permit a utility firm to earn excessive profits, the unnecessarily high rates may prove more costly to the community than competition. One may conclude from Barnes's comment that inefficient regulators are not actually protecting the public when they prevent entry; indeed the opposite outcome results.

According to Lee Loevinger, regulation is not an "effective or efficient" alternative to competition.[51] In effect, Loevinger is claiming that regulation is clearly inferior to competition and cannot provide those benefits available from competition. This is a remarkable statement, given that Loevinger was a commissioner of the Federal Communications Commission when he wrote these comments.

The existence of competition is an admission that regulation by law is ineffective.[52] Behling contends that the agitation that existed during the 1930s for municipal competition, for laws less favorable to monopolized industries, and for public ownership confirm dissatisfaction with the imperfections of the system of regulation. The public's dissatisfaction with the situation existing in the 1930s in public utility regulation is reflected in the following statement:

> It is not surprising that there is developing an insistent demand for greater reliance upon competition as a supplement to regulation, not because it is the preferred method of organization and control for these [electric utility] industries, but because regulation has not been equal to the task set before it.[53]

Table 5–3
Public Service Commission Policies toward Competition between Utility Firms in 1971

State	Commission Policy toward Direct Competition
Alabama	No policy
Alaska	Seeks to eliminate
Arizona	Not permitted
Arkansas	Not permitted
California	Probably not permitted
Colorado	No policy
Connecticut	Actively discourages
Delaware	No jurisdiction
Florida	Not permitted
Georgia	No policy
Idaho	Not permitted
Illinois	Not permitted
Indiana	Not permitted
Iowa	No jurisdiction
Kansas	Not permitted
Kentucky	Allowed in some cases
Louisiana	Not permitted
Maine	No established policy
Maryland	No response
Massachusetts	Not permitted
Michigan	Opposed to extension of competition
Missouri	No jurisdiction over existing competition between private and municipal utilities
Montana	No jurisdiction
Nevada	Not permitted
New Mexico	Not permitted
New York	Would allow competition if considered useful
North Carolina	North Carolina courts have held that municipally owned electric systems are free to compete
North Dakota	Not allowed
Ohio	Not sanctioned
Oregon	No response
Pennsylvania	Not encouraged or advocated
Rhode Island	Legislature would not permit
South Carolina	Not permitted between private utilities
South Dakota	No regulation
Tennessee	Not permitted
Texas	No regulation
Utah	Not permitted
Vermont	Not permitted
Virginia	Not permitted
West Virginia	Permitted if existing service is inadequate
Wisconsin	Permitted if existing service is inadequate
Wyoming	Not permitted

Source: Mail questionnaire sent to regulatory commissions.

One may conclude that the failure of regulation is certainly an important justification for admitting competition and an important cause of emerging pressures to allow competition.

Present dissatisfaction with the regulatory process and its outcome may be at a peak.[54] Unfortunately the institution that is failing (regulatory), through the group administering control of the process (the public utility commission), is empowered to prevent or affect entry of a new firm as a remedy to its own failure. This lack of checks and balances probably looms even larger if Behling's statement is correct that the mere presence of competition indicates a failure of regulation. One might ask what the propensity of regulators will be to allow the entry of competition when such an action demonstrates regulation to be a failure.

Some Attempts at Entry

Between 1911 and 1941, there were at least 120 reported cases in which the desirability of competition in gas and electricity had been an issue before a state commission.[55] Although these data are somewhat old, they do reflect two truths: many seem to be unconvinced of the validity of natural monopoly theory, and entry into the utility industries has actually been sought and will continue to be desired in the future.

Why Competition Has Ceased in Some Cities

Given the power of public utility commissions over new entry into the electric utility business, research was undertaken to ascertain in a rigorous way the actual impact of regulatory attitude on direct competition.[56] While there had been forty-nine cities with direct electric utility competition in 1966, that number had dropped by at least seventeen cities by 1979. Why had competition been lost in certain cities?

Table 5–4 presents communities in which direct competition existed in 1966, the year in which competition was discontinued, and the circumstances surrounding the rivalry in certain situations. Some data for the analysis were obtained from mail questionnaires in May 1979 to the forty-nine cities that had direct competition as of January 1, 1966. Follow-up questionnaires were sent to nonrespondents in April 1980 and again in September 1980. This information was incorporated into table 5–4. Information from an additional mailing in January 1981 supplemented the data.[57] The most important relevant result is that the data provided some support for the hypothesis that hostile public utility commissions are associated with the demise of competition. Where the public utility commission was judged to be hostile toward direct competition, cities were more likely to lose competition than in cases where that condition did not exist. The research also reveals that there is no support for the hypothesis that either growing or stagnant cities are associated with viability of competition. Nor does self-reliance in supply appear to have any significant relationship with the viability of competition; that is, generating firms were no different from purchasing firms as far as the viability

140 · *Unnatural Monopolies*

Table 5–4
Communities with Competition as of May 1982

Alabama	**Ohio**
Bessemer (1971)	Brooklyn[d]
Tarrant City	Cleveland
Troy[a]	Columbus
	East Cleveland[e]
Alaska	Hamilton
Anchorage (1973)	Newton Falls
Spenard (1978)	Piqua[b]
	Pomeroy[c]
Illinois	
Bushnell	**Oklahoma**
Jacksonville (1973)	Duncan
Indiana	**Oregon**
Fort Wayne (1975)	Keizer (approx. 1967)
	Portland (after 1966, date unknown)
Iowa	Salem (approx. 1967)
Maquoketa	Springfield (1976)
	The Dalles (1976)
Kentucky	
Paris	**Pennsylvania**
	East Stroudsburg
Maryland	Stroudsburg
Hagerstown (1970)	
	South Carolina
Michigan	Greer
Allegan (1968)	
Bay City	**South Dakota**
Bessemer (1978)	Sioux Falls (1976)
Dowagiac	
Ferrysburg	**Texas**
Traverse City	Commerce (1979)
Zeeland	Electra
	Floydada
Missouri	Garland (1973)
Kennett	Lubbock
Poplar Bluff	Seymour
Sikeston	Sonora
Trenton	Vernon
	Winters (1978)

Note: Year competition discontinued is in parentheses.

[a]Direct competition comes about whenever annexation takes place; the cooperative retains its customers unless consumers elect to receive electric energy from the city.

[b]Direct competition exists in areas contiguous to the city but not within the city limit.

[c]Columbus and Southern Ohio Electric Co. has been serving a small number of customers in Pomeroy for many years. The company explains that shared areas more appropriately describes the situation than competition. Since both firms in Pomeroy are now owned by the same company, studies are in process to determine if it economically feasible to eliminate one of the firms in the market.

[d]The city of Brooklyn, Ohio, reports that a monopoly firm served the city on April 14, 1981; whether competition ever existed in 1966 is unclear.

[e]The city of East Cleveland, Ohio, reports that a monopoly firm served the city on April 17, 1981; whether competition even existed in 1966 is unclear.

of competition is concerned. In addition, the research showed that commissions take a more negative stance toward competition in larger cities than in smaller cities. Finally, there is no support for the hypothesis that unprofitable operations are more likely to cease competing.[58]

Public Utility Commissions: Their Attitudes
Toward Competition

Above all, it is the public utility commission's stance toward competition that most affects the viability of competition in markets where it exists. Whenever commissions are hostile to direct competition, such competition exists in a precarious state. Although competition may endure over a long time period, its survival is always uncertain since the commission will remain intolerant toward direct competition. Consequently at some point in the future, competition probably will be discontinued at the whim of the commission. This situation highlights the importance of considering provisions that would separate or balance powers between the regulatory function of existing firms and the mechanism whereby new firms are permitted to compete. If some regulators do view direct competition as an admission of their failure adequately to provide the regulatory function, they may be more hostile to competition whenever entry is attempted. They are, in a real way, forced to pass judgment on their own effectiveness, a situation that might impede the admission of direct competition when it is warranted.

Other Research Concerning Direct Competition

Direct competition between electric utility firms does not lead to more excess generating capacity than exists in a monopoly market.[59] Pricing behavior with two competitive electric utility firms tended to show that direct competition can exist in a single city without the concern of price wars, which are an important part of the theory of natural monopoly.[60]

A number of case studies show that direct competition actually improved the performance of the utility firms, as well as generated salutary effects on consumer welfare.[61] Two detailed case studies in particular discuss the favorable effects of the direct competition, one focusing on Lubbock, Texas, and the other on Sikeston, Missouri.[62]

The case studies show that effective competition can and does exist. Price wars do not seem to be a serious problem, better consumer service occurs with competition, competition in electric utilities can occur over a very long time, better consumer prices evolve with competition, and consumers prefer competition to monopoly. Generally consumers tended to feel that they benefited from direct competition.

In surveying managers in cities with two directly competing electric utility firms, several interesting results emerged.[63] Some managers said that they benefited from the direct competition, but others said that competition caused problems for them. The benefit came from the stronger incentive to be efficient; the problems came from the additional trouble and work from more planning in order to meet the competition. The trouble did not seem to be any different from the competitive difficulties involved in any industry whenever a firm needs to combat a competitor. Monopoly is obviously much easier than competition; firms must work much harder when they compete. Some managers charged that direct competition results in wasteful duplication and inefficiency, one of the traditional arguments presented by proponents of natural monopoly. Obviously they had not developed sophisticated cost comparisons on which to base these kinds of judgments; they had no real knowledge about the extent of X-inefficiency existing within their firms. They were merely articulating the conventional wisdom that the utility firms have handed down from generation to generation. Nor are these attitudes unbiased. Both their firm's interests and their personal interests would be enhanced if monopoly existed. Any rational firm would rather have a monopoly than be forced to compete against another business.

Conclusions

Research examining some key components of the natural monopoly theory shows that direct competition in electric utility markets leads to substantial benefits for consumers. These benefits include lower operating costs and lower consumer prices. Perhaps readers should be reminded that the results are based on data from firms engaged in distributing as well as generating electricity. The results seem to support the proposition that distribution can be deregulated, although some have held to the proposition that this function constitutes a natural monopoly.[64]

The attitude of hostility toward direct electric competition is one limiting factor to the expansion of direct competition in the United States. Public utility commissions are powerful influences, and empirical data show that their hostility toward direct competition tends to undermine its continued existence in actual markets.

John Ryan, former chairman of the Indiana Public Service Commission, believes that natural monopoly theory does not justify limiting competition:

> The natural monopoly argument in favor of utility regulation is the poorest possible excuse to limit competition. It is the essence of natural monopoly that competition is self-limiting, that economies of scale are so pervasive and consistent that only one producer can endure. If this indeed applies, why are

public utilities so afraid of competition? Their plants are in place; they have a clear lead in production and distribution. If natural monopoly conditions exist, competition will simply fail.[65]

Ryan advocates a free enterprise alternative of more competition.

Edison Electric Institute argues that one problem with examining the proposals for deregulation is that they do not provide much explanation of how they would operate or how they might be implemented.[66] Yet it should not be necessary to present any grand plan of how competition would actually take place if it were not vigorously opposed. In Hagerstown, Maryland, direct electric utility competition emerged a long time ago because an electric railway was generating surplus electricity, which it began to sell to consumers.[67] Entry into the industry is clearly possible under similar conditions if entry were permitted. Indeed Mitchell's proposal to establish energy industrial centers is compatible with allowing the industry to change by evolution.[68] Ryan mentions a similar procedure, which is extremely interesting. He says that franchise protection should be removed from the utilities to allow competition. At the same time, rate control should be relaxed so that companies can make unilateral adjustments; these rates, however, would be subject to regulatory review. This change would allow present companies and potential competitors to adjust prices to market conditions. From these steps, progress toward full deregulation would be started.[69] The essential point is that the market will evoke entry as appropriate conditions emerge in a market. It would probably be a very serious error for one to set up plans for structural changes in the electric utility industry.

Dissatisfaction with existing public utility regulatory mechanisms and outcomes is quite general at this time. As remedies are considered to reform existing regulatory arrangements or as plans for deregulation are made, direct competition should be considered as a serious option. In this light, entry into the electric utility industry should be deregulated. Existing competition indicates that such a change could significantly improve electric utility performance.

Notes

1. See Edison Electric Institute, *Deregulation of Electric Utilities—A Survey of Major Concepts and Issues* (Washington, D.C., 1981), *Alternative Models of Electric Power Deregulation* (Washington, D.C., 1982), and *A Survey of Deregulation Experience in Selected Industries* (Washington, D.C., 1982).

2. See Walter J. Primeaux, Jr., *An Examination of Direct Electric Utility Competition: Some Perspectives on the Natural Monopoly Myth* (New York: Praeger, forthcoming); and "An Assessment of X-Efficiency Gained through Competition," *Review of Economics and Statistics* 59 (February 1977):105–108.

3. See William H. Shaker and Wilbert Steffy, eds., *Electric Power Reform: The Alternatives for Michigan* (Ann Arbor: University of Michigan, 1976); Pennsylvania Electric Utility Efficiency Task Force, *Report to Lieutenant Governor William W. Scranton* (Harrisburg: Commonwealth of Pennsylvania, March 1983), vols. 1–2.

4. Pamela Sherrid, "Live Wire," *Forbes,* September 27, 1982, pp. 84–85.

5. Walter J. Primeaux, Jr., "A Reexamination of the Monopoly Marketing Structure for Electric Utilities," in *Promoting Competition in Regulated Markets,* ed. Almarin Phillips (Washington, D.C.: Brookings Institution, 1975), "A Duopoly in Electricity: Competition in a 'Natural Monopoly,' " *Quarterly Review of Economics and Business* (Summer 1974):65–73, and *Examination of Direct Electric Utility Competition.*

6. See Primeaux, "Reexamination of the Monopoly Market," and "Some Problems with Natural Monopoly," *Anti-trust Bulletin: The Journal of American and Foreign Trade Regulation* 24 (Spring 1979):63–85; J.L. Ryan, "Let Us Try Free Enterprise—Regulation Has Failed," in Shaker and Steffy, eds., *Electric Power Reform*; and Primeaux, *Examination of Direct Utility Competition.*

7. B.N. Behling, *Competition and Monopoly in Public Utility Industries* (Urbana: University of Illinois, 1938).

8. Leonard W. Weiss, "Antitrust in the Electric Power Industry," in Phillips, *Promoting Competition,* and "The Possibilities for Competition in the Electric Power Industry," in Shaker and Steffy, *Electric Power Reform.* See also Sherrid, "Live Wire."

9. Congressional Budget Office, *Promoting Efficiency in the Electric Utility Sector* (Washington, D.C.: Government Printing Office, November 1982).

10. John H. Landon and David Huettner, "Restructuring the Electric Utility Industry: A Modest Proposal," in Shaker and Steffy, *Electric Power Reform.*

11. Edward Berlin, Charles Chicchetti, and William Gillen, "Restructuring the Electric Power Industry," in Shaker and Steffy, *Electric Power Reform.*

12. Neil Mather, "If Generation Is Deregulated, Publicly Owned Distribution Systems May Be Viable," in Shaker and Steffy, *Electric Power Reform.*

13. Weiss, "The Possibilities for Competition," in Shaker and Steffy, *Electric Power Reform.*

14. Linda Cohen, *A Spot Market for Electricity: Preliminary Analysis of the Florida Energy Broker* (Santa Monica, Calif.: Rand Corporation, 1982).

15. Ibid., p. 50.

16. Ibid., p. viii.

17. Ibid., p. ix.

18. Roger E. Bohn, Michael C. Caramanis, and Fred C. Schweppe, "Optimal Pricing of Public Utility Services Sold through Networks," working paper (Cambridge: Division of Research, Harvard University, January 1983).

19. Ibid., p. 62.

20. R.E. Bohn, R.D. Tabors, B.W. Golub, and F.C. Schweppe, "Deregulating the Electric Utility Industry" MIT Energy Laboratory Technical Report, No. MIT-EL 82-003 (January 1982).

21. Bohn, Caramanis, and Schweppe, "Optimal Pricing," p. 63.

22. B.F. Hobbs, "A Spatial Linear Programming Analysis of the Deregulation of Electricity Generation" (Paper presented at the Twenty-eighth Annual North American Meeting of the Regional Science Association, Montreal, Canada, November 1981).

23. B.F. Hobbs and R.E. Schuler, "Estimating the Economic Consequences of Competition in the Distribution of Electricity—An Application of Location Theory" (Paper presented at the Twenty-eighth Annual North American Meeting of the Regional Science Association, Montreal, Canada, November 1981).

24. Shaker and Steffy, *Electric Power Reform.*

25. E.J. Mitchell, "Lower Power Costs through Private Industry Generation: A Proposal," in Shaker and Steffy, *Electric Power Reform.*

26. Ibid., p. 267.

27. Primeaux, "Reexamination of the Monopoly Market."

28. Primeaux, "Some Problems with Natural Monopoly."

29. Primeaux, *Examination of Direct Electric Utility Competition.*

30. Harvey Leibenstein, "Allocative Efficiency vs. 'X-Efficiency,' " *American Economic Review* 56 (June 1966):392–415.

31. F. Stewart Brown to the author, July 20, 1969.

32. Oregon is one state that has discontinued electric utility competition.

33. Primeaux, *Examination of Direct Electric Utility Competition.*

34. Walter Primeaux, Jr., Robert S. Herren, and Daniel R. Hollas, "Characteristics of Viable Competition in the Municipal Electric Industry," unpublished manuscript.

35. Another reason for not using the privately owned firms in the sample is that those firms typically serve more than a single community. The competitive area served by these multicity privately owned firms is quite small in relation to their whole service area. Consequently the competitive effects on the cost functions of these firms would probably be quite small because of the nature of the existing competition.

36. A more thorough explanation of the matching procedure and its rationale is presented in Primeaux, "Reexamination of the Monopoly Market."

37. Ibid.

38. The results are quite robust in that the competitive variable used to indicate the cost effects of competition was statistically significant at the 1 percent level.

39. Primeaux, "Assessment of X-Efficiency Gained through Competition."

40. *Electric Power and Government Policy* (New York: Twentieth Century Fund, 1948).

41. These results do not mean that the competitive firms in the sample necessarily operated at minimum costs. Indeed it may be possible from an engineering point of view that they too could lower costs and operate more efficiently. What the results do mean is that the competitive firms actually achieved lower costs than the monopoly firms in the sample. Thus, competition has reduced X-inefficiency as competitive firms achieve lower costs per kwh sold. These conditions are ignored in Hobbs and Schuler, "Estimating the Economic Consequences of Competition," and in Hobbs, "Spatial Linear Programming Analysis of the Deregulation of Electricity Generation."

42. Walter Primeaux, Jr., "Deregulation of Electric Utility Firms: An Assessment of the Cost Effects of Complete Deregulation vs. Deregulation of Generation Only," working paper no. 905 (September 1982).

43. Ibid.

44. Primeaux, "Assessment of X-Efficiency Gained through Competition."

45. Primeaux, *Examination of Direct Utility Competition.*

46. Patrick C. Mann and John L. Mikesell, "Tax Payments and Electric Utility Prices," *Southern Economic Journal* (July 1971):71.

47. All firms did not generate their power requirements, but the majority of firms did. All firms in the sample were engaged in distribution.

48. Behling, *Competition and Monopoly*. Behling credits regulatory commissions with contributing to the monopolistic structure as it currently exists.

49. Ibid.

50. Irston R. Barnes, *The Economics of Public Utility Regulation* (New York: F.S. Crofts & Co., 1947).

51. Lee Loevinger, "Regulation and Competition as Alternatives," *Antitrust Bulletin* 11 (January–April 1966).

52. Behling, *Competition and Monopoly*.

53. Ibid.

54. Primeaux, "Reexamination of the Monopoly Market."

55. Henry Kohn, Jr., "A Reexamination of Competition in Gas and Electric Utilities," *Yale Law Journal* 50 (1941):875–879.

56. Primeaux, Herren, and Hollas, "Characteristics of Viable Competition in the Municipal Electric Industry."

57. Because of the nature of the problem, nonparametric (chi-square) statistics were used in the analysis.

58. For case studies concerning the termination of direct competition, see Primeaux, " Duopoly in Electricity," "Dismantling Competition in a Natural Monopoly," and *Examination of Direct Electric Utility Competition*.

59. Walter Primeaux, Jr., "The Effect of Competition on Capacity Utilization in the Electric Utility Industry," *Economic Inquiry* 16 (April 1978):237–248.

60. Walter Primeaux, Jr., and Mark Bomball, "A Reexamination of the Kinky Oligopoly Demand Curve," *Journal of Political Economy* (July–August 1974):851–862.

61. Primeaux, *Examination of Direct Electric Utility Competition*; and Richard Hellman, *Government Competition in the Electric Utility Industry: A Theoretical and Empirical Study* (New York: Praeger, 1972).

62. Jan Bellamy, "Two Utilities Are Better Than One," *Reason* (October 1981): 23–30.

63. Primeaux, *Examination of Direct Electric Utility Competition*.

64. Primeaux, "Reexamination of the Monopoly Market," and "Electric Utility Competition Is Feasible."

65. Ryan, "Let Us Try Free Enterprise," p. 90.

66. Edison Electric Institute, *Deregulation*.

67. Walter Primeaux, Jr., "The Decline in Electric Utility Competition," *Land Economics* 51 (May 1975):144–148.

68. Mitchell, "Lower Power Costs through Private Industry," and Primeaux, "Reexamination of the Monopoly Market."

69. Ryan, "Let Us Try Free Enterprise."

Comment

William W. Berry

D eregulation and competition in the electric utility industry would increase efficiency in the development of new generating capacity, in the operation of utility plants, and in the use of available capacity to meet regional electricity demands. Deregulation and competition also would allow the electric utility industry to build the new generating capacity that will be needed to serve future electricity demand. These gains cannot be achieved fully under regulation—not because of any failures or lack of interest of the regulators but because of the intrinsic nature of the regulatory system.

Construction Cost and Operations

Under regulation, the incentives to control construction costs and to design performance characteristics that will reduce the life cycle cost of electricity are indirect and far weaker than they would be with competition. Many small utilities lack the skills to build complex power plants efficiently. As a result, there are large differences in the cost of new generating units that cannot be explained by any differences in objective circumstances. With competition, there would be strong, direct incentives for efficiency in construction, and new units would be built by the companies that could offer capacity at the lowest life cycle costs.

Under regulation, financial difficulties and changes in demand forecasts often force costly delays in plant construction. Under the plan of deregulation I have proposed, independent competing generating companies that secured sufficient long-term contracts for capacity from a proposed unit would be able to obtain financing and complete the unit on the least costly schedule.[1] The risk of changes in expected demand would be borne by distribution companies.

Even with the long-term contracts that are needed to permit financing of central station generating units, the deregulated industry would have stronger incentives for operating efficiently than the regulated industry. Generating companies would be able to profit by surpassing performance standards that would be specified in contracts between them and the distribution companies. Furthermore, the performance of a generating company's existing units would affect its competitiveness in selling capacity from proposed new units.

Meeting Demand Efficiently

In the plan of deregulation I have proposed, there would also be substantial efficiency gains in the use of available generating units to meet regional electricity demands. The present system, in which each utility control center coordinates the use of its generating capacity to meet electricity demand in its area, is not good enough. There are about 160 control centers, around ten times too many. The incentives for trading among them are too weak, and the difficulties in forming power pools are great. Even in power pools there are typically problems in building the transmission lines needed to make the best use of the pool's capacity. Under the present industry structure, electricity is often supplied by more costly units while more efficient generators sit idle.

In the deregulated industry I envision, the generating units in each of about a dozen regions would be used at maximum efficiency by a regional energy broker. The energy broker would also own the transmission system and have incentives to strengthen its capabilities to allow more efficient use of generating capacity. With deregulation there would be efficiency gains, or at least no efficiency losses, in planning to meet new electricity demand and in coordinating the development of new generating and transmission facilities.

Building New Capacity

Deregulation would allow the utility industry to build the generating capacity the United States will need in the coming years. After the sharp energy price increases of the 1970s, the growth of electricity demand slowed but did not cease, as was true of nonelectrical energy. Electricity demand after the 1973 Arab oil embargo grew by 2.9 percent a year through 1980, or slightly faster than the growth of the total economy.

Although there are widely divergent electricity growth projections for the 1980s and 1990s, probably there will be significant growth that cannot be met fully by increases in conservation and load management or by nonutility generators of electricity.

Under present regulation, electric utilities generally are not being allowed to earn a return equal to the market cost of capital. They therefore have an incentive to minimize their capital investments. A capital minimization strategy will keep rates lower and improve utilities' financial positions in the short run. But such a strategy is likely to lead to unnecessarily high electricity costs as utilities eventually must resort to inefficient stopgap measures to avert incipient shortages and as greater use is made of uneconomic oil- and gas-fired capacity. Capital minimization also will impose an important hidden cost by constraining productivity improvements, technological innovation, and economic growth.

With deregulation and competition, the price mechanism would be freed to play its proper role in balancing supply and demand. In my proposal, competing generating companies would be under no obligation to build new capacity but would offer to do so when the price of new capacity was bid to a level that offered the prospect of profit. Distribution companies would retain an obligation to serve and would seek to purchase the capacity to fulfill that responsibility. They would have to be able to pass through to customers capacity costs set in a free competitive market, as utilities already do with respect to most costs for goods and services.

In addition to the market for purchases of new capacity, there would be markets for secondary trading in long-term capacity and for short-term or spot transactions. These markets would allow distribution companies to adjust to variations in demand and offset forecasting errors.

In theory, the disincentive to build new capacity could be eliminated under the present regulated system if regulators allowed utilities to earn a market return on their investments. But in practice, whenever utilities face cost pressures that require rate increases, that result is unlikely—even if the increases are less than inflation. Regulation is part of the political process and inherently responsive to pressures to keep rates low in the short run. Those pressures are intensified by popular dislike of monopolies and an inchoate, but fundamentally correct, belief that utilities could and should be more efficient. Unfortunately there is little understanding that the inefficiency that people sense is basically the fault of the system itself, not of the utilities or their regulators. The problem is fundamental and can be corrected only through fundamental structural change.

Structural Change

I believe that deregulation and competition are possible only in electricity generation, which accounts for the bulk of the cost of electricity. To permit competition in generation, the present vertically integrated electric utility industry must be separated into competing generating companies and regulated distribution companies linked by energy brokers owning and operating the transmission system. These components can be institutionally separate while remaining physically linked as the nature of electricity requires.

There are numerous examples of independent distribution companies that obtain their electricity from other companies providing generation and transmission services. The linkage between independent generating companies and the transmission system would be provided by the energy broker, which would make the market for, and be a party to, contracts between generating and distribution companies, in addition to the role as controller of the region's generating capacity.

This type of market, with numerous buyers as well as numerous sellers of generating capacity, is important to avoid giving the energy broker monopsony powers, as suggested in some deregulation proposals. It also allows the responsibility for maintaining adequate service to be fixed on the distribution companies, which alone would remain under state regulation.

The vertical separation of the electric utility industry would have far-reaching implications. The managements of the generating companies would become more entrepreneurial, and the ownership of the companies would shift in response to the new balance of risk and reward. Generating companies would find themselves in differing competitive positions based on the age, performance, and fuels of their existing units. The various risks related to capacity development could be clearly allocated and probably better controlled. Most important, electricity users would be better off as efficiency gains from competition offset the effect of pricing generation in a free market.

Transitional Steps

A change of this magnitude probably cannot and should not occur in one leap. Rather, there are steps that can be taken immediately to provide some of the benefits of deregulation and competition and to ease the transition to full deregulation of electricity generation:

> The Federal Energy Regulatory Commission (FERC) should reduce its regulation of wholesale power sales among utilities and allow shareholders some benefit from power transactions.

> FERC should approve contract rates that will allow separate generating companies actually to earn their authorized rate of return.

> FERC and state regulators should expand that use of performance-based rates of return and other measures that simulate market-like incentives.

> Congress and state governments should ease their controls over utility structures to help clear the way for consolidation of utilities that are below an economic size and allow other reorganizations that foster operating efficiency. That would mean amending or repealing the outmoded Public Utility Holding Company Act.

> The federal government should get on with the job of phasing out wasteful subsidies and preferences for government and cooperative electric systems.

The Public Utilities Regulatory Policies Act should be amended to allow greater utility participation in large, unregulated generating units.

Competition in Electricity Distribution

The implications of the deregulation that I envision are quite different from those that would result if Walter Primeaux's analysis is correct. Primeaux advances the thesis that electricity distribution is not a natural monopoly and that competition is possible among distribution companies and, presumably, among vertically integrated utilities. I find this proposition implausible and the evidence offered in support of it unconvincing.

For competition in distribution to be economic, the resulting efficiency gains at the distribution level would have to be large enough to more than offset the substantial increased cost of building and operating duplicate distribution systems. Although there are identifiable potential efficiencies in the construction, operation, and dispatch of generating units, it is difficult to see the nature of the efficiency gains available in electricity distribution. Even assuming the efficiency gains reported by Primeaux in cities with competitive distribution systems, there is no showing that these gains exceed the additional cost of duplicate distribution systems and result in a net economic benefit. Furthermore, it is unlikely that the existence of two distribution systems within a geographical area would provide a basis for effective competition over an extended period or that the multiple distribution systems that would permit numerous competitors could be economic.

Primeaux's analysis is also weakened by its focus on municipal electric systems, which do not behave in the same ways as investor-owned companies and whose costs probably do not include the full cost of capital. Capital costs would be most affected by duplicative facilities so that any understatement of those costs would distort the analysis.

In addition to these problems, the municipal distribution systems evaluated by Primeaux are small in comparison to the average utility. The average system with competition considered by Primeaux had annual sales that were less than 7 percent of the 1982 sales of the one-hundredth largest utility and only about 0.3 percent of the 1982 sales by Vepco. It may be that the systems he considered are too small to take advantage of all the available economies of scale. I do not believe that the analysis of these small municipal systems demonstrates that it would be economic to install the duplicate facilities necessary for competition among, say, Vepco, Carolina Power and Light Co., and Potomac Electric Company over an area of 63,000 square miles in five states and the District of Columbia, or even in compact areas that are much larger than those considered by Primeaux, such as New York City.

Conclusion

While electricity distribution, in my judgment, remains a natural monopoly, competition is clearly possible in electricity generation. The breakup of the vertically integrated industry that will permit this competition will be legally and politically difficult. But these difficulties are not insuperable, particularly if we move to the new structure by intermediate stages that are meritorious in their own right. The present regulated system is not working well. No doubt it can be improved. But even if it is, we need competition where it is possible. Competition is not just better than bad regulation; it is better even than good regulation.

Note

1. William W. Berry, "The Deregulated Electric Utility Industry," *Electric Rate-making* 1 (June 1982) and "The Case for Competition in the Electric Utility Industry," *Public Utilities Fortnightly* 110 (September 1982).

6
Cable and Public Utility Regulation

Charles L. Jackson

> The onus is on us to determine whether free societies in the twenty-first century will conduct electronic communications under the conditions of freedom established for the domain of print through centuries of struggle, or whether that great achievement will become lost in a confusion about new technologies.[1]

Of the welter of new communications technologies available today, cable creates the most confusion among those who discuss policy. The confusion arises not because of the technical complexities of cable—the concept of cable is simple. Rather, cable combines economic aspects of distribution utilities and newspapers with the tradition of broadcast regulation. Cable offers a new start to those who dislike today's commercial broadcasting. Cable has begun to introduce formidable competition to existing broadcasters and even some miniscule competition to local telephone companies. With all these factors combining to push for regulation, it is no surprise that cable has come to be regulated at the local, state, and federal levels.

At first it may seem out of place to have a chapter on cable television as part of a book on public utility regulation. After all, while cable is regulated, it is not subject to full public utility regulation. But there are those who would subject cable to such regulation. And appearances aside, cable is regulated much like a public utility. Municipal franchises are required. Rates are regulated, although usually without formal consideration of a rate base and the allowed rate of return.

The economic and legal attributes usually called on to support public utility regulation include: the existence of a natural monopoly, a firm whose unit costs decline over the relevant scale of production; the provision of an essential service associated with the public interest; and a holding out to serve the general public or the dedication of a business to a public use. Traditionally, many industries possessing these attributes have been regulated as public utilities (water, gas, electric) or as common carriers (railroads, trucking, telephone, telegraph). Most of the concerns about the need to regulate cable stem from the fact that it appears to have some of the same characteristics as other regulated industries. It is primarily a distribution system (like the gas or electric company); uses wire (like the telephone or telegraph company); depends on the grant of a franchise (like the telephone company); exhibits economies of scale over a limited range of outputs; and provides services that may be deemed important if not essential (extension of television coverage). The regulatory impulse is quickened by cable's tie to broadcasting. Broadcasting is regulated, so it seems natural enough to regulate related enterprises. Cable, a multichannel broadcast service, is more like broadcasting than broadcasting itself. After all, if the state can regulate someone providing a single channel of television, does not the state have all the more right to regulate someone providing twenty channels of television?

Despite these forces tending toward public utility regulation of cable, I believe that such regulation is ill considered and that, by and large, society would be better served by less, rather than more, regulation of cable.

Cable and Cable Regulation

Cable technology grew out of the need to provide low-cost television reception services in remote communities. The easy way to provide such low-cost service is to erect one expensive, but sensitive, antenna capable of pulling in distant signals well and to amplify that weak signal and share it among all the viewers in the community. This shared antenna approach worked out to be far less costly than having each household build its own antenna.

The television signals are distributed from house to house by a network of cables—hence the name *cable television*—which is organized much like the water system with the signals flowing out from a central location. Once the cables are in place, they can carry more than just over-the-air television signals. The supply of television programming originally grew to fit the limited over-the-air distribution system. But as cable has grown, cable-only or cable-directed services have sprung up. Their growth has been helped by the communications satellite that substantially lowered the cost of building a nationwide network.

It costs about $500 per household passed by the cable to build a cable system. If half the households subscribe to cable, then the system costs $1,000 per subscriber. In comparison, in a household with two color television sets, the consumer may have $500 to $1,000 of additional investment in the television system. The cable system must also pay for the programming it buys and resells to viewers. Rates for cable service vary, but generally basic service—retransmission of the over-the-air signals—costs about $10 per month. Adding a pay movie channel, an all-news channel, and a sports channel might increase the monthly rate to about $20 per month.

Cable is regulated by the local, state, and federal governments. Local governments grant franchises to use public rights-of-way. They usually require the cable company to pay franchise fees and frequently extract other tangible benefits from the cable company, such as requiring it to provide free cable television service to fire stations and schools. In most states, the state role is limited. But the federal role makes up for any lack of activity by the states. The federal government regulates and controls much of the activity of cable companies. Federal regulations include technical standards, limits on the franchise fees cable companies can pay, and must-carry rules that tell a cable system which over-the-air signals it must carry if the broadcaster requests carriage. Federal copyright law also contains a compulsory license provision that gives cable operators the right to retransmit television programs without the permission of the copyright owner.

Although this sounds like a lot of regulation, it is instructive to go back to the discussions of cable regulation that occurred in 1972 or 1973. Then the federal government was also in the business of telling cable systems which over-the-air cable signals they could not carry and which movies they could show on pay channels, and it imposed far more detailed technical regulation. By the standards of 1973, cable television has been deregulated.

Generic Alternatives to Cable

How does cable fit into the communications market, and how does it compare with competitive technologies and services? Three key services regularly

Table 6–1
Alternative Local Distribution Systems for Three Key Applications

Burglar alarms

  Leased private lines from telephone companies
  Standard dial-up telephone lines
  Master antenna systems
  Private radio systems
  Campus industrial park cable systems

Electronic newspapers/videotex

  Switched telephone service
  Multipoint distribution service (MDS)
  Television teletext signal
  FM subcarrier
  Master antenna TV (MATV)
  Direct satellite services

Pay video programming

  Leased point-to-multipoint service (Telco)
  Multipoint distribution service (MDS)
  Direct broadcast satellites (DBS)
  Pay television broadcasting (live or recorded)
  Master antenna TV (MATV)
  Videotape/video cassette (rentals/sales)

used as examples of the need for regulating cable systems are alarm services, electronic newspapers, and pay video programming. Table 6–1 shows the range of distribution alternatives serving each of these services.

Here I systematically consider communications needs and alternatives and show the range of local distribution alternatives available. Within this context, I consider how well alternative local communications systems can meet specific needs. I discuss several generic communications needs—low-speed data, high-speed data, and video communications—and the alternatives for meeting them. I then turn to specific communications needs, such as burglar alarms, pay television, and voice telephone services, and the alternatives for meeting them.

Communications Applications

As shown in table 6–2, communications applications can be grouped into a few broad generic categories that together include most of the economically important communications needs. Table 6–3 shows how these generic data communications applications encompass a wide range of specific needs.

Table 6–2
Generic Communications Applications

Low-speed data

    Teletypewriter communications
    Remote meter reading
    Paging
    Signaling for utility load shedding

Voice communications

    Telephone communications
    AM radio broadcasting
    FM radio broadcasting

High-speed data

    Rapid office-to-office transfer of computer files
    Transmission of compressed digital video

Video

    Pay television
    Nonpay television

Other

    Subvoice bandwidth analog communications used for slow-speed facsimile
    Equipment control
    Analog communications using a bandwith wider than voice but narrower than video to carry stereo program signals to radio stations

---

Table 6–3
Specific Communications Applications

Low-speed data

   Burglar alarms (other emergency alarms)
   Teletype communications
   Data terminal entry (human to computer)
   Utility load monitoring
   Utility load shedding
   Paging service

Voice communications

   Ordinary local telephone service
   Access to long-distance services
   Mobile telephone service
   Mobile vehicle command and control
   Radio broadcasting (voice and music)
   CB radio
   Intercoms

High-speed data

   Data terminal response
   Facsimile
   Computer file transfer

Video

   Television broadcasting
   Pay television
   Security monitoring
   Teleconferencing

Communications services can be compared on the basis of a number of important criteria. First, what is the bandwidth or data rate—the information capacity—of the communications? How many bits per second can be transmitted through that link? How many video or voice channels can that link carry at the same time?

Second, how reliable is the communications link? Is it likely to be working when needed? For example, the telephone network is, as a whole, enormously reliable. It is an extremely rare occasion that a telephone company's central office goes down, denying telephone service to all telephones in a neighborhood.

A third measure of a communications link is the quality of the link. Is it relatively free of noise or static? Is the error rate on data links low or high?

A fourth attribute important for communications technology is its inherent privacy. Everyone is familiar with the fact that CB radio has little or no inherent privacy. To get privacy, one must send in code or jargon. In fact, all broadcast systems and cable must obtain their privacy through scrambling techniques. In contrast, the telephone network offers moderate privacy since tapping the telephone requires access to a cable or specific line pair. Fiber optic technology (not yet widely available) would seem to have even higher inherent privacy, since it will be more difficult to tap than either traditional telephone lines or cable television.

A fifth attribute of communications systems is their universality. How completely do they cover their desired market? One of the competitive strengths of the proposed DBS system is pay television coverage to an entire time zone in the continental United States from a signal satellite.

A sixth criterion, cost, would appear to be an essentially self-explanatory attribute. However, one must recall the many dimensions of cost. A communications system may be relatively cheap when providing service to a few locations, but expensive to extend to additional locations. Conversely, a communications system may have low average cost for serving a large number of locations.

Directionality is a seventh important quality. Are communications links two way or one way? The speed or immediacy of a communications link can be an important factor in assessing the value of that link. For example, telegrams are faster than letters, but slower than telephone calls. For many data, television and audio program distribution needs, physical transport of materials (computer tapes, computer disks, video tapes, videodiscs) can provide reasonable speed at lower cost than electronic alternatives.

Ease of use is an eighth key attribute of communications sytstems. For example, over-the-air broadcasting is a far more convenient video program distribution mode than is cable television, since one can move television sets from one room to another without rewiring.

A ninth attribute, connectability, is most apparent in the telephone and postal systems network: a user can send a message to virtually any other location in the country or in the world. Thus, these communciations services have wide connectability. In contrast, many other two-way services have limited connectability; customers can reach only a small range of the potential universe of recipients with whom they would like to communicate.

The final characteristic important to communications services is the mobility of the communications facility. Carphones and Sony Walkman FM radio sets are as mobile as is reasonably possible. An intermediate level of mobility is provided by more traditional broadcast services, such as television broadcasting services, or the instructional television fixed service (ITFS). In these services, receivers normally operate at a fixed location for the duration of a program. But receivers can be moved quickly and easily from one location to another without extensive work. At the other extreme are found waveguide systems, such as telephone network or cable television, in which cables must be mounted on poles or buried in conduits to connect the receiving terminal with the transmitting location. Clearly these systems are almost completely fixed.

Table 6–4 presents a comparison of three communications technologies: cable TV, multichannel multipoint distribution service (MDS) or ITFS technology, and switched telephone service. The table makes one key point: no single technology is dominant on every attribute. Cable television provides higher aggregate bandwidth to any single location than does MDS or switched telephone service. In contrast, multichannel MDS offers a relatively low-cost way of providing video communication to a small number of widely dispersed points within a metropolitan area. MDS receiving stations can be relocated far more easily than can cable television systems or telephone cable.

Common Carriers

Existing telephone companies are a major source for a wide variety of local communications services. Their facilities are universal and use a familiar technology. Legally and technically, telephone companies can meet almost every local communications need.

The heart of most existing telephone company local distribution facilities is the local plant used for telephone service and other voice services. This plant consists primarily of cables containing many pairs of wires, each of which has the capacity to carry a single voice channel—roughly 4 kilohertz

Table 6–4
Comparison of Three Local Communications Technologies

Attribute	Cable TV	Multichannel MDS	Switched Telephone Service
Bandwidth	High[a] (200–400 MHz)	Medium (30–40 MHz)	Low per circuit; high in aggregate
Reliability	Medium	Medium	High[a]
Quality	High[a]	High/medium	High/medium
Inherent privacy	Low	Low	Medium[a]
Universality	Medium	High	High[a]
Cost	Medium/high	Medium/low[a]	Medium
One way/two way	Mostly one way	Mostly one way Two way possible	Two way[a]
Ease of use	Immediate	Immediate	Immediate
Network connectability	Low	Low	High[a]
Mobile or fixed	Fixed	Fixed (but easily relocated)[a]	Fixed

[a]The technology that is dominant on that attribute. For example, the telephone network is best for two-way communications; cable has the highest raw bandwidth; multichannel MDS is the easiest to construct quickly.

(kHz) of bandwidth. These loops are also capable of carrying data signals at medium speeds (up to 56,000 bits per second). Currently efforts are underway to develop practical technology for combining voice and data on these pairs. Although the capacity of each pair of wires is small, the total capacity of hundreds of thousands of such pairs is enormous, exceeding the capacity of even the largest existing cable system.

Telephone companies are not restricted to voice services. They can build wideband facilities and offer services on them. Telephone companies already offer a wide range of high-speed data and wideband analog services, which are primarily point-to-point private line services. Some companies also offer point-to-multipoint video services by leasing multiple channels to firms that use those channels to provide cable service. And Illinois Bell once offered Picturephone services, a switched video service.

Telephone companies provide mobile telephone and paging services using radio facilities for local distribution. The Federal Communications Commission's (FCC) cellular order sets aside 20 megahertz (MHz) of spectrum for use by telephone companies to provide advanced mobile telephone service. This substantial capacity will allow telephone companies to offer a wide range of voice and data services with great flexibility.

Mobile telephone service and paging service is also provided today by radio common carriers (RCC), carriers that specialize in local signal distribution by radio. Twenty MHz spectrum for use in cellular mobile radio is also available to this group of operators.

As fiber optic technology develops, it may become an economical replacement for the copper wire pairs now used by the telephone companies. If this occurs, the local telephone system will be capable of supporting full video transmission. "Dial-a-Movie" could replace "Dial-a-Joke." Admittedly implementation of this possibility lies years in the future.

One alternative to local distribution is direct satellite service. As a common carrier, Satellite Business Systems (SBS) offers intercity voice and high-speed data service using satellites and small transmit-receive stations located at customers sites, thus bypassing altogether the need for local distribution.

Voice Communications Needs

In addition to the wide range of voice-grade local distribution services provided by telephone companies and other common carriers, there are several other alternatives. For many point-to-multipoint operations, radio broadcasting (both AM and FM) remains the dominant alternative. Private radio systems, both mobile and fixed, provide an excellent and widely used alternative for voice communications. It is hard to overstate the importance and capacity of private radio systems. Radio-based systems are flexible and efficient. Although the FCC has allocated only a small part of the total radio spectrum to private radio systems, it is about the same size as the entire useful bandwidth of a cable system. New technology will make it possible to use higher regions in the spectrum and thus will expand the capacity available to private radio systems.

Video Services

Video distribution deserves special consideration since video, particularly retransmission of television broadcasts, is the heart of the cable business. Originally, cable began as the only video distribution facility in communities lacking over-the-air broadcast service. As recently as the mid-1970s, cable was the only practical alternative to traditional television broadcasting. Today, however, there are several methods for local distribution of video signals (see table 6–1). More alternatives are technologically feasible and are awaiting regulatory approval. And since technological innovation has not ceased, we can reasonably expect other alternatives to be developed in the future.

Television broadcasting remains the primary method for local distribution of video signals. Broadcasting's great advantages over cable are its low cost and wide coverage.

MDS, created by the FCC in 1972 as a common carrier, provides television broadcasting at microwave frequencies. MDS requires a direct line-of-sight transmission path from the transmitter to the receiving antenna. Two channels in each market currently are available for MDS operation. The FCC recently added eight more channels to the MDS service and allowed ITFS licensees to rent their channels to commercial users. Depending on how many ITFS channels are rented out to commercial users, the number of MDS-like channels available for local video distribution will jump to between ten and twenty.

In fall 1982, the FCC granted eight applications for authority to construct and operate direct broadcast satellite systems. Current technology will allow construction of broadcast satellites that can transmit three television channels directly to home receivers. The footprint (area served) of a single satellite would cover a single time zone. Of course, satellite broadcasting is not simply a local distribution service. Rather it combines the long haul and local distribution tasks into a single step. This service has just begun operating in the United States. The technology is proved and available and will soon be serving many consumers.

Physical distribution of recorded materials, such as video discs and videocassettes, is another important alternative. While it is slower and less convenient than electronic signal distribution for movies, recordings offer a wider choice of materials and scheduling flexibility. In this respect, cable systems are to cassette rental firms as newspapers are to libraries.

All of the video distribution alternatives discussed so far are currently available alternatives—systems that can be built with today's technology. But there is no reason to believe that technological progress in electronics has stopped; indeed there is every reason to expect more progress. In particular, technology will be developed to use higher regions in the spectrum. CBS, for example, recently experimented with terrestrial television broadcasting at 12 billion cycles per second (12 GHz). There are no fundamental limits preventing broadcast operations at such higher frequencies. It is difficult and expensive to-day to build radio transmitters and receivers that work at these frequencies. But that was once true of broadcasting at UHF frequencies. And it was less than a decade ago that broadcasting at MDS frequencies became possible.

Technological innovation is not restricted to over-the-air systems. Improvements in telephone company local loop plant could provide it with video local distribution capability.

Nonvoice, Nonvideo Communications Needs

Multiplexed broadcast signals provide a major alternative to cable for local digital signal distribution at low to moderate speeds. Most familiar of these multiplex technologies is the FM subcarrier technique (sometimes called SCA), which allows an FM broadcast to carry a second signal in addition to the normal stereo broadcast. Receiving the SCA signal requires special equipment and cannot be done by a normal FM receiver. SCA channels have been used for a wide variety of applications, including distribution of Muzak, data broadcasting, electronic newspapers, and transmission of programming to AM broadcast stations.

AM broadcast signals can carry a multiplexed data signal of a few bits per second.[2] Although this is a limited rate, the local coverage provided by AM signals is essentially universal, reaching every room in every building in a community. Thus, data signals multiplexed onto AM broadcast are well suited to such applications as emergency notification or electrical utility load management. Utility load management also can be done using electrical power lines to carry communications signals.[3] Power lines themselves provide a limited communications capability that power companies frequently use for internal communications.

The FCC has proposed allowing television broadcasters to use time division multiplexing to insert data into an otherwise unused protion of the television signal. Such multiplexed data transmission capability will be substantial. The FCC's proposal would allow each television broadcaster to transmit data at an average rate of about 100,000 bits per second or 12,000 characters per second. This works out to more than 3,000 characters of text per day for each household in Washington, D.C., from each television station.[4] If the same text were to be delivered to every household, as with newspapers, one television channel could deliver about a billion characters per day.

All of the alternatives, as well as a few others, are displayed in table 6–5. The table first groups alternatives by legal organization, that is, true common

Table 6–5
Potential Communications Alternatives to Cable Television

Common carriers

Telephone companies
  Switched telephone service
  Leased low-speed data lines
  Leased high-speed data lines
  Leased point-to-point video service
  Leased broadcast video facilities
Traditional mobile telephone service
  Paging service
  Cellular mobile service
Nontelephone common carriers
  Mobile telephone service
  Paging
  Cellular mobile service
  Satellite carriers—high-speed data to end-use site

Quasi-private carriers

Multipoint distribution service
Digital termination service
Miscellaneous common carriers

Private carrier-like entities

FM radio station subcarriers
AM radio baseband signaling
TV broadcast videotex capability
Direct broadcast satellites
SMRS (special mobile radio service)
Shared mobile repeaters
Shared microwave systems

Private systems

Private radio systems
  Private mobile radio
    Pure dispatch operators
    Interconnected with telephone system
  Private microwave
    Operational fixed service to hotels/motels
    Corporate voice service/data service
    Corporate video
    High-speed data
  Private satellite networks
  ITFS capability
    4-channel education TV systems (two way possible)
    Cheaper than cable in low-density areas
Private point-to-point optical systems
TV broadcasters
AM radio broadcasters
FM radio broadcasters
Direct broadcast satellites
Private waveguide systems
  Master antenna TV (MATV)
  Satellite fed MATV (SMATV)
  Power line carrier
  Campus cable (MIT, Duke)
  Ethernet, Wangnet, GE Net

(Table 6–5 continued)

Other alternatives

Direct satellite services
CB radio
Video recordings
Physical transport of discs, tapes
U.S. Postal Service

Future alternatives

Multichannel MDS
Packet radio-AlohaNet
Telephone company fiber optic local loop
Use of higher frequencies
  12 GHz broadcasting
  60 GHz point-to-point links

---

carriers, entities much like common carriers, and private systems. It then lists the alternatives within each category. Table 6–6 recasts these alteratives in terms of the generic communications needs they serve. Examination of the tables shows that there are alteratives today to every service offered by cable; there will be more alternatives in the future. Given competitive alternatives and the rapid technological change occurring in communications, treating cable as a monopoly seems inappropriate and counterproductive.

Table 6–6
Generic Needs and Noncable Alternatives to Meet Them

Low-speed data

   Leased telephone lines, switched telephone service, paging service, satellite service, FM sub-carrier, AM baseband signaling, TV videotex, private radio systems, physical transport (if immediacy is not important)

Voice communications

   Switched telephone service, AM broadcasting, FM broadcasting, leased point-to-point lines, mobile telephone service, cellular mobile telephone, DTS carriers, private mobile, private microwave, tapes and records

High-speed data

   Leased telephone lines, satellite service, DTS, TV teletext capability, private microwave, ethernet, wangnet, GE Net, physical transport of discs, tapes

Video

   Telco point-to-point service, Telco leased multipoint facility, C-band satellites, DTS systems (teleconference-quality video), television broadcasting, MDS, DBS, MATV, SMATV, video recordings

Video Alternatives in Portland, Oregon

Today Portland, Oregon, has only five over-the-air broadcast stations. Additionally, the signal of a station in Salem, Oregon, reaches Portland. There are currently applications pending at the FCC for four more full-power stations in Portland, all UHF. One of these applications is for a frequency not assigned to Portland by the FCC, so I am not certain that all four can be granted. By the end of ten years, those three or four licenses will have been granted. Portland could have many more new UHF stations. In the early 1950s, the FCC cleverly designed the UHF table of assignments to reduce the cost of UHF television receivers. But this reduction in the monetary cost of receivers was achieved at the sacrifice of many channels of communications. Channel 4, in the VHF band, was assigned by the FCC for use in sixty-three cities. Yet channel 40, in the UHF band, was assigned for use in only twenty-three cities—only about a third as many possible stations as are available on channel 4. New technology allows us to build UHF television receivers at reasonable cost that are compatible with more intensive use of the UHF television band. If we were to adopt such technology, Portland could have ten to fifteen full-power UHF television stations. Combining those with the existing five VHF stations leads to a total of from fifteen to twenty full-power, over-the-air television stations in Portland.

Low-power television offers another route to additional television outlets in Portland. There are currently thirty-three applications at the FCC for low-power television stations in Portland. These applications are for only thirteen different channels, so, clearly, there are overlapping and conflicting applications. Without studying these applications in detail, I would estimate that about ten of them can be granted. If we installed improved UHF television receivers, we would increase the number of possible low-power stations to between fifteen and twenty-five.

MDS uses microwave frequencies (2,150 MHz) to carry television signals. Currently only one MDS station is licensed in Portland. But the FCC has just transferred eight other, essentially idle frequencies to the MDS service. The FCC might be able to expand the number of such channels to between thirty and sixty. If that were done, then around forty MDS channels would become available in Portland.

Television broadcasting can use other parts of the microwave spectrum besides the MDS frequencies. The Japanese have experimented with broadcasts in the super high frequency region (SHF). CBS has requested permission from the FCC to experiment with broadcasts in this region. I think it unlikely that the FCC will set aside frequencies in this range for television broadcasting, but it could allocate a band capable of supporting twenty SHF television stations in Portland.

Direct broadcast satellites (DBS) provide another source of television channels. Probably one or two broadcast satellites will be providing service to

Table 6–7
Video Channels in Portland, Oregon

	Now	*Probable 1992*	*Achievable 1992 (with FCC push)*
Full-power TV	5	9	15
Low-power TV	0	10	20
MDS	1	8	40
SHF broadcasting	n.a.	0	20
Direct broadcast satellite	0	6	25
Cable	Building	108	108
Total	6	141	228

the West Coast, including Portland, by 1992. Since each system will have three or four channels, between three and eight DBS channels will be available in Portland by 1992. If the economics supported more DBS systems, the frequencies are available for more channels—up to a maximum of about twenty-five. In this case, the binding constraint is likely to be the marketplace, not the FCC's rules.

Cable television will increase substantially the television channels in Portland. Portland has already granted cable television franchises. Construction of a 108-channel system serving all households in the eastern franchise area (with three-fourths of the Portland population) was finished in early 1984. Fifty-four channels are currently activated and the cable is in place for the other fifty-four channels. An older system, originally built in 1952 and with a thirty-six-channel capacity, serves the west side of Portland. Every household in Portland will be passed by either one system or the other. I doubt if the 108-channel system will add any capacity in the next decade; the thirty-six channel system probably will upgrade capacity when the supply of programming expands. Table 6–7 presents the information on video alternatives in Portland in summary form.

Beyond 1992: The Long-Run View

The projections for 1992 are based on today's technology. But we are in a period of rapid and intense innovation in electronics and communications. Our understanding of the fundamental laws governing communications is remarkably mature. Innovation is proceeding rapidly in the key technologies supporting communications systems. New transmission media such as fiber optics and radios capable of operating at higher frequencies than are practical today promise major expansions of capacity, far beyond those I outlined. Improved electronics will expand the performance of existing communications channels. Addition of storage capability to home terminals will double or triple the effective number of channels. Such use of electronic storage was begun recently when ABC received permission from the FCC to offer pay television at night. Video cassette recorders in each subscriber's home record the pay signal for later playback.

By 1992, improvements in integrated circuits will allow us to compress the bandwidth of a television signal to such a degree that broadcast-quality television could be transmitted in a band only a quarter the width of today's television channels. All these are improvements we can count on. But it is instructive to go back a decade and look at the Sloan commission study on cable television or a little further back and look at the 1968 report of the President's Task Force on Communications Policy.[5] Neither report discussed fiber optics or multichannel MDS as a competitor to cable television. The Sloan commission felt that it was "at least conceivable" that the capacity of urban cable systems could rise as high as eighty channels. Similarly, improvements in television distribution may arise in ways we can no more foresee today than these commissions foresaw as they studied the problem. The discussion here of cable alternatives describes only lower bounds on what we can achieve.

There is no doubt that policies that have restricted the growth of cable television and have limited the number of over-the-air broadcast stations to levels far below the levels technology allows are responsible for whatever scarcity exists today. In fact, cable is primarily a response to these restrictions. If enough full-power and low-power stations had been licensed, there never would have been a need for cable to fill in the gaps and expand coverage.

Cable Television and the Telephone Industry

The most interesting interplay between cable television and public utility regulation today is the ongoing fight over cable's role in the carrying of voice and data signals. This conflict is taking place in several places. At least one telephone company temporarily refused to allow a cable company to use the telephone company's poles and underground ducts if that cable company was going to offer data service. Utility commissions, state legislatures, the FCC, and the Congress have all been drawn into a fight over the proper range of services cable systems are to be allowed to offer.

On one side are the cable industry and its allies. They would prefer cable to be allowed to offer any service that is technically feasible. On the other side are the telephone companies and the state regulators. Their positions cannot be characterized so neatly. Some state regulators want cable restricted to one-way video services. Some telephone companies want cable restricted from offering any service the telephone company can offer. Some telephone companies also want to be deregulated if a cable company begins to compete with them.

It is too early to predict confidently the outcome of this conflict. Both telephone companies and cable companies have entrenched core businesses (switched voice in one case, broadcast video in the other) that are hard for the other side to take away. I expect the regulatory boundaries that reserve services either to cable companies or to telephone companies will gradually break down over the next ten to twenty years.

Conclusion

Cable manifests many aspects of those firms regulated as public utilities. But cable also differs in two major ways. Cable is an information service—and now, with the coming of satellite services, a publisher. Cable is also part of the rapidly evolving electronics industry. The rapid changes in the underlying technology put cable in a different spot than water and sewer utilities.

Cable's role in information services prompts many to suggest a separation of content from conduit, to suggest that cable be made a common carrier of sorts. Thus, one answer to the conundrum posed by cable is a structural change for the industry—and perhaps more regulation. Another answer is that supported by the cable industry: deregulation of cable except for the federal limits on franchise fees and for a federally enforced franchise renewal expectation.

There are two polar models for cable regulation: the monopoly public utility, an entity not much different from other telecommunications common carriers, and the deregulated cable company, which behaves like a newspaper. Treating cable as a public utility is difficult enough today. It will become more difficult as communications and electronic technology continues to improve.

The precise evolution of cable will depend in large part on its regulatory environment. If cable firms are free to enter, explore, and test new markets—withdrawing when results are unsatisfactory and staying and profiting when results are good—then cable may well evolve into the major local communications highway some futurists foresee. But if cable is locked into any market it enters, with cable firms forced to support failing services, while other firms can pick and choose among services, or if cable is held to public utility regulation and limited rates of return in the few areas in which it succeeds, then it will be significantly handicapped and far less able to evolve to its potential. If cable becomes bound by regulation, the big losers will be not the cable companies and their investors but the public, which will be denied services and job opportunities that the cable industry otherwise would have created.

Two issues seem to be paramount in any discussion of cable: access and competition with the telephone companies. Those who advocate common carrier status for cable do so because they fear that otherwise the cable operator would unfairly deny access to the television channels on the cable system. However, this threat is essentially entirely speculative. I would be more concerned about the threat of limits to access if the cable industry were a monolith or even it were as concentrated as the postdivestiture telephone industry is. But the cable industry is diffuse. The largest cable operator has less than 10 percent of the market; the top four firms in the industry hold less than 25 percent of the market. The programming supply market is more concentrated. There are only a few major suppliers of satellite video services. One firm, HBO, has more than 50 percent of the pay movie market. While preventive measures may seem sound, in this case it seems more prudent to wait until the problem manifests itself before taking corrective action. Because the cable industry is diffuse, we have an opportunity to observe a wide range of behavior, and the harm done by any single abuse is limited.

The antitrust laws also can deal with many of the problems of access. Indeed, the suit by Turner Broadcasting against Westinghouse is cited as an example of the need for access regulation.[6] Of course, it can also be cited for just the opposite proposition: that there already is a forum for dealing with the access problem, and no new remedy is required.

Cable will be surrounded by a host of other video distribution systems and information systems. These alternative systems will put economic pressure on cable to carry the most attractive package of programming for its subscribers, and they will limit any denial of information flowing from an abuse by cable of its central position in local electronic information distribution.

We should regulate cable companies the same way we regulate newspapers—with no special rules flowing from their status as information conduits. Newspaper delivery trucks and newspaper route carriers use public rights-of-way. But such use of a public right-of-way does not transfer into regulation of the newspaper. It merely shows up as roadway regulation of the trucks as trucks. The *Washington Post* delivery trucks have to obey the speed limit, just like everyone else. If the regulatory problem is the safe use of the streets and public rights-of-way, we should direct attention toward that problem rather than regulating a particular use of the streets. If necessary, perhaps a new common carrier—a public utility—should be formed to operate conduits under the street. But the utility should be kept as narrow and as focused as possible. There is no need to make the cable company a utility when we can have a pole and conduit utility.

A company could be formed to operate poles and conduits in the community as a common carrier. Any cable company wishing to enter business would purchase duct and pole space from this utility. If, as many claim, public regulation of cable flows from the need to maintain safe streets and to coordinate use of public rights-of-way, then it should be possible to accomplish these regulatory aims without regulating cable companies at all. Of course, if the regulator's real aim is to control electronic publishers, then this alterative will be unattractive.

Even with a pole and conduit utility, cable television would still display some economies of scale and considerable sunk costs that could not be recovered if a firm discontinued business. These conditions mean that the cable industry is not readily contestable the way trucking or airlines are, at least not by competitors using cable technology. Even with a pole and duct utility and true open entry in the cable industry, cable's competitors would be likely to be the video technologies on the competitive fringe—direct broadcast satellites, video recordings, multichannel MDS—rather than competing cable networks in a community. Given this economic structure and the incentives facing both municipalities and cable companies, I doubt if the political system will focus on the fundamental problems for our system created by city franchising of cable companies: a government license to a form of publisher.

I predict that the major political fight about cable regulation over the next ten years will center on determining the extent that the cable company is permitted to offer services traditionally offered only by the telephone industry, and vice versa. Cable provides the opportunity to bring major competition into the local communications market. Such competition would provide the occasion and the need to deregulate the comparable offerings of the local telephone companies.

I doubt that the political system is willing to seize the nettle and quickly deregulate cable television even though such deregulation would serve both First Amendment interests and the long-run interests of cable viewers. Rather, I expect that the transition will be slow and will take many steps. As the economic pressure on cable from the new technologies increases, cable companies in turn will fight harder to remove uneconomic regulation. Similarly, as the perception of a competitive video distribution market grows, the politics of cable regulation will change; people will become more willing to accept reductions in cable regulation.

Notes

1. Ithiel de Sola Pool, *Technologies of Freedom* (Cambridge, Mass.: Harvard University Press, 1983).

2. Altran Electronics Division of McGraw-Edison has developed a distribution automation load management system using low-data-rate quadrature modulation of an AM broadcast station's carrier. This system provides extremely robust and widespread coverage of urban areas.

3. American Science and Engineering, Cambridge, Mass., has developed a load-management and load-control system that uses AC power wiring to carry low-data-

rate control signals to appliances and meters. A number of utilities have installed and are currently using this technology.

4. The calculation is:

$$\frac{100,000 \ (\text{bit/sec}) \ \times \ 86,400 \ (\text{sec/day})}{[\ (8 \ \text{bits/char}) \ \times \ (300,000 \ \text{households})\ ].}$$

5. See *On the Cable: The Television of Abundance,* Report of the Sloan Commission on Cable Communications (New York: McGraw-Hill, 1971), p. 37. See also *Final Reort: President's Task Force on Communications Policy* (Washington, D.C.: Government Printing Office, December 7, 1968).

6. Turner's lawsuit was filed March 3, 1983, in Atlanta: *Cable News Network* v. *Satellite News Channels and Westinghouse Broadcasting and Cable* (Case No. 83-430, N.D. Georgia, Atlanta Div.).

Comment

Ithiel de Sola Pool

C harles Jackson's chapter is a superb analysis of the available technologies of communications, but at the end it falls into an ideological trap. What Jackson's discussion does well is something that needs to be done more often. Too much public policy is made by lawyers and economists who do not understand the technological alternatives with which they are playing. As Jackson notes, the history of broadcasting regulation is a star example. The "scarcity" that exists and that for sixty years has resulted in a tightly regulated, politicized, oligopolistic, and indeed trashy system of broadcasting is the result of regulatory policies adopted by political decision makers, not a result of technological constraints to which the decision makers thought they were responding. There were alternatives of which they never dreamed.

Indeed the contention that no central decision maker is likely to be as wise as is the collective process of many small decisions made by millions of people over time is a shared conviction of most contributors to this book. The errors that have been made by many well-intentioned regulators that could have been avoided in a diffused system of decision making are repeatedly illustrated in the chapters that deal with past regulation. I join with Charles Jackson in warning that most of the proposed schemes for regulating cable are ill advised, shortsighted, and based on lack of understanding of where the technology is going. In particular, the bills proposed in 1984 in both houses of Congress would saddle us with a disastrous quarter- or half-century of stupidity much as we have had with broadcasting, until technology worked us out of a politicized system that we need not get into. And the bills proposed by the cable industry and by its critics are equally disastrous in these respects.

What then is wrong with Jackson's simple formula, "Don't regulate"? It assumes that there is always a choice between doing nothing (allowing the incremental processes of pluralistic decisions to work) and making a central decision. Political processes favor that kind of simple two-valued formulation of alternatives, and that is one of the problems with politics as a decision process. We get into silly debates, as though such an on-off choice existed. We insist on characterizing people as conservatives or liberals as though serious substantive decisions can be made by ideological formula.

Pluralistic unregulated decisions are always made within the context of an accepted system of rules of the game, which for shorthand we label by such terms as *the law* or *property*. For reasons of stable planning, these are not designs that should be changed frequently or lightly, but they are matters of decision. It is not the case that there is just one natural system of law or property; there are structural choices that have to be made about the legal or property system. Those are political decisions.

So all of us in this book probably would agree that in designing a system of cable or of telecommunications in general, one goal should be to minimize the amount of governmental day-by-day decision making, administrative supervision, licensing, or rate regulation. We should, as Jackson argues, create as fluid as possible a situation for entrepreneurs to experiment with novel marketing ideas and novel technologies. It is a marvelously fertile field for innovation and progress, and furthermore it is one that touches on the special issues of the First Amendment.

In this field, however, as in every other field of policy, there arise certain decisions that cannot be made pluralistically. The reasons for that are several; Jackson lists some of them, such as natural monopoly and essential service affected by the public interest. There are others, too, such as the one I have stressed—the need to define the set of enforceable rights in which people trade. In these comments I will not address the issue of why such decision situations arise. The point is that there are situations in which some central decision maker does have to reach a decision that will affect the interests and welfare of millions of people. In our democratic society, two principles ought to govern such decisions over and above the cost-benefit considerations for the particular subject matter. One is that such decisions are properly made by democratically chosen government authorities, not private monopolists (hence the antitrust laws). The other is that the decision should be made in such a way as to minimize regulatory processes and encourage pluralistic decision making.

All of this bears vitally on the present situation of cable. We are moving in an ill-considered and thoughtless way into a system that depends in detail on government-granted monopoly franchises, in which the present political debate is about whether the Federal Communications Commission (FCC) should take over the regulatory powers from the cities, not over what the structure of the system should be. There is nothing in the law of nature that says a cable franchise should be for a 100-channel system. It could be separate channel by channel, separate for the carrier plant from the channels, sold at auction, or granted by formula. There are arguments for and against every solution. The one thing that is not possible is to make no decision and leave it to pluralistic processes. For various reasons it is not acceptable to allow anyone who wants to string cables over or under the city streets to do so where they want, when they want, and to whom they want. That being the case, decisions have to be made politically.

By failing to face up to those essential political decisions and how they can be made in ways that minimize government administration and maximize the prospects for pluralistic entrepreneurial use of the available new technologies, Jackson misses a great opportunity and ends with a weak set of conclusions from what starts out as a brilliant presentation.

He makes a passing remark about the possible desirability of a new common carrier to operate conduits under the street and leaves it there unconsidered except for expressing a perhaps well-founded distaste for making that the job of present cable companies. He casually concludes that the major problem of cable regulation over the next ten years will be determining how far cable companies will be allowed to offer services that have traditionally been offered by the telephone systems. I differ; that will be a problem but far less important and controversial than another one. The main problem is that if no change occurs, cable systems will acquire de facto a politically unacceptable degree of monopolistic control over the contents of what people can communicate in this country.

I am not arguing with Jackson's list of the technological possibilities for a pluralistic communications system. Furthermore, I believe that in the end technology will overwhelm the monopolistic powers that cable systems are acquiring. Twenty-five years hence we may find ourselves in a new movement of deregulation and divestiture of which the cable systems will be the victims as we allow other new means of communication to flourish. The fact remains that between now and that future we are moving inadvertently into an undesirable and politically nonviable situation of concentration of political power over communications.

Whatever the prospects for the long run, the picture that is emerging for the next couple of decades is that the dominant successful second carrier (besides the telephone company) in U.S. cities will be a cable system. As Jackson points out, it will not be the most efficient system for each communications function, but as a package it seems likely to be the dominant alternative. This major communications facility will be run as a monopoly in each city, and the monopolist that runs it will be chosen by a highly political franchising process. That is bad enough, but now we come to the truly ominous prospect: the cable monopolist will make the most of the monopoly and therefore become a self-interested controller of what any publisher or producer can put on cable in that market. Americans will not long tolerate a situation in which a politically chosen company in each city can decide which videotex service, movie series, or news program can get effectively published in that city. To argue, as Jackson does, that there are some more expensive ways or new ways in the future to bypass the enfranchised cable monopolist is no answer. Would we allow city governments to choose and enfranchise the city's monopoly newspaper and dismiss objections by saying there are other ways of delivering the news? That clearly would be intolerable.

Jackson and I agree that the wrong solution to this prospective problem would be the establishment of a system of government-administered fairness and balance requirements or even a rigid prohibition on cable companies experimenting with content offerings. But it is highly irresponsible not to recognize that the pattern that seems to be evolving is one of a highly politicized system with substantial control over effective publication of major types of material. It is also poor policy analysis not to ask what the alternative structures of cable property rights can be to minimize those dangers and to maximize the amount of pluralistic unregulated decision making over cable use.

This is not the place to put forward panaceas, but it must be noted that most people who are thinking about these matters tend to look for systems in which by one means or another entrepreneurs other than the enfranchised monopolist can lease cable time to provide competitive and alternative services to the public. To label such property schemes regulation and property schemes in which the city or some other political authority bestows an exclusive control of content on their chosen agent nonregulation is clearly obfuscation.

7
Telecommunications: After the Bell Break-up

Peter Samuel

"If it works, don't fix it." That is the comment most often made currently about the present reorganization of the U.S. telephone system. People are not pleased by what is happening with the breakup of Bell.

Americans have had a love-hate relationship with Ma Bell, as if she were a rather formidable mother-in-law. They have hated her for her power and size and impersonal character. But they have loved her for her efficiency and reliability. To Americans who have traveled, it has been obvious that Bell as a telephone service was without a rival. When forced to make international comparisons, Americans had to concede Ma Bell was good. It is hardly surprising given this ambivalent attitude to Bell during her lifetime that Americans have mourned her passing and that they praise her more in death than they did when she lived.

But nostalgia is no basis for policymaking. Bell cannot be brought back to life. Her demise was the product of a variety of forces, some within the control of public policy, some outside it. It was partly populist trustbusting that got Ma Bell in the end. The Department of Justice's endless antitrust action against Bell finally wore her down. Blocked from exploiting her inventions of solid state physics outside telephony, the management of Bell was chained by the court. Bell Labs invented the transistor and many other key components of computers and modern electronic circuitry, but as a regulated utility Bell was prevented from harvesting the fruits of its labors. So it was partly pursuit of commercial freedom that motivated Bell to propose the present breakup, the divestiture, to the Justice Department.

Even if the United States had not had an antitrust policy, however, Bell probably would have broken up around now. Such vast centralized organizations are increasingly hard to manage. More important, technology has changed so that commercial pressures have been at work to create a more diversified and less centralized telephone system. For a start, it is not just telephone anymore. Although voice telephone is still the major form of telecommunication, there is an increasing range of things we want to transmit other than talk: video pictures, facsimile reproductions, and written characters and numbers (data), as well as other communications like alarm signals. Moreover, technologies for communication have proliferated, and specialization in the different technologies is occurring. There is a vast scope for innovative ways of combining the high technology and offering different packages of services. So it is natural to expect a proliferation of businesses, eroding the dominance of the old monopoly.

Complicating the telephone scene have been a variety of regulators, with different constituencies and different philosophies, therefore working often at cross-purposes with one another. The Justice Department has focused on antitrust issues. The Federal Communications Commission (FCC) has been seeking movement toward more competition. It has been described as having a philosophy of deregulation, though a cautious and limited deregulation. Third, state public utility commissions, susceptible to consumerist political pressures, have been standing ready to move in on regulatory ground vacated by the federal authorities. Fourth, the judiciary has been reshaping telecommunications, especially in the person of Washington Judge Harold Greene, whose judgments and threat of judgment have played a major role in refashioning the telephone industry. Fifth, federal politicians have stood ready to enact new laws at the behest of special interest groups who feel disadvantaged by change, while invoking the public interest and exclaiming ferociously on behalf of the supposedly helpless and ever-victimized common person. The move toward deregulation will lead to soaring telephone bills, say these politicians. Even more than higher telephone charges, the politicians have raised the ogre of tariff charges leading to older people's being forced to disconnect their telephones. Universal telephone service is under threat, they allege.

The U.S. telephone business is in an odd situation. Bell has broken up and competition is increasing, but the revised tariff arrangements necessary to put that competition on a fair and rational basis are being deferred. Under threat of legislative and judicial obstruction, the FCC has been repeatedly forced to defer—at least for residential and single-line business users—the new pricing arrangements that many believe are essential to make competition work properly.

The regulated, Bell-dominated telephone system apparently developed massive cross-subsidies. People paid too much for long-distance calls, and the profits there paid for basic connection to the system, for which there has been no charge. Now that there is competition, these huge cross-subsidies are unsustainable. American Telephone and Telegraph (AT&T), at its present long-distance tariffs, is bound to lose market share heavily, since it is charging too much. At the same time local telephone companies are being prevented from introducing (for single-line customers anyway) access charges or flat rate monthly fees to cover the costs of connection to the national telephone network. The current situation is a messy mix of incompatible politics and economics. Strong financial pressures already exist to let prices adjust, and these are bound to intensify.

A freer, more competitive telecommunications industry should be good for the country. Of course, the new world of competition and choice is more work for consumers. It is always easier for consumers to have their decisions made by a paternalistic monopoly. But just as people manage to make choices among complex and changing offerings of different features, quality, and prices in cars, insurance policies, home computers, and newspapers, so they will adapt to competition in telecommunications.

A competitive industry will be better for consumers for several reasons. It will be more efficient, delivering more services for less cost. Regulated monopolies are inevitably controlled by some form of cost-plus pricing system, which provides no incentive for minimizing cost. Bell, like all other huge protected monopolies, was comfortable. It almost never fired anyone. It built durable products. It was expensive. These features are all typical of a regulated utility, which is not much concerned about cost, since its revenues are controlled according to some cost-plus-a-reasonable-profit kind of formula. Since it was not allowed by regulators to benefit in its profits from taking a prudent risk, it naturally tended to invest its way out of risk taking. It overbuilt everything.

Take, for example, the microwave towers that Bell builds (solid pyramidal structures) as compared to some of MCI's towers (light guy-wired structures). The latter are built with cost in mind, the former with engineering excellence as the primary concern. In a competitive environment, the players are forced to think more of the economic trade-offs involved in their engineering and to economize. In the regulated environment, costs are less constrained.

Competition is beneficial mainly because it tends to drive prices down toward real costs and makes cross-subsidies unsustainable. For years, the Bell system made a virtue out of its free services like directory assistance that save consumers from using the telephone book or maintaining a list of numbers. These services have been free of direct charge to the subscriber but cost somewhere in the region of 40 cents to $1 per call serviced to the telephone company. The cost of these services was loaded onto telephone bills somewhere else. That lack of a direct charge meant the service was used wastefully. People made little attempt to record numbers. There was no scope for anyone to try to run a competitive and more efficient directory assistance service. And the telephone company had no measure of the real economic demand for these services. Now that there is competition in long-distance telephony, AT&T cannot afford to load the directory assistance costs onto its calling tariffs. It is proposing a 75 cent charge for long-distance directory assistance calls, and the local companies are starting to charge for local directory assistance calls, as they should. People will have an incentive to record numbers and will use the service only when it is worth 75 cents to them, approximately its cost. Also, companies now have an incentive to find a more efficient way than AT&T's for giving people numbers because they might be able to make money at less than 75 cents per call.

Competition has dynamic benefits too, as economic theory can demonstrate. Greater profit goes to those who seize the opportunities of economic new technology, and losses are in store for those who fail to adopt them. But perhaps some history is more persuasive than theory.

Telecommunications: A Brief History

Western Union has a grand place in U.S. history. It was the world pioneer of the first form of telecommunication, the telegraph. Western Union was splendidly entrepreneurial in developing Samuel Morse's invention in the 1840s. His tapping of Morse code dots and dashes down an electrified cable was a revolutionary advance over horseback delivery of messages or the use of carrier pigeons. Western Union was rewarded for its entrepreneurial dash and its good judgment with virtual domination of the telegraph industry. It continued for some time as an innovator and entrepreneur. It developed telegrams, then teleprinter machines, and eventually telex. Out of Western Union's technology grew whole new industries, including stockbrokerage and commodities trading. The railroads and newspapers grew with telegraph service.

But Western Union, like most other monopolies, grew complacent. Eventually the company made a catastrophic business mistake in 1876 when it turned down the offer of the telephone patent. Alexander Graham Bell and his father-in-law did not think they would have the cash to develop the telephone, so they offered to sell it to Western Union. Smug at the command of their enormous telegraph system, Western Union's chief executives sneered at Bell's telephone and lost forever the opportunity to remain at the forefront of telecommunications. That is not unusual. IBM, after all, did not invent the personal computer. Two brilliant college students in a garage in San Francisco did and went on to become Apple Computer.

It has been in periods of untidy, tumultuous competition that products have been democratized and have gone through their most rapid rate of growth and innovation. For most of its history, the telephone has been governed by a near-monopoly market situation and strong government regulation, but it has had bursts of freedom. From 1876 to 1894 Bell had the monopoly, due to patent law. During those years and growing from nothing, its rate of growth averaged 16 percent a year.

Normally one would thereafter expect a declining rate of growth, but the patent monopoly had in fact been inhibiting the development of telephony. The Bell chiefs at first saw the telephone only as an instrument for business use and for the very rich. They made little attempt to sell it outside inner-city areas. (Bell was never as limited in its outlook as the British Post Office, which was granted a telephone monopoly in that country. One of the commissioners of the British Post Office at first dismissed the telephone as a gimmicky U.S. invention that the old country had no need of "because we have a quite adequate supply of messenger boys here.")

In the United States, the real takeoff of the telephone business occurred in 1894, when the Bell patent expired and independents were able to enter the business in competition with Bell. Thousands of entrepreneurs rushed in to wire up small stores and began to make telephones available to the middle class in their homes. Between 1894 and 1907, open competition promoted an annual growth rate of telephones in the United States of 27 percent. By the end of that period of open competition, there was one telephone for every 14 Americans compared to one per 250 thirteen years earlier.

Historians describe the flowering of telephone competition:

> The effects of competition in telephony were striking. Between 1893 and 1907, when the independent [telephone] movement reached its peak in relative terms, the number of phones in the U.S. increased from 266,000 to 6.1 million. Of these 3.0 million were independent and 3.1 million were Bell phones; Bell's market share had fallen from 100 percent to 51 percent. Although its market share had been cut in half, Bell did react vigorously to the new competition by cutting its charges to its subscribers and by adding more than ten times as many phones during 1893–1907 as it had put into service in the era of its monopoly from 1876 to 1893.[1]

But Bell-AT&T (it formally became American Telephone & Telegraph in 1900) did not like competition. It had been making profits of 40 percent on capital in its patent monopoly period. After 1900, the hectic competition from the independents reduced its rate of return to around 8 percent. It saw an easier and more profitable life through a restoration of monopoly. Government regulation was to be the key. Under the influence of financier J.P. Morgan, AT&T brought in a new chairman, Theodore Vail, who began a massive buy-up of independent telephone companies and a propaganda drive against the supposed wastefulness of competition. That campaign bore fruit in 1910 with a law to bring telephony under the regulatory control of the Interstate Commerce Commission (ICC), and competition was effectively ended for more than half a century.

Under Vail (1908–1913), the growth of the number of telephones dropped from 27 percent annually to 8 percent annually. From 1914 on under ICC control and from 1934 on under FCC control, annual growth was between 4 and 5 percent.[2] During the competitive telephone period, between 1894 and 1907, quite a lot of service duplication developed; about 15 percent of AT&T's subscribers in 1909 had lines and telephones from a second telephone company.[3]

During this same period, AT&T's telephone revenues per station were halved by competition; they went down from $76.41 in 1894 to $35.71 in 1909.[4] Competition pushed prices down and boosted service dramatically up. Monopoly saw slower growth of telephone service and higher prices and profits for Bell.

Recent Semideregulation

Following some sixty years (1908–1968) of heavy regulation and controlled monopoly in the telephone business, we have moved into an era of semideregulation. In the past fifteen years, deregulation of entry into telephony has occurred. Deregulation has progressively removed restrictions that had prevented new firms from entering into three areas of telephone business: (1) the sale of customer-premises telephone equipment like telephone sets and private branch exchanges (PBXs), (2) the provision of long-distance service, and now (3) with various kinds of bypass of local lines, there is new entry of business and hence competition end to end.

So far, this deregulation is only partial, since many prices continue to be regulated at the federal and state levels. There are also severe restrictions on what AT&T and the local telephone companies can do and how they are to be organized. At the federal level, the continuing regime of regulation is justified by the fear that, during the transition to a competitive structure, the old Bell companies will engage in predatory pricing and cross-subsidization internally to destroy their new competitors. Intrastate telephone service meanwhile remains under the firm control of state public utilities commission (PUCs), which have shown no strong philosophical commitment to deregulation. So it is quite inaccurate to describe the present state of the telephone business as the product of deregulation.

Semideregulation has enormous problems of its own. The continued partial regulation of the dominant companies creates great uncertainties and introduces new distortions into the business. The uncertainties result from the constant changing of pricing plans and timetables for their introduction as the FCC battles politically with Congress and the various telephone interests and is subject to court interventions also.

The distortions introduced by attempts at continued public-utility-style regulation of telephone company prices have been pointed out by Nina Cornell, Michael Pelcovits, and Steven Brenner.[5] Under regulation, the local companies have been entitled to recover all their historical book costs, plus an allowed rate of return on investment. Their proposals for new flat rate monthly access charges are based on an embedded cost, plus rate-of-return calculation that is likely to produce inflated rates. Under regulation the companies have almost certainly overinvested in plant and also not written off their investments quickly enough. At these "utilities" there have been none of the block write-offs of historical costs that competitive commercial companies engage in when they find that new lower-cost technology has reduced the earning value of their capital plant. However, as long as the local companies are being regulated, they will be operating in that peculiar regulators' cocoon in which there is the standard allowed return on every historical cost, however foolish it was or however inadequately it has been depreciated. Thus, regulation is keeping up prices.

Nina Cornell and her associates do not attempt to quantify the extent to which the local telephone companies' book costs may be exaggerated and their access charge proposals thereby inflated. They suggest the matter is so complex and untestable that "the issue of historical subsidy flows will probably never be resolved."[6] Cornell and her associates are probably wrong in their provocative guess that there has been no substantial cross-subsidization at all from long distance to local telephony. But they are probably correct in saying that a continuation of standard rate-of-return regulation on historic cost-type price setting will lead to uneconomic charges for local service. And they could be right in saying that the regulators, instead of withdrawing from their mistaken price controls, may be tempted to compound the distortions of their regulation by interfering against competitive market-based alternative technologies. In other words, there is always a danger that semideregulation may retreat into regulation, leaving deregulation to be regarded as no more than a mistaken idea that is blamed for everything that went wrong. The idea of telephone deregulation as a future all-purpose scapegoat is the gloomy prognosis.

On a more optimistic note, it is possible that some kind of compromise between politicians' wanting to keep local access charges down and the regulators' overemphasis on historic costs may turn out not to differ too much from economic charges that might be produced in a competitive marketplace.

Although there is now competition in long-distance service and in supply of equipment and enhanced services, regulators continue to hold to the basic premise that local telephone service remains a natural monopoly. (Local service refers to the basic copper wireline cabling connection between the consumer's house or business and the local central office switches within a local dialing area.) The idea of natural monopoly is the rationale for the special controls over local telephone companies by the FCC and state regulators. Indeed it was the rationale for the enforced divestiture of the Bell system. As part of the deal with the Justice Department to allow AT&T to enter competition, AT&T was to spin off its utility-type operations, with the assumption that they would continue as regulated monopolies.

At first glance, local telephone service is the closest thing we have to a natural monopoly utility. Millions of miles of copper cables link each house to a telephone exchange or central office, where the dial tone either allows callers to actuate switches that put them through one network or another, or else the dial tone connects the caller to someone else in the local exchange area.

This natural monopoly, the local telephone company, is under challenge too. The advances of solid state physics and fiber optics that have conjured up the electronic chip and lasers and made possible manufacturing techniques of vast precision at microscopic scale provide new means for busting the telephone trust.

Most of the new telephone technologies get subsumed under the heading "telephone bypass." Actually there is no reason why bypass of the local telephone company should not occur with old copper wire, indeed with the existing wires already strung on poles or running in ducts beneath the street. Because there are a lot of spare copper telephone cables in most streets, no great expense would be required to give many subscribers a second local service. The local telephone company has been doing exactly this for years in supplying telex lines. They have been taking a regular telephone cable, almost always an idle one awaiting demand for extra service, and have connected it to the circuits of Western Union, RCA, or whichever telex service a consumer subscribed to. It would be just as simple for a consumer to be given a direct connection to MCI, AT&T, Allnet, USTS, or any other telephone company one wanted a connection with. The direct access line would be in the nature of a private line in the sense that it would not access the local telephone company switch. In places where there are no spare telephone cables, new cables could be strung overhead or pulled through underground ducts. AT&T has proposed in Manhattan to bypass New York Telephone Company by this means of private conventional wirelines, since it regards the $6 monthly access charge by the local telephone company as too expensive.

There is no reason there should not be competing local service by means of multiple ownership or leasing of local loop copper wire either. Phillip Freedenberg, a telephone consultant in the Washington, D.C., area, says he expects that as deregulation evolves, a lot of commerce in existing telephone plant will develop.[7] He foresees complicated multiple operations at the local level. He envisions the local telephone companies realizing that they can generate extra revenues by encouraging competitors to buy up or lease from them surplus local loop cabling, even switches and central offices. He draws an analogy with the airlines business under deregulation in which competing companies sell and lease one another planes, do ticketing and servicing of one another's aircraft, handle luggage, and ticket passengers for a fee.

New Technologies

New technologies are usually a driving force for competition and a challenge to established companies. Telephony provides a good example of this impact of technology on business. MCI's growth began based on special expertise in microwave links. SBS got into telephone service by satellites.

Coaxial cable, the 3/8 inch thick cable consisting of a core wire surrounded by an outer conducting sheath, is an old new technology that can be used to bypass the local telephone company. It is primarily installed to provide cable television. Telephone conversations can be added to the video signals carried by coaxial cable because it has a generous bandwidth. MCI is testing a complete system it has dubbed cablephone in several cities that uses coaxial cable to bypass the local telephone company and provide direct access for its subscribers, avoiding the need for them to pay the access charges. In New York City, Manhattan Cable has been offering private line coaxial cable connections between downtown and uptown office buildings for a mixture of voice telephone and data. There are no technical obstacles to interconnecting with public switched networks. The Washington-area subsidiary LDD (local digital distribution) of the Boston-based telephone manufacturer M/A-COM has for sale a device called CAPAC (cable packet communications system) designed to interface between coaxial cable and telephone systems. In some areas, regular copper-pair telephone lines are of poor quality because of their age, the large number of splices, or multiple unused ends (like dead-end streets). Consequently coaxial cable often will give a clearer voice signal and will be cheaper than fixing the copper telephone wires.

Given that cable television goes to some 40 percent of households and that increasingly the systems are two way as needed for telephony, there is great technical scope for the cable companies to become second telephone companies. That they have shown no great enthusiasm to do this so far is partly attributable to regulation. The cable companies are fearful of coming to be regarded as common carriers subject to FCC regulation.

But if regulatory hurdles can be jumped, telephone (and data) use of some of the bandwidth of coaxial cable may become a profitable extra service offered by the local cable television company.

The world's first electronic communications link, between Washington, D.C., and Baltimore, was a telegraph, a copper wire carrying a battery-powered electrical current and strung on wooden poles. Built to the design of Samuel Morse, it carried the code that bears his name. Telecommunications nearly became a government monopoly in this country. Morse's first line was built with $30,000 appropriated by the Congress, and it was from the Capitol that Morse transmitted the first telegraph message to Baltimore: "What hath God wrought." Morse wanted to sell the telegraph patent and rights to the postmaster general. He was turned down because this civil servant did not believe telecommunications had any potential. It was left to the Magnetic Telegraph Company to take over the Washington-Baltimore telegraph line and extend it to New York City.[8]

Along the route pioneered by Morse's telegraph where copper wires proliferated and then were displaced by coaxial cable and microwave dishes, alongside the tracks of the Pennsylvania Railroad (now Amtrak), history is turning full circle. The installation of fiber optic cable along that route signals the end of telecommunications dependence on electrical and radio waves now that light waves in a strand of glass will carry most telephone conversations. In 1880 Alexander Graham Bell patented a photophone that used light reflected from the sun by a parabolic mirror to carry a sound signal. It did not work well and was abandoned in favor of the electricity in a wire that has been the basis of telephone technology in its first hundred years. The return to light as a medium for voice communication had to wait for the development of an especially pure kind of light, the laser in the 1960s (Theodore Maiman of Hughes Aircraft was the inventor), and for improvements in purity of glass manufacture by Corning Glass Works in the 1970s.

Fiber optics is a logical extension of the trend in radio communications toward making use of higher and higher frequencies of electromagnetic waves. The great characteristic of fiber optics is its carrying capacity. Tiny hair-fine paired threads of super-pure glass can carry 4,000 telephone conversations simultaneously. Cable less than half an inch thick, bundling forty such glass pairs together, can carry over 100,000 conversations. Moreover, light signals carry farther than electrical signals, so over a given route only about a quarter of the repeater or booster devices are needed. Consequently the immediate application of optic fiber is in long-distance telecommunications on densely trafficked trunk routes, of which the Washington–New York–Boston corridor is a prime example. With just one fiber optic cable the thickness of a finger, buried alongside 4,000 miles of railroad tracks, MCI can build a capability east of the Mississippi comparable with AT&T's network and multiplying manyfold its existing microwave network.

On the Washington-Baltimore route, both AT&T and MCI currently operate fiber optic trunk cables. Also planned is one leg of a local Washington-Baltimore network being constructed by Institutional Communications of Bethesda, Maryland.[9] The approximately 100 mile network mainly within the metropolitan area of the twin cities will aim at the business of companies with yearly telephone bills of $10,000 or more. The concept is an outgrowth of an unsuccessful cable television bid. Using fiber optic technology, the system is designed to bypass the local C&P Telephone company and hook customers directly into long-distance companies—SBS, MCS, Sprint, AT&T, and ITT.

Burying Cable

David Macaulay is a draftsman with a good eye for how buildings are built and a genius for making the inside details of construction interesting. One of his best books, *Underground*, describes with drawings what lies beneath the streets under manholes from which steam blows, into which people with ladders descend, and through which cables are drawn from giant spools.[10] The maze of fascinating pipes underground in large cities includes ducts built for great clusters of different colored wire pairs of plastic-covered copper wires. As the drawings of Macaulay illustrate, the space under city streets is a large-scale ants' nest of passageways. Despite modern digging machinery, the network is quite expensive to tamper with.

There is much discussion about fiber optic cable revolutionizing the economics of cable-based communications. But the reality is that, for many applications, no matter how cheap and how efficient the cable gets, the costs of breaking ground, placing ducts, and restoring the roadway will continue to pose the biggest financial problem. Cable stock costs themselves are trivial compared to these other costs.

According to a study of telephone manufacturer M/A-COM DCC, the costs of building underground ducting in city areas are about $20 to $25 per foot. So where cable has to be put in new ducts, whether cable can be reduced in cost from $5 a foot to $2 is immaterial. The cost of hanging cable from existing poles is much less than ducting. Hanging cable from existing poles costs about $4 or $5 a foot in an average cable system, about one-fifth the cost of building underground ducts. Laying cable underground in open suburban areas, where ducts are not needed and cable can be buried behind mechanical plows, costs about $10 per foot. Even there the cost of installation is greater than that of fiber optic cable itself. Coaxial cabling costs per subscriber range between $180 and $540. Only a lucrative new business, such as video entertainment, will justify new cabling to households and telephony will have to be an add-on use to someone else's cable system.

As far as businesses in established city centers are concerned, the key issue is whether the competing new cable technologies can get into the existing underground ducts, given the vast expense of new ducting. So far the local telephone companies have virtually monopolized the telephone ducts. In most places, however, state utility laws require them to share their ducts on a reasonable rental basis. Getting the courts or PUCs to ensure such sharing when the local telephone company owns the ducts is often held to be a problem. Consider, however, that the new technologies of coaxial and optic fibers mean the old ducts can carry cabling with vastly greater capacity than the bundles of copper pairs they were often originally built for. Thus, the dominant local telephone company should need progressively less duct space for its own purposes. It should be able to rent or sell ducts to its competitors and should be keen to do so if it is seeking to maximize its income.

A substantial proportion of U.S. homes are being wired with coaxial cable for home entertainment. Each of these cable systems has a great hunk of bandwidth to allow telephone circuits to be inserted. Thus this essentially entertainment medium provides enormous potential for competing telephony. But a variety of problems have stopped this competition to date. Cable television companies are principally entertainment oriented, and most have not pursued alternative possibilities wholeheartedly. The cable needs to be two way to work telephone, though most new systems are two way. Perhaps most important, the cable companies are afraid of being regulated as common carriers if they accommodate telephone traffic.

If cable companies do get into telephony, that raises the question of whether existing restrictions on local telephone companies that prevent them from offering coaxial cable services will be justifiable. Eli Noam suggests that regulations prohibiting local telephone companies from going into cable should be lifted in places where there is an established cable company permitted to use part of its cable bandwidth for telephone service. Says Noam, "By pitting large carrier systems against each other, one encourages a dynamic development of technology and applications, and at the same time reduces the need for regulation."[11] One problem that might hinder dynamic competition between telephone companies and cable operators alike is that both have developed a monopoly mentality. In New York City in 1983, some of the cable franchise selectees in previously uncabled boroughs threatened to pull out of New York because Merrill Lynch and others were planning to install cable through the franchise areas to link a proposed Staten Island teleport (a collection of satellite-earth stations) with their customers. The cable television operators seemed to think they were getting some monopoly right to lay cable in these boroughs and that the city would protect them from competition. Indeed they seemed to believe the city would keep out any kind of high-bandwidth cable medium. In this case, the cable in question was fiber optic, not coaxial, and best suited to data, not video entertainment, yet the franchised cable companies wanted the city to prevent even this form of competition, indicating how deeply cable television companies believe in their monopoly entitlements even when it is not written into their agreements with cities.

For their part, cities have shown little interest in competition, probably in the instinctive understanding that where there is competition, there is less monopoly profit to be skimmed off by government officials in the franchise bidding process and less of a case for regulation afterward. Around the country skirmishes have been occurring between city regulators and apartment owners about satellite master antenna television (SMATV) or minicable networks. It makes economic sense for an apartment owner or condominium association having a master antenna to sell signal to nearby apartment blocks. They can legally do this if they can avoid any public property. If the cable has to go over or under even the tiniest public alleyway, they can be held in breach of cable television franchise regulations under the monopoly mentality with which these are administered. Thus we have yet another case of local regulations hindering economical and service-rendering systems.

Local Glass Fibers

Some of the local Bell companies are starting to use fiber optics on the subscriber side of the local exchange or central office. This provides an economical way of connecting into various local distribution points or remote terminals from which conventional copper-pair connections are made. The system is called Fiber-SLC (subscriber-loop carrier) and was first installed at Chester Heights in the suburbs of Philadelphia.[12]

The system is analogous to a tree, with fiber feeders corresponding to the trunk and the traditional copper-pair wires comprising the individual branches. There is an important reason in many suburban areas to go from bundled copper-pair feeder cables to optic fibers. Where these feeder cables are slung aerially between posts and are sometimes as much as an inch thick and require steel rope for support, these old-fashioned feeders are an aesthetic horror. Maintenance, too, is a problem since street trees must be pruned constantly to accommodate the aerial wires. Fine glass-fiber cables will help get these feeder trunks undergound.

There is no immediate need for the local telephone company to extend optical fibers right to people's houses, unless these companies are allowed to cater to new demands for more than just telephone service. As long as regulators prevent telephone companies from offering extra communications services, such as alarm and security links, remote meter reading, data channels for home computers, and video or television, fiber optic cable has far more capacity than is needed currently. Even old copper-wire pairs are being conditioned so they can carry data and voice telephone simultaneously under a system called local area data transport (LADT). Already a telephone line can carry computer signals with the use of a modem that is a big seller to home computer owners. A modem converts digital (or on/off)-style computer data to analog (or wave)-style voice line signals so regular copper-pair telephone lines can be used as data links.

In New York City there is a furor about the New York Telephone Company's creation of a new area code for Queens, Brooklyn, and Staten Island. It is a long-distance call to dial under the East River from Manhattan. Los Angeles has already been split into several area codes. The enormous demand for extra telephone lines seems largely to be the result of people getting modems for personal and home computers, facsimile machines, and database terminals in offices. The local telephone companies are running out of numbers. Competition in the local loop may turn up more innovative ways of connecting New Yorkers on either side of the East River than requiring them to dial long-distance codes.

Wireless Telephony

Even more exciting than the improvements in various kinds of wires is the expanding potential of telephone systems using various kinds of radio waves— telephones that are wireless.

An ideal telephone system would apply the telephone number to the person, not the place. In other words, people's telephones could accompany them wherever they are so that callers would not have to leave messages or call another number to reach people away from their home or place of work. It could have an on-off switch so people could not be bothered if they preferred. The system could also have an automatic call forwarding to a message taker or an answering machine. The telephone would be designed so consumers could use it to establish a data link for their portable computers. The ideal telephone would end a lot of current practices: leaving a message to return a call, only to find that the caller is not by the phone, so one has to ask a secretary to take the message requesting the caller to call again, and so on.

The ideal telephone would be able to accompany users wherever they choose. The telephone should be accessible, and the user should be able to make calls from anywhere, any time—at home, in the office, commuting, walking, driving, interstate, in a plane. The ideal personal telephone would be small enough to carry in a briefcase or handbag or even to fit in a pocket.

The first serious technology for widespread personal telephony of this kind is cellular radio-television service, often abbreviated as cellular. Its key characteristic is the use of relatively high-frequency, low-power radio signals. Higher frequencies produce more directional, less diffused signals, and the low power means that the signal does not go too far and does not need much electricity. The relatively low electricity demand and small battery requirement makes it easier for engineers to design a compact, light, and portable phone. The small geographic spread of the signal allows scarce radio frequency slots to be reused many times over in one metropolitan area. The confined spread of the radio signal does mean that the system requires a great number of interlinked system transmitter-receivers (transceivers in the jargon). With 666 radio frequencies available, about half that many conversations can be carried on simultaneously without interference with or from immediately adjacent signal cells. And in nonadjacent cells, the signal frequencies can be reused. More telephone traffic can be accommodated by a process of cell splitting, which means adding new transceivers within the old cell area and reducing signal power so that frequencies can be reused more often. An automated control system is vital to the smooth operation of the system. The control system must keep track of the various mobile telephones so it knows where to direct incoming calls. Also vital to the system is a signal strength monitor that could help hand off a conversation from one transceiver to another, as the mobile telephone moves out of range of one and into range of an adjacent one. This hand-off (as in a relay race) as the mobile telephone moves from cell to cell can be accomplished so smoothly that talkers would not even notice the change.

Carphones have existed for years, but they have had poor-quality signals. Worse, they have had such large reception areas that frequency reuse has been impossible within a metropolitan area, resulting in a service available for only a tiny elite. There have been only 150,000 conventional carphone users in the United States, whereas many millions, perhaps even tens of millions should be able to use cellular. The old carphones were an inherently elitist technology because they allowed only a small number of users. But the new cellular technology should develop into a mass product. The old carphones also use too much power to be portable, but cellular telephones could be built so they could be carried on the person.

The United States has been slow to use cellular. Almost fifteen years of studies, experiments, hearings, and other excuses for inaction by the FCC have delayed its introduction by more than a decade, so that Japan and Western Europe have had the opportunity to jump ahead. Cellular telephones represent one of the major opportunities for bypassing local telephone companies and interconnecting with them. A person using a cellular phone to talk to someone interstate, directly connecting with a long-distance carrier, is using cellular as an instrument of bypass of the local wireline company. If a caller uses cellular to speak to someone on a regular local telephone, it is being used as an instrument of interconnection. One might, of course, talk to someone else on a cellular phone. Those three ways of using a single system point to the practical difficulties, not to mention the inequities and inefficiency, of moves to restrict or levy charges on local telephone bypass.

Car Cellular First

Most industry observers think the bulk of bypass action initially will be in carphones or mobile phones because it is much less demanding to manufacture a telephone that can work from a car than to make one to be carried around. In the car, the telephone can draw on the car's power supply (12V), the transceiver unit can be located in the trunk, and the roof can be used for an antenna. In a truly portable system, the telephone has to carry its own power and antenna. Nonetheless, such a system is being produced, and a U.S. company is leading the way. Motorola of Chicago started to sell the world's first truly portable telephone, the Dyna-TAC 8000X, in March 1984. Under 2 pounds in weight, it measures 8 inches by 2 inches by an average of 3 inches deep. The device sells for around $4,000. Jim Caile, Worldwide Marketing Support Manager, of Motorola claims it will fit in his pocket, clearly an excellent start as a portable telephone.[13] It is good for twelve three minute calls on a battery charge and can be plugged into a special vehicle adapter for recharging or use on a car power supply.

A new Washington, D.C.–based company, Millicom, got a lot of publicity in 1983 with a rather similar-looking portable telephone that the company said would sell for $1,000 and rent for $28 a month. In spring 1984, it was announced that Millicom would not manufacture the device itself but was in partnership with the large radio manufacturer E.F. Johnson, a Western Union subsidiary. According to Tom Asp of E.F. Johnson, the Western Union portable cellular telephone will be ready for sale early in 1985 and will sell for "between $3,000 and $4,000."[14]

Portable telephones based on cellular concepts will not be a fad like CB radio, whose weakness was that with it one could talk only to other CBs. Using cellular portables, consumers will be able to dial directly into the regular telephone network, and portable telephones will be accessible from any telephone in the United States. Telephone numbers will increasingly be attached to people, not the places they inhabit.

People will take their telephones with them to work, home, and even out of town. People will be able to reach cellular portable telephone users wherever they are (although these telephones come with a switch to indicate a busy signal if one does not want to take the call). They will work just about everywhere in the home, in the street, and in cars but not so well in the interiors of office buildings. They probably will not work at all in elevators or subways and certainly not in planes, although in planes there will soon be a satellite-based system. Cellular will not be quite the ubiquitous means of communication, but it will be a massive advance on the wireline fixed telephone we now know. A numbering system has yet to be devised to allow users to operate their cellular telephones out of the metropolitan area in which they live, so as yet the systems being built cannot service so-called roamers, people from another city.

No one can say with certitude how ubiquitous the mobile telephone will become because much depends on the competitive environment established and whether the new technologies are allowed free rein. A great deal depends on the price of cellular telephones and how well they work in the hands of ordinary nontechnical people. At one extreme are authorities who believe cellular is such a powerful technology that it will replace the present wireline system and become the dominant form of telephony. One expert, Stuart Crump, Jr., says that wireless telephones will displace the wireline ones "within about twenty years."[15] At the other extreme are skeptics who predict that cellular will be a small add-on type service, always likely to be minor in scale compared to the wireline system. William Newport of the Chicago Advanced Mobile Phone Service, Inc. (AMPS) says that cellular will never seriously encroach on the wireline system, citing parallel improvements to the wireline service that will enable it to compete and maintain its market dominance.[16] A detailed survey of cellular demand by Herschel Shosteck, using data about the interest in cellular phones at different prices, shows price to be the key.[17] In surveys of business, Shosteck finds less than 10 percent of businesses interested in cellular telephones at total costs of $100 and more per telephone per month. At $50 a month he finds 25 percent of businesses interested. For households, Shosteck could find no measurable demand at $75 per month but substantial demand developing at $50. Says Shosteck, "What we see here—in the case of both business and, in particular, household demand—is a tremendous price sensitivity. The extensive use of cellular radio will not occur until prices are low enough to attract a lot of people to purchase the service."

But will the prices go down? We know not to put too much faith in the pronouncements of companies hungry for publicity. Millicom's $1,000 portable telephone of mid-1983 has turned out to be a $3,000-plus E.F. Johnson product. It is still early in the marketing phase for portables, however, with only Motorola actually having one for sale. Motorola's Edward Staiano says he expects portables to drop down through the $1,000 barrier "before the end of the decade."[18]

Mobile or carphones will comprise the great bulk of the early sales. By early 1984, in the Washington, D.C., area the cheapest mobile cellular telephone being offered cost $1,495, while most sold in the low- to mid-$2,000 range. At a financing rate of 14 percent, that meant a monthly leasing charge of about $32 for each $1,000 worth of equipment, so an average mobile telephone in 1984 cost the consumer about $70 to $80 per month on the equipment. On top of that was a monthly flat access charge of $25 and a charge of 40 to 45 cents per minute in business hours, and 25 to 27 cents off-peak. At these rates, cellular telephones look more like a technical curiosity for the wealthy. Indeed, big government monopolies overseas have catered precisely to these elite groups in selling cellular phones. In Australia, for example, the system was launched at a monthly rate of A$150 (comparable to $170 U.S. dollars at the prevailing exchange rate), with calls costing extra. The system has gotten a mere 6,000 subscribers in three years.

The instinctive Bell company approach appears to be similar: to build a gold-plated system and to price it accordingly, the way the government monopoly telephone systems overseas have done with cellular. That kind of high-priced cellular telephone system will not become an item of mass ownership and use. It is competing with telephones at home or in an office that have a basic monthly cost of $30, with pagers that some retailers now sell for $99.50 to purchase and cost $5 per month to use, and with payphones that cost mere coins.

If we were left to the mercies of government telephone systems and government-supported monopolies, I could end this chapter here. None of the already operating cellular systems overseas has become a mass-user system, none has even stimulated the development of portable telephones as opposed to carphones. But with the help of competition, there is hope that costs will be driven down and that major marketing efforts will find a rapidly broadening customer base. One optimistic line on cellular's potential is the statement that "cellular phones have the potential to do to the wireline phone system what the jet aircraft did to the railroads."[19]

After Cellular Digital Phones

Some point out that the present cellular telephone systems are far from the end of the technological road. Indeed, cellular as now being celebrated incorporates a rather old-fashioned FM analog-signal system, although its solid state construction and sensing and hand-off systems represents state-of-the-art electronics. Two more advanced systems are being mentioned that would use the same general principles of low-powered signals, multiple reuse of frequency, and automatic hand-off that the new FM cellular uses, but they would use more advanced signal techniques. These are (1) amplitude compandored sideband (ACSB), which promises to increase six-fold the number of channels available because of narrow-frequency spacing, and (2) digital signaling. Soldiers in several Western armies have been using tiny digital radios for several years. These radios cost approximately $10,000 each.

International Mobile Machines Corp. of Philadelphia, M/A-COM of Boston, and Digital Data Corporation are collaborating to develop a mass-marketable digital radio telephone. The sound wave of a voice varies continuously and in analog electronics is reproduced by an amplitude-modulated or a frequency-modulated system. Instead digital systems use sampling techniques to measure every sound wave and report its features in strings of 1s and 0s—binary bits of data. Digital phones eventually should be cheaper than analog ones and smaller because they do not need one hard-to-miniaturize component, a duplexer, which allows one to hear and speak simultaneously.

In a digital radio telephone, that process can be done in the solid state circuitry using logic chips. The military began using communications digital because it makes security easier, a feature that could be important to the future of cellular radio telephones. The present generation of analog-FM cellular cannot give any assurance against determined eavesdropping, whereas digital signals can be encrypted securely. IMM Corp. plans to market its digital telephone, the Ultraphone, in 1984 as a stationary unit in remote places and in 1985 as a pocket telephone. The unit is described as cigarette-pack sized. It is expected to sell eventually for $1,000 or less per unit.

A number of other simpler radio-telephone systems use long-established technology and just require relaxation of regulations. Mobile radio—specialized mobile radio (SMR) in the jargon—has been around for years providing company vehicle fleets with communications via a home-base radio. Regulations have prohibited sale of the service to outsiders. In 1982 the FCC took the first step toward deregulating mobile radio by allowing its owners to handle interconnect arrangements with the telephone company for their customers as long as they do not make a profit. We can hope that mobile radio as a commercial service will not forever be left to philanthropy and may one day be allowed to assert itself in the world of profit.

Another simple and attractive service struggling through the FCC's regulatory maze is personal radio communications service (PRCS), a kind of long-range cordless telephone. Being pushed by General Electric but a relatively simple technology that scores of others can produce, PRCS would use a small base station on the user's premises, as with a cordless phone, but whereas the cordless phone will only work at a range of a few hundred feet, the PRCS would work out to about five miles. The GE design provides for ranges of ten and fifteen miles through use of cheap repeaters stuck on buildings between the base station and the mobile unit. The promise of PRCS is its simplicity and cheapness—$500 for the base station and mobile unit, which means the system would cost less than $20 per month to lease. It will be a strong competitor with cellular radio for those whose work has them moving in a defined area within a metropolitan area and who want a cheaper mobile telephone service. It will make use of the local telephone company for switching and will mostly help people who currently use payphones and pagers.

Japan has a personal radio service with some of the features of cellular radio telephone but with less automation. Consequently it requires somewhat more work by the user but costs less. There is obviously huge scope in a deregulated environment for experimentation and entrepreneurship to find the right combinations of services and cost that people want. Cellular in the United States must conform to national technical specifications laid down by the FCC. Such specifications have the advantage of resulting in equipment that should be able to be used nationwide, and there may be economies of scale in production for a national market. It will also tend to freeze the technology, so progress will depend on whether the FCC allows other kinds of wireless telephone (SMR, PRCS, digital) to innovate freely.

Fixed Wireless

A number of wireless telephone and telecommunications systems that compete with the regular wireline service are being introduced for offices. Unlike the mobile systems just discussed, these are fixed wireless systems. Licenses have been issued for hundreds of common carrier digital termination systems (DTS), alternatively known as digital message service (DEMS), a sophisticated switching and communication system based on a microwave-frequency broadcast of radio signal in digital packets.

Designed for use within a metropolitan area, DTS operates in the frequency levels used in communications satellites (10.55 to 10.68 GHz). The general trend of radio technology, especially in congested U.S. radio-frequency fields, is toward development of new systems with radio signals of ever higher frequencies in search of new spectrum space. The technical corollary of ever higher frequency is ever tinier wavelength. The smaller wavelength signals have some drawbacks in that they are intensely directional and more easily interrupted by rain. A great advantage of using these smaller wavelength signals, however, is that equipment components, especially antennas, can be made smaller.

DTS is called a point-to-multipoint system in that one central node—the control center, switching point, and interconnection with local and long-distance telephone—sends and receives simultaneously many signals to many different subscriber points within an arc. It uses sophisticated packets or bursts of addressed messages, assigns frequencies on demand, and multiplexes (intermixes) signals, techniques designed to make maximum use of scarce frequency and expensive equipment.

At the subscriber end there will be 2 foot diameter dish antennas either on roofs or inside windows with a view toward the central transceiver. Range can be up to 10 or 15 miles. The subscriber equipment for a small office costs about $10,000, equivalent to half the cost of the PBX (private exchange), which such an office usually buys. Use of DTS microwave radio may justify itself in an office that has, for example, a facsimile machine, a computer terminal, perhaps ten outside telephone lines, and a lot of business to conduct with a head office elsewhere.

Jerome Lucas of Telestrategies, Inc., a Washington-area telecommunications consultant, shows a graph at telecommunications conferences that indicates 550 miles as the cutover point, after which DTS and satellite are cheaper than the Bell system's leased lines and use of its Digital Dataphone Service (DDS).[20] There are plenty of companies with substantial communications traffic extending 550 miles or more.

Cost is not by any means the only attraction of the new local telecommunications technologies. Local telephone companies have great difficulty physically providing high-speed and broad-bandwidth service suited to modern office needs. The new technologies usually allow quicker connection than the local telephone company and better quality. Error rates are usually a fraction of those experienced on regular lines, which makes for clearer voice channels and fewer computer glitches.

In 1982 and 1983, the FCC was taking applications for DTS and allocating licenses. But building of systems has been extremely slow, primarily because of uncertainty over the future prices of local-wire telephone lines. Investors do not want to commit themselves to the new technology until they have some grasp of the prices that will be charged by the competition.

Point to Point

Much simpler systems such as the old point-to-point microwave still have great potential in many places for bypassing the local telephone company. Using new very high signal frequencies, some simple, lightweight, and quite inexpensive new point-to-point microwave systems are being introduced. GEMLINK, a General Electric system in the very high 23 GHz frequency, is a leading example. It can use a pair of 10 pound dishes that look like car headlights and can be bolted onto a 1½ inch water pipe. Good anywhere that one can get a line of sight between two points up to 6 miles apart (depending on rainfall patterns), the GEMLINK system costs half the amount that it costs to lease Bell lines and will cost perhaps a tenth or less in capital and installation costs. Old-fashioned low-frequency microwave was simply uncompetitive in such applications, and, in any event, there usually is not the radio spectrum available.

Lasers and Other Light Links

Just as light can be used inside a very pure glass fiber to communicate, so it can also be used in beam forms. The Central Intelligence Agency (CIA) was the first major user of laser communications because of its need for security. Electrical signals in wires and broadcast can be tapped in many ways without the user's being aware of it, but a highly focused light beam like a laser cannot be intercepted without breaking the link, so it is ideal for security. Consultants around the CIA's area in northern Virginia have quietly taken to laser links too, sometimes termed atmospheric optical communcations. The first highly publicized private-sector laser communication system was in midtown Manhattan where retailer JCPenney connected two buildings a block apart in 1983. They use it for videoconferencing, but such links can be used for connecting telephone PBXs, facsimile machines, computers—any instrument that produces digital signal. The laser equipment looks like a large telescope and is usually mounted inside a window near the ceiling.

To date, laser communications have no licensing or regulation. No government agency asserts any jurisdiction over light beams. As of 1985, engineers need only to find a line of sight between two buildings and install the gear at either end. Limitations include haze and fog, which can block the beam and cut the communications link. Absolute maximum recommended range at present is 10 miles, but the shorter the range, the less the link will be interrupted in poor atmospheric conditions. So far most laser links have been used for ranges of half a mile or less. Users speak highly of their lasers, saying they were cheap and quick to build and work extremely reliably except in dense fog.

Other light systems are regarded as having potential, too, in the variety of systems that can provide a bypass of the local telephone company. On-the-premises satellite earth stations are another system for bypassing the telephone company. Most of the present ones have to be so large that they cannot be fixed to the roof for fear of being blown away by high winds. They tend to be installed in parking lots or on the ground. In the $20,000 to $50,000 price range, these systems make sense only for the very high volume communicators. Two developments are making satellite antennas more affordable: the size of antenna needed is diminishing as the new generations of satellites go to higher radio frequencies and power, and teleports are being created whereby firms band together to share satellite antennas, their office complexes designed around them. Merrill Lynch and others in New York City are building such a teleport on Staten Island, supporting a large office-industrial park of communications-intensive companies. The same system is linked by a cable system to companies downtown. Satellite communication makes most sense where information is broadcast to a number of parties simultaneously or where it spans a continent or an ocean.

Bypassers

There is a rich mix of technologies and new opportunities to spur telephone competition. Interest will center heavily on how the old monopoly, the local wireline telephone company, will be bypassed and who will be the bypassers. One of the largest bypassers could be AT&T itself, wanting direct connection to its large long-distance customers. That seems likely to happen first in Manhattan where AT&T will bypass New York Telephone Company with leased lines into many of its corporate customers. But until pricing of access charges is clarified (and that will not be at least until after the FCC and the new Congress are able to address the issue in 1985), there will be great uncertainty and hesitation. MCI, GTE-Sprint, SBS, Western Union, Allnet, and other national long-distance carriers in competition with AT&T are concentrating now on developing their intercity systems, making it clear there will be assured competition in the telephone business. It is unclear how much they will compete with local telephone companies by going the last mile to the customer or bypassing the existing system, but a large proportion of this country's big corporations, state governments, and state agencies are seriously committed to various local networks and systems that bypass the local telephone company.

For those who welcome such competition and diversity and prefer a system offering multiple ownership and choice, the old monopoly is gone forever. Bypass cannot be stopped in the United States, which is not to say that mistaken attempts will not be made to stop it.

The FCC says it favors economic bypass and opposes uneconomic bypass. Economic bypass refers to bypassing the local telephone company based on lower costs, reflected in lower prices for telecommunications service as compared to those charged by the local telephone company. Uneconomic bypass refers to telecommunications bypass of the telephone company because its prices are higher even though its costs are lower. The incentive for this kind of bypass arises usually out of regulations that distort prices, preventing them from reflecting costs because of enforced cross-subsidies, or because of restrictions on the local telephone company providing the service. Since there is no way of knowing in each case whether bypass is economic or uneconomic, the only logical policy is to remove the obstacles to competition and the demands for cross-subsidies that are the real source of uneconomic pricing and behavior. Then the market will sort out the uneconomic from the economic bypass proposals.

The old hothouse of monopoly in which U.S. communications has been coddled and restricted, spoilt and stunted, this controlled environment has produced artificial subsidized and also high-cost services that are threatened by competition. In particular the fixed costs of connecting a subscriber to the local telephone exchange (or central office) have traditionally, under the regulated monopoly setup, been covered in large part by artificially inflated toll charges for long-distance calls. Competition drives a business to charge prices that are quite closely related to costs; that is one of its great virtues and justifications. In telephony, competition means that long-distance calls are going down in price and local access charges have to go up. Those in the media and politics who want a cheap jeer at telephone deregulation talk only about the charges that are going up.

The prospect that local charges will have to rise creates a constituency agitating for politicians and other regulation-minded persons to obstruct the workings of the marketplace by demanding new forms of controls. The great battlecry is the imperative of defending universal service. It is cast in terms of the Robin Hood tale of virtue being with those who say they are looking after the poor. It is the familiar morality tale employed by so-called liberals against any budget economizing or greater reliance on the market.

Again and again it is being said that telephone competition favors the rich and business. That will be true at first. Businesses and the rich will be the first big users of the new telecommunications, partly because they are big users of communications. The same is true of all new devices. It was the rich who first got electricity in their homes, first got washing machines, and first bought automobiles. The rich were the first who were prescribed antibiotics. All these gadgets and technologies took time and development to become generally affordable items that could be widely owned and used. They were pioneered on the rich and on businesses, which could afford their initial high prices. It will be the same with the new communications technologies. But technology trickledown works. We all have electricity in our homes now, at least in the United States.

A large part of the reason why the United States has benefited by new and productive technology has resulted from the extent of competition. Competition has forced constant change, economizing, and improvement by service providers and manufacturers. Communications is particularly in need of competition and entrepreneurship. And it is especially ill served by bureaucracy and government planning.

A spectacular array of new technologies and new opportunities is now available. There are quickly changing costs and ingenious new ways of doing things. The bottom-line question always is what that heterogeneous crowd of hundreds of millions of consumers will pay for. The free market's trial and error system is essential. Some services and systems have to be allowed to fail so that successes can be found. Because people do not know what they will want until they are offered it with some flair, imagination, and indeed overstatement, competitive marketing is vital. Most of the world does not have this in telecommunications. Entrepreneurs who can make the correct judgments about what services will sell will prosper. Those who turn out to be wrong will falter and perhaps fail. The dynamic field of communications is, above all, a place where people should be expected to put their money where their mouth is and to lose it if they misjudge either the costs and technology on the supply side or the consumers' needs on the demand side.

The breakdown of the telephone trust, the collapse of the old natural monopoly of telecommunications, is already wreaking major changes. Much of this is seen in the furor over access charges, the new flat rate charge that will begin to be phased in to cover the costs of connection to the telephone system. Under the regulated regime and the Bell monopoly, these fixed connection costs—called nontraffic-sensitive costs in the telecommunications jargon—were not charged directly to consumers. Instead Bell made about $10 billion a year of monopoly profits on long-distance calls. Also for many years it profiteered in renting its equipment, mainly plain telephones, to people at high rents (like $3 per month rental charges on a telephone instrument that costs $25 and lasts twenty-five years). With these monopoly profits, basic service—connection to the telephone system—was heavily subsidized. The egalitarian social goal of universal service was served by this cross-subsidization. As a result, the United States has the most telephones per capita in the world. There are close to as many telephones as people in the United States and almost as many telephones in the United States as in the rest of the world put together. According to the 1980 U.S. Census, 98 percent of U.S. households have a telephone, so we are presently as close to the ideal of "universal service" in this country as we are likely to get.

For most people the telephone is an essential part of modern life. Most use it in work. Social life usually depends heavily on it. We make and maintain friendships and relationships with it. And it is an emergency lifeline to the outside world to call for help in time of crime, fire, or medical emergency. The efficiency with which it is managed to meet human needs will have an enormous impact on living standards, productivity, and the quality of life. More, it will vitally affect the creation of new jobs, the nature of jobs, where it is practical for Americans to live and work, and how they work.

That is why the pricing of telephone service and its competitiveness is so important. Under the Bell-FCC telephone trust, Americans have paid a price for this profiteering on behalf of universal service. Long-distance usage has been discouraged because it has cost more than it would have in a more competitive market. Business location decisions, economic activity, communications, and transport decisions have been distorted as a result. Various attempts have been made to estimate the cost of the mispricing caused by the pursuit of universal access.[21] They vary enormously but run into billions.

Opportunities

Enormous benefits and changes can be wrought by lower, more realistic telephone charges and the new services. We get a glimpse of that from some advances already made. Consider the impact of just one innovation, the automatic collect call system. The system is already a major factor in the deurbanization of the United States. Now it is possible to run national businesses by a trout stream in Vermont, or in the dry heat of high New Mexico, or in South Dakota. Mail order (toll-free telephone order business) has been growing at twice the rate of retail sales generally, in large part because of lower rates in the context of a modern nationwide telephone system. Factories in remote areas can sell directly to customers with national advertising and by taking orders with toll-free long-distance telephone calls. It must be a major factor in the historic turnaround registered in the 1980 census. For the first time in more than a century, the country's rural population increased faster than the population of the cities and towns.

Telecommuting

Telecommuting is another phenomenon that modern telephony (and the computer) can make possible. With telephone access into remote computers and databases and portable terminals with acoustic coupler modems, people can draw text and data from their offices down the telephone line and feed their work back down it again with the flick of a switch.

This communications revolution is just beginning. The word *revolution* can be used in misleading hyperbole. A revolution can be taken to suggest a reordering of society that happens all of a sudden, as in a political revolution. The communications revolution that is being wrought by the great advances in solid state physics and the manufacturing advances of microcircuitry looks more like a revolution akin to the industrial revolution. It may take as long. The communications revolution may be the dominant force for change over some decades. it will take that much time because there are so many interdependencies and chicken-and-egg situations. It is frequently said, for example, that high-speed equipment (such as facsimile or telecopier machines) will not be developed for mass production until there is a high-speed data network. But such a network will not be built until there are machines to be put on either end of it. Much of the same situation may exist with databases or electronic reference services. They have large fixed costs, so it is hard for them to build a mass customer base enabling them to charge affordable prices without first suffering many years of losses. Free markets and tax write-offs of losses do enable such obstacles to be overcome, but often only with time.

Machine-readable bar coding of supermarket products took a long time to become used at checkouts. Debit cards and point-of-sale terminals also took time to attain widespread use. Electronic banking remains an idea still. This is not to say these changes will not happen, only that they can be delayed or held in suspense for long periods, waiting for an entrepreneurial leap between interdependent needs.

In most places in the world, fear of profit seeking has led to nationalization of telecommunications and their monopolization by government organizations—the worst imaginable situation. Government monopolization guarantees minimum choice, minimum efficiency, minimum adaptability, and minimum responsiveness to public need. Power rests not with the public, free to take their business elsewhere, but with a nonresponsible, externally unchallengeable management that is often heavily beholden internally to an employee labor union with its own monopoly powers. U.S. populism led to what was fortunately a slightly lesser evil than overseas government telecommunications monopolies—an incomplete but heavily regulated private monopoly. That this monopoly and this regulation is now breaking down should be the cause of great celebration.

Notes

1. Sidney Ratner, James Soltow, and Richard Sylla, *The Evolution of the American Economy* (New York: Basic Books, 1979), p. 340.

2. From John R. Meyer, Robert W. Wilson, Alan Baughcum, Ellen Burton, and Louis Caouette, *The Economics of Competition in the Telecommunications Industry,* a Charles River Associates Research Study (Cambridge, Mass.: Oelgeschlager, Gunn & Hain, 1980), p. 30.

3. Ibid., p. 31.

4. Ibid., p. 33.

5. Nina Cornell, Michael Pelcovits, and Steven Brenner, "A Legacy of Regulatory Failure," *Regulation* (July–August 1983).

6. Ibid., p. 42.

7. These predictions were made by Phillip Freedenberg to me in an interview at MACOM DCC, as well as in two telephone interviews in the spring of 1984.

8. David Hounshell, *Telegraph, Telephone, Radio and Television* (Washington, D.C.: Smithsonian Institution National Museum of History and Technology, 1977).

9. *Telephone Bypass* (February 1984):15.

10. David Macaulay, *Underground* (Boston: Houghton Mifflin, 1976).

11. Eli Noam, "Toward an Integrated Communications Market: Overcoming the Local Monopoly of Cable Television," *Federal Communications Law Journal* 34 (1982):209, 246.

12. Irwin Welber, "Technology for the Loop," *Bell Laboratories Record* (September 1982).

13. Telephone interview with Jim Caile of Motorola in January 1984.

14. Conversation with Tom Asp of the Mobile Telephone Systems Division at E.F. Johnson, April 23, 1984.

15. Stuart Crump, Jr., editorial, *Communications News* (August 1982).

16. William Newport, "Resale *Will* Be a Profitable Business . . . and How You Can Get into It," *Personal Communications* (May–June 1983):12–15.

17. Herschel Shosteck, "How Real Is the Demand for Cellular Service?" *Personal Communications* (May–June 1983):24–26.

18. *Radio Cellular News* (April 1984):6.

19. Craig R. Johnson and Mark A. Swift, "Is the Wireline Telephone System Obsolete?" *Personal Communications* (July–August 1983):20.

20. Jerome Lucas, president of Telestrategies in Virginia, showed the graph at a conference of Telestrategies, New York, January 1983.

21. See James Griffin, "The Welfare Implication of Externalities and Price Elasticities for Telecommunications Pricing," *Review of Economics and Statistics* 64 (February 1982):59–66.

Comment

Patrick K. Wiggins

A s a former state regulator, I must confess a certain ambivalence toward Peter Samuel's chapter. On the one hand, he has produced a useful journalistic survey of the state of postdivestiture telephony. He has amassed a formidable amount of information about the state and history of the industry and has conveyed something of the excitement that captures it today. The descriptive reporting in the chapter is well done. The analytical part of his work, however, is not as successful. As an analytical work, Samuel's piece is unbalanced and simplistic and suffers as a result.

Social Debate

Samuel's chapter is a statement in favor of continued, quickened deregulation in telecommunications. He seems to advance the following themes:

Regulation is bad and free market competition is good.

Regulators, especially state regulators, are wrongheaded and would muck up the advancement in telecommunications by clinging to a moribund system of regulation.

Advances in telephony are fueled by marketplace competition and will continue if regulatory hurdles are not thrown in the way.

In response, one simply cannot argue for either regulation or deregulation without stepping directly into social debate. The language at times may be economic, but the fight is social. Thus, in critiquing either regulation or deregulation, one should be specific about the definition of social good one is advancing. Otherwise the public debate will proceed as if the participants were speaking in tongues.

In making his statement for deregulation, however, Samuel fails to state clearly his definition of social good. For example, is the promotion of competition a social good in itself, or is it instead the promotion of a mechanism for achieving a variety of social goods? If the latter, what exactly are these desired goods? A balanced analysis should begin with such definitions.

A balanced analysis should also identify the stakes in the debate. In reading Samuel's chapter, one infers that at stake is whether and how soon the public will reap the benefits that competition in telecommunications can bring. There is more at stake, here, however, than just the marketing of telephone equipment and services.

Samuel is correct that poor regulatory decisions can delay the introduction of new telephone services and products to the consuming public. He is also correct in observing that we are moving from a mostly regulated telecommunications industry to a mostly competitive one and that this transition will benefit the public. And he is correct in arguing that the sooner we can become mostly competitive, the better; that unneeded regulation must be avoided; that in many situations historical rate-base regulation will be unnecessary; and that mindless barriers to entry and competition must not be tolerated. Samuel is right about all of this, just as he is right that the complexion of today's marketplace is at stake.

Embracing these shibboleths is the easy part. More difficult is to determine a course by which we can achieve this desired marketplace without hurting those who may not be able to afford the high-tech wonders we eagerly await. To chart this course, we need to identify what public good we would promote through unleashing competitive forces and to acknowledge at least that competition may have adverse social consequences. We need to identify what we are trying to accomplish.

Samuel does acknowledge briefly that not everyone will immediately benefit from competition. He observes that initially only the rich will be able to afford many of the advances in telephony but suggests that eventually the benefits of new technology will trickle down to the poor. Thus, at least the children or grandchildren of today's poor will benefit from today's competition. It puzzles me that an apparent champion of individualism would retreat into collectivism in explaining away these concerns about equity in the pricing of telephone services.

But I do not mean to be captious. In fact, competition as a mechanism is generally to be preferred to regulation. However, some see competition as an end in itself, and others who call for competition actually have something else in mind. Moreover, the values I believe normally to be served by competition might in fact be sacrificed by cutting loose AT&T too soon or by not protecting the local telephone company during the transition from a mostly regulated to a mostly competitive telecommunications system.

Social Concerns

There are persuasive economic arguments in favor of competition as the most effective mechanism to ensure the most efficient allocation of goods and services within markets. My preference for competition, however, rests on slightly different judgments and assumptions. For me, two principles seem basic to our notions of government: government should accord its citizens the greatest opportunity for self-advancement, and government should reward and encourage successful risk taking in the marketplace. Freedom from regulation is freedom of opportunity and freedom to take economic risks for the promise of economic gain. The promotion of these freedoms seems essential to individual advancement and to the economic vitality of society. Thus, without regard to economic efficiencies, I favor competition over regulation.

This personal social philosophy has to do with what I perceive to be at stake here. What is at stake is not whether some businessperson will enjoy the benefits of cellular radio within the next two years or whether some inter-exchange carrier will be able to use a cable television company to bypass the local telephone company. Instead two things are really at stake here: the economic and social infrastructure of our society in the year 2000 and the socially just treatment of today's poor in the provision of telephone service.

Social Structure

The information age will dramatically reshape society. As an extension of the industrial revolution, the information age should continue social trends begun in the nineteenth century. One trend has been to shift the work force from both agrarian activity and manufacturing to the provision of services, with some 65 percent of the work force now engaging in the production of services.[1]

The social trends accompanying these shifts in the work force are worth noting. As Eli Ginzberg has observed, "Although this transformation has been brought about largely by mechanization, it has been accompanied by social trends so pervasive that they must be included among the causes of the transformation as well as among its effect.[2] He identifies among these trends the rising of the age of entry into the labor force and the requirement of higher levels of training to perform jobs. Ginzberg then makes an observation that policy-makers in the area of telecommunications would do well to consider:

> A disquieting feature of these dynamic internal shifts in the labor force has been the persistence of high levels of unemployment among its less educated members. Such unemployment raises the question of how any society can function effectively over the long run without bringing all its adult members into its economic life, able not only to work but also to buy.[3]

We can expect profound social changes to occur during the next fifteen years. If the past is any indication of the future, we can expect that the access to education and information will remain a key to upward mobility among the citizenry. Thus we must be careful not to allow a caste system to evolve in which there are basically two classes: the information rich and the information poor. Many state regulators believe that one key to avoiding such a caste system is to maintain a universally affordable, public-switched telephone system. Thus some state regulators see the stakes being not just the marketplace of today but the social infrastructure of tomorrow.

Social Contract

Throughout Samuel's chapter there are references to alleged cross-subsidies among kinds of services, such as between long-distance and local service. He suggests that these subsidies be ended, even if local telephone rates rise. The subsidy issue will be addressed later. Here I simply wish to note why regulators believe that doubling or tripling local telephone rates would be bad.[4]

First, such increases would threaten universal service. State regulators generally believe that access to the public-switched telephone system should be promoted, not discouraged.

Next, long-distance companies may owe it to the local telephone companies to pay more for the long-distance link to a particular customer, such as a large business, than it would cost them if they bypassed the local telephone company. As Samuel notes, technological developments are making long-distance and other types of telecommunications services competitive. This in turn is putting financial pressures on the local telephone company, which will ultimately result in significantly increased local rates. High-volume users who can now demand lower rates for services they purchase seem outraged at the attempt by the local companies and state regulators to stifle their use of bypass facilities so that "excessively" high rates can be applied to them. They have short memories.

One of the advantages of the old vertically integrated, regulated AT&T was that significant funding of Bell Labs came from local telephone bills.[5] As a result, Bell Labs had the luxury of being theoretical.[6] Bell Labs made many of the breakthroughs in telephony that now would allow high-volume users to bypass the local telephone company. Given the fact that subscribers to the local telephone company helped pay for the technological developments that allow bypass, why does it outrage some that the local companies would attempt to delay the use of these developments to the extent that use would injure those who cannot afford either to bypass or pay the increased rates resulting from the bypass?

Continuing in this vein, one could view the old integrated telephone systems as grounded in a social contract among all users. Under the contract, technological developments were achieved that allowed the system to mature and grow away from its basically regulated, imperfect nature. Unfortunately, the local system built under the contract was very expensive and is yet to be paid for. Isn't it a breach of that contract to use the technology developed by that system to repudiate one's obligation to pay for the plant already purchased under the contract?

This analysis may not be persuasive. Nevertheless, a balanced view of the regulatory dilemma would at least identify the concerns of the various participants. Moreover, a balanced treatment should recognize that there is no simple, valid solution to the problem of equitably pricing telephone services during this transition from a mostly regulated to a mostly competitive system. The problems we face are not susceptible to purist solutions, and that sense of balance is lacking in Samuel's discussion.

Social Subsidies

A sense of balance is also missing from Samuel's presentation of other matters. For example, he asserts that long distance subsidizes local telephone service. One can reasonably argue just the opposite: that in fact local service subsidizes long distance. For example, the local system would have been built much less expensively were it not for long-distance service requirements.[7] The local folks would have bought a compact economy car to run around town in rather than a deluxe touring limousine suitable for transcontinental trips.

Long-distance revenues do provide significant support to local telephone service. Whether this support is a subsidy depends on how you allocate joint costs between long-distance and local service. For example, if the local company's switch handles both long-distance and local calls, how do you allocate that investment between the two? Any method of allocation is arbitrary. As more than one regulator has observed, "Costs are as costs are defined."[8] Thus any definition of telecommunication costs for the purpose of allocation is an exercise in the formulation of social policy.

In one sense, this talk about subsidization is irrelevant. Discussion of cross-subsidies is basically a discussion about costs and allocation of costs. Designing appropriate rate structures for long distance is not a costing problem but a pricing problem. How much can a firm charge customers for various types of telephone service without triggering undesirable responses in the customer?

A short explanation is useful here. As Samuel notes, local telephone companies are subjected to rate-base regulation. Under this system, the company's revenue needs are determined, and then the search is on to determine how to collect these revenues from the company's customers. This latter problem is a pricing problem or, in regulatory terms, a rate-structure problem. Historically in designing rate structures for telephone services, companies have taken advantage of the fact that demand for long-distance service and local service is largely inelastic with respect to price. Technology, however, has changed the price demand curve by dramatically reducing the cost to a consumer of bypassing the local telephone company. As a result, in any given market, demand from a particular customer may drop to zero at current rates. Unfortunately, we cannot identify which customers currently are being induced to bypass. The threshold of economic bypass varies with each market and each customer so it is difficult to find appropriate price levels when pricing telephone service for large-volume users.

When rates are discussed in terms of underlying costs, the problem typically is identified as one of fairly allocating and recovering nontraffic-sensitive (NTS) costs. Historically NTS costs have been recovered through usage-sensitive pricing. An alternative approach is to charge all or some NTS costs to end users through a flat charge. That approach is favored by the FCC, AT&T, and other long-distance carriers and by Samuel as well. This flat charge, called customer access line charge (CALC), is the "new" pricing arrangement "many believe essential to make competition work properly," as identified by Samuel. State regulators and key members of Congress from both parties have blanched at the imposition of CALC.

There are legitimate concerns about implementing the CALC. First, through the CALC, the FCC would have imposed a local rate increase on subscribers to local service using the rate structure it chose in order to implement that increase. This offends state regulators. Without regard to whether the NTS should be recovered from local customers, state regulators would at least like to design the rate structure through which the recovery was effected. Next, many regulators find that a flat charge violates their notions of fairness. For example, it would be imposed whether the subscriber made long-distance calls; also it would be imposed on both the customer in the large city who has access to numerous competitive long-distance carriers and on the customer in rural areas who does not.

Another equally troubling concern about the CALC was that AT&T and the FCC proposed a shift of some $4.3 billion of NTS costs to local ratepayers without any guarantee that AT&T would effect a dollar-for-dollar reduction in its long-distance rates. In fact, before the residential CALC was deferred, Vermont state regulatory agenices petitioned the FCC to reduce AT&T's long-distance rates in step with the imposition of the CALC.[9] At the time of the filing, there had been no move by the FCC or AT&T to seek such a reduction.

Antisocial Conduct

As a final example of imbalance, Samuel identifies the probable incentives for AT&T to divest itself of its local telephone companies but neglects to mention why the Department of Justice (DOJ) subjected AT&T to "good old populist trustbusting." The reason is that the DOJ believed that AT&T for years had used systematically its control over local-exchange telephone companies to inhibit competition against AT&T in other areas such as long distance and the provision of terminal equipment. AT&T denied these charges. At trial AT&T moved to dismiss all charges at the close of the DOJ's case. Judge Harold Greene denied the motion.[10] No one has ever accused AT&T of being illiterate, and they certainly could read the writing on the wall. In addition, they were no doubt concerned about various legislative proposals being considered by the Congress, as well as what the courts might do with the FCC's Computer II decision. They decided to settle. A balanced view of the breakup would have given serious attention to both AT&T's anticompetitive behavior over the years and the legal and regulatory uncertainties that AT&T attempted to control through the settlement.

Conclusion

It would be inappropriate to criticize Samuel for a lack of balance without at least mentioning that his views do reflect conventional wisdom and that my views do not. What is important here, however, is not the relative popularity of our respective views. Instead readers should understand that the debate over the future treatment of telecommunications is a social debate with important social implications. Economists, accountants, technicians, regulators, politicians, attorneys, journalists, and a host of others bring to the debate perspectives peculiar to their training. Some of the participants in this debate are better skilled than others at predicting the consequences of various courses of action, but the selection of one set of consequences over another is a social decision based on value judgments. When these participants go beyond identifying consequences to advocating them, they move into political advocacy.

In our system of government, the selection of one set of social consequences over another is political decision making and thus is relegated to the political arena. This means that we can expect legislators, executive agencies, judges, regulators, and others to stay involved in this transition from a mostly regulated to a mostly competitive telecommunications system. Given that the nation's future social structure is being forged in this process, we should welcome the demagoguery, not resent it.

Notes

1. This work force information is drawn from Eli Ginzberg, "The Mechanization of Work," *Scientific American* 247 (September 1982):67. Statistical data on the nation's work force may be found in *Bicentennial Edition Historical Statistics of the United States, Colonial Times to 1970*, pt. 1.

2. Ginzberg, "Mechanization," p. 67.

3. Ibid.

4. There is general agreement that local telephone rates will rise during the next five years, although there is significant controversy as to how much and why. Generally, state commissioners fear doubling or even tripling of basic rates by 1989 and tend to blame the increases on federal decisions. Not surprisingly, the FCC denies that federal decisions have or will contribute so dramatically to local rate increases. See, for example, FCC, *Analysis of the Effects of Federal Decisions on Local Telephone Service* (December 21, 1983). The FCC foresees in 1989 roughly a 50 percent increase in local rates for residential customers who purchase their own telephones. This would amount to a compound annual growth rate of about 6 percent per year. The FCC's report, however, has not gone without criticism. See U.S., House, Committee on Energy and Commerce, *Report on Local Telephone Rate Increases* (January 1984). This staff report, using Michigan as an example, corrects for alleged errors in the FCC analysis and computes a doubling of local rates.

5. In 1981, the Bell Operating Companies (BOC) contributed about $600 million to Bell Labs. This amounted to about 2.5 percent of their gross operating revenues. These BOC funds constituted "about 80% of the Research and Systems Engineering functions," which includes basic research. See testimony of John H. Gibbons, director, Office of Technology Assessment, before the Committee on Science and Technology, U.S. House of Representatives, June 9, 1982.

6. Bell Labs has prided itself on its commitment to basic research and suggested in the news media that this function would be sacrificed by the divestiture or proposed congressional legislation, or both. See "Bell Labs—The Threatened Star of U.S. Research," *Business Week,* July 5, 1982, and "Scientists Mold Industry at Big Bell Labs," *New York Times,* May 27, 1982.

7. For a discussion of how the exchange plant was built more expensively to accommodate long-distance service, see Richard Gable, "Allocation of Telephone Exchange Plant Investment," in *Adjusting to Regulatory Pressures and Market Realities,* ed. Harry M. Trebing (East Lansing: Graduate School of Business Administration, Michigan State, 1983), p. 452.

8. For a discussion of the problem of determining the reasonableness of rate increases for local service in the light of a standard based on the principle of economic cost causation (service components should pay the costs they impose on the system), see William Melody, "Cost Standards for Judging Local Exchange Rates," in *Diversification, Deregulation, and Increased Uncertainty in the Public Utility Industries,* ed. Harry M. Trebing (East Lansing: Graduate School of Business Administration, Michigan State, 1983). Of particular interest here are Melody's comments with respect to cost causation for exchange costs:

> Unfortunately, there are no detailed studies of the specific characteristics of the cost causation pattern for exchange facilities. However, on the basis of existing information relating to (1) the design and cost characteristics of exchange plant; (2) the failure of the cost separations methodology to recognize exchange plant cost causations; and (3) the results of the cost-of-service studies that have been performed, it would appear that local service is more likely to be subsidizing toll than vice versa. We do not know the

magnitude of the subsidy because the current accounting system, cost allocation methods, and other information sources do not permit calculation of the magnitude.

9. "Petition to Prescribe Just and Reasonable Message Toll Rates," and "Memorandum in Support of Petition to Prescribe Just and Reasonable Message Toll Rates," filed July 15, 1983, FCC Docket No. 78-72, Phase I: In the Matter of MTS and WATS Market Structure, filed by the Vermont Department of Public Service, and the Vermont Public Service Board.

10. *United States* v. *American Tel. and Tel. Co.,* 524 F. Supp. 1336 (D.D.C. 1982).

Index

About the Contributors

Malcolm B. Allen, Jr., is an attorney with Holme Roberts & Owen. He received his J.D. degree from the University of Denver College of Law.

William W. Berry is president and chief executive officer of Virginia Power Company. He has written several articles for *Electric Rate Marketing* and *Public Utilities Fortnightly.* He received his M.S. in economics from the University of Richmond.

Sue D. Blumenfeld is an attorney in the Washington, D.C., office of Willkie Farr & Gallagher. She received her law degree from Rutgers-Camden School of Law.

Linda Cohen is a research associate in the economic studies department at the Brookings Institution. She received her Ph.D. in social sciences from the California Institute of Technology.

Nina W. Cornell is an economist with Cornell, Pelcovits & Brenner Economists Inc. She has published a number of articles on regulatory and natural resource issues. Dr. Cornell received her Ph.D. in economics from the University of Illinois.

Thomas Hazlett is assistant professor of agricultural economics at the University of California at Davis. He is the author of numerous papers and monographs and a contributing editor of *Reason* magazine and senior editor of the Manhattan Report on Economic Policy. He received his Ph.D. in economics from the University of California at Los Angeles.

Charles Jackson is a principal in Shooshan & Jackson, Inc., an adjunct professor at the Duke University Institute of Policy Sciences and Public Affairs, and a fellow of the Annenberg Washington Center. He received a Ph.D. in communications and operations research from the Massachusetts Institute of Technology.

Leland L. Johnson is a senior economist at The Rand Corporation. He received his Ph.D. in economics from Yale University.

William Mellor is deputy general counsel for legislation and regulations at the U.S. Department of Energy. He received his J.D. degree from the University of Denver College of Law.

The late **Ithiel de Sola Pool** was a professor of political science at the Massachusetts Institute of Technology. He received his Ph.D. in political science from the University of Chicago.

Walter J. Primeaux is professor of business administration at the University of Illinois at Urbana-Champaign. He has published in the leading economics journals. His Ph.D. is in economics from the University of Houston.

Peter Samuel is a correspondent for *The Australian* newspaper and a contributing editor of *Reason* magazine. He also writes weekly for the *Washington Inquirer* and has written for *Defense Week* and *Human Events*. Mr. Samuel has an honors degree in economics from Melbourne University.

Douglas Webbink is an economist at the Federal Trade Commission, Bureau of Economics, Division of Regulatory Analysis. He is the author of articles and reports on such subjects as the use of the frequency spectrum, common carrier regulation, the semiconductor industry, and competition in the energy industries. He received his Ph.D. in economics from Duke University.

Patrick K. Wiggins is an attorney. He received his J.D. degree from the University of Florida.

About the Editor

Robert W. Poole, Jr., received two engineering degrees from the Massachusetts Institute of Technology. He worked in the aviation industry for three years and has spent ten years doing research on public policy issues for a variety of research organizations. He is president of The Reason Foundation and editor of *Reason* magazine. Mr. Poole is also editor of *Instead of Regulation: Alternatives to Federal Regulatory Agencies* (Lexington Books, 1982) and *Defending a Free Society* (Lexington Books, 1984).